# Voice of God
## Traditional Thought and Modern Science

# Voice of God

## Traditional Thought and Modern Science

Edited by
Baidyanath Saraswati

D.K. Printworld (P) Ltd.
New Delhi

in association with

N.K. Bose Memorial Foundation
Varanasi

**Cataloging in Publication Data — DK**
[Courtesy: D.K. Agencies (P) Ltd. <docinfo@dkagencies.com>]

**Voice of god :** traditional thought and modern science / edited by Baidyanath Saraswati.

p. cm.
Contributed articles.
With special reference to India.
Includes bibliographical references.
Includes index.
ISBN13: 9788124604724
ISBN10: 812460472X

1. Philosophy and religion. 2. Philosophy and religion — India. 3. God. 4. Religion and science — India. 5. Religion and sociology — India. I. Saraswati, Baidyanath, 1932-

DDC 201.61 22

**ISBN13: 978- 81-246-0472-4**
**ISBN10: 81-246-0472-X**
*First published in India in 2009*


*Published by*:
**D.K. Printworld (P) Ltd.**
*Regd. office* : *'Srikunj'*, F-52, Bali Nagar, New Delhi - 110 015
*Phones* : (011) 2545 3975; 2546 6019; *Fax* : (011) 2546 5926
*E-mail* : dkprintworld@vsnl.net *Web* : www.dkprintworld.com

*in association with*

**N.K. Bose Memorial Foundation**
B-8/9, Bara Gambhir Singh, Varanasi - 221 001 (UP)
*Phone* : (0542) 227 5289

*Printed by*: D.K. Printworld (P) Ltd., New Delhi.

# Contents

# Introduction

*Baidyanath Saraswati*

THE N.K. Bose Memorial Seminar on *Traditional Thought and Modern Science* began with the *Concept of Death* (November 2002), followed by the *Concept of Life* (November 2003), and structured by *Five Senses* (2004). The next theme, in this series is *God and His Kindred*. We seek to approach various traditions, offering different kinds of intelligibility (2005), which we now take into comprehension in its entirety.

**Theme**

The Indian picture of God is fascinating, having a *thousand names* and a thousand forms, each having a definite form and specific function. At the conceptual level, God's unfolding comes from the concept of *Brahman* (*brih*, expand), along which comes the notion of *nāda* — *Śabda-Brahman*, the cosmic sound. Related with the notion of sound is *bindu*, the dimensionless point — literally a drop. The Indian concept of zero (*śūnya*) denotes the notional place as well as the void, that is, the absence of the notional place. Generally, the concept of zero when applied to *Brahman*, the Absolute, is unthinkable in itself. Metaphysically, it is identified with both fullness and emptiness. Fullness is the non-dual infinity of *Brahman*. The Universe that is unborn and that which is born is full. The opposite of fullness is emptiness. The description of *Brahman* as full-and-empty shows that it is beyond the dialectical opposition between time and timelessness, formed and unformed, mortal and immortal, actual and beyond, and so on.

The relationship between the unmanifest *Brahman* and the manifest universe is formed by a divinity called God. As an aspect of *Brahman,* God is transcendent, and as an architect of the universe it is *immanent.* The *Brahman* is without name, without form and without function, but is called the God of creation (Prajāpati Brahmā), the God of life-sustaining force (Viṣṇu), and the God of dissolution and death (Mahākāla Śiva). One God assumes many forms, out of nothing and nowhere. There are many gods and goddesses with many names, many forms and functions, and yet they are not viewed in terms of *Alpha* and *Omega.* In fact, they are so much a part of the form and function of the observable universe that with the extinction of the universe they all dissolve in the same manner and at the same moment as the universe dies. With the passage of time and as a result of cross-cultural encounter the literature on the concept of the universe grew up as a highly complex text. In this process, the philosophical concept of God merged into one single entity having many names and forms, each venerated in communion with the Ultimate.

All religions accept the concept of God, but all philosophies do not agree on God as the highest manifestation. Thus, some may say the "Death of God," some deny "God as creator and arbiter of the Universe." Semitic religion makes absolute difference between God and man. Man is a created being, and hence, has only one life till his "physical death," i.e. he is in a kind of suspended animation till called on the *Day of Judgement*, before the tribunal of God, to be assigned to Heaven or everlasting Hell. In contrast, the Eastern religion conceives the finite spirit as more intimately related to God, and in some forms, such as in the Advaita Vedānta, even identified with God. Death does not mean the end of man's career in worldly life. In fact, this life is just one link in the series of births and deaths, before and after. The law of *karma* (action) operates, and determines the kinds and varieties of different births and status of the individual soul.

Theologians and philosophers, in the East and the West, have tried to prove God's existence and his nature by appeal to scriptures, as also arguments, although among themselves they are not in complete consensus. The cosmological, teleological, and ontological proofs, in various forms, have been interpreted to assert the *Reality of God.*

**Texts of God**

In the prayer to Agni, the *Ṛgveda* reveals: "O God, you are our providence, our Father. We are your brothers; you our source of life. You are called Father, you carry us forward. Supremely wise, you teach the simple wisdom."

The *Kaṭha Upaniṣad* says: "Above nature, the unmanifest seed, above the manifest seed, God. God is the goal; beyond him nothing. God does not proclaim Himself. He is everyday's secret, but the intellect of the sage has found Him. Above the unmanifest is God — unconditioned, filling all things. He who finds Him enters immortal life, becomes free."

The Buddhists adopted a large number of deities from other religions; they are essentially atheistic. Their deities do not, by any means, represent the highest existence. They think of standing below the Buddha, protecting the Buddha and the Dharma. Gods are above the realm of human beings, but the Buddha-realm is above all existence, and it is the human beings, not the gods, that are able to reach this state. The Buddha is viewed, in Hinduism, as the 9th incarnation (*avatāra*) of Viṣṇu.

The Jains do not believe in God as an Almighty, perfect, conscious soul to be a creator. Great is the power of purity and truth. No external God creates and sustains the world, no means of redemption outside themselves. Salvation is believed to terminate the cycle of births and deaths, and reincarnation, when the soul is finally liberated to eternal bliss and infinite knowledge.

The Zoroastrians have their own cosmology. Ahura Mazda is the supreme Lord of everything; the pure eternal omniscient and powerful Creator of the world, out of whom everything proceeds, depends, and is ruled. Evil, belonging to cosmic dynamism as a person, as a concrete object, rules the universe with the same energy as God has. God remains beyond the destructive, which cannot rise above the level of existence itself.

The Judaism, religion of the Jews, was founded by Moses. The supreme deity of this religion is Yahveh (also called Jehovah) who revealed this faith to the most pious member of the chosen people on the earth. He revealed to him the secret of divinity, along with the codes of the proper conduct. Yahveh gave Moses the rules of social life in the form of Ten Commandments. Judaic God is just and merciful. He is the perfect one, who created the world in six days. Jews believe in the continued existence of soul, after the death of man.

The Christian story is derived from Greek logic. It has a climate of opinion on an unquestioned fact that the world and man in it had been created in six days by God, the Father, an omniscient and benevolent intelligence for an ultimate. Although created perfect, man had, through disobedience, fallen from grace into sin and error, thereby incurring the penalty of eternal damnation. Yet happily a way of atonement and salvation had been provided through the propitiatory sacrifice of God's only begotten Son. God is love. God is, in fact, community. Man was made in God's image. God is simple. God is pure Act, the changeless one. God is pure potency, which is pure non-being. God is historical. The Christian belief in the incarnation of God in Jesus should be understood as God continuing to make the world by redeeming it; God continuing to make human life.

The Islamic story, the complete and total doctrine of the nature of God in Arabic, refers to Allāh, the Supreme Reality, who is not only transcendent and immanent, infinitely beyond, but also infinitely close to man, majestic and merciful. He is Absolute, infinite and the source of goodness. He is the *origin* and *end* of all things.

The Nihongi, or Chronicles of Japan (CE 720), began with a history of the creation and the generation of gods. Of old, Heaven and Earth were not yet separated and the *In* and *Yo* (feminine and masculine principles) not yet divided. They formed a cosmic mass, like an egg, which was of obscurely defined limits, and contained germs. Purer and clearer part was thus drawn out and formed Heaven, while the heavier and grosser elements settle down, and become Earth. Heaven was formed first, and Earth was established subsequently. Thereafter, Divine Beings were produced between them.

The Altaic people are a linguistically related group, including Turks, Mongols, and Turks-Manchus, In their perception God and Devil are identified with the "First Man."

The "Primeval Man" creates God in his own image. Xenophanas remarked long ago that the complexion of Nigro God was black and their noses flat; that Thiracion Gods were ruddy and blue eyed; and that if horses, oxen and icons only believed in gods and had hands with which to portray them; they would doubtless fashion their deities in the form of Horses, Oxen, and icons. In modern Egypt, the magician still works his old enchantment by the same ancient means; only the God by which he conjures is different. The man who knows the most great name of God can by the mere utterance of it kill the living.

The Dinka in Africa worship innumerable deities, and yet affirm that "divinity is one." What they mean is simply that there is one divine power, one absolute reality, perceived in many different aspects, like light refracted in many colours; it is a matter of perception.

## The Goddess

In the beginning God was a woman. Persistence of Goddess religion for 3,000 years began in the Late Paleolithic, the Ice Age. Goddess religion was earth-centred, not heaven centred, of this world, not other-worldly, body-affirming, not body-denying, holistic, not dualistic. The Goddess was immanent, within every human being, not transcendent; and humanity was viewed as part of nature, death as a part of life. Her worship was sensual, celebrating the erotic, embracing all that were alive. The religious quest was above all for regeneration of life, and the Goddess was the Life-force. The Goddess had been a model of woman's nature in all its fullness.

## The Celestial Deities

The Sun, the Moon, the Stars, the Spirits and the Demons of the primitive man belong to "Super-human Forces," elevated high up, infinite, eternal and powerful. Celestially structured supreme primitive divinity tends to disappear with the creation of God-centric religion. The conversion to Christianity does not stop a Tribal approaching the old God, saying: "Now we have tried everything, we still have you to help us." And they sacrifice a white cock to him. "God thou art our creator, have mercy on us."

The message of all the sacred traditions is more or less the same. Man is a thinking animal, having a mindset, raising ontological questions, builds up theories (cosmological, ontological, teleological), and forms his own conclusions: Who is God? Is He perfect? Does He care about human beings? Is man one with God? From where does God come out? At the level of physical appearance, is there a personal God? Is God Indefinable? We bow down to Him, Great Sage! Faith in God remains very strong. God is the base of reality. He dissolves the distinction between subjectivity and objectivity, and unites, Spirit and Nature.

Truly speaking, we do not know what God is, except that he has thousands of names, he has created man and all that exists in his own image, that in the beginning, he created the Heaven and the Earth, and Men and Animals, following the ways that he has made. If you admit all this, how can you be sure that there is nothing behind the curtain? The *Sacred Science Review* raises such questions. Think: What, if there is no God? Who plays with the Nature? Also, who said that it was very good?

Essentially, the Sacred originates with the recognition of a directing consciousness beyond apparent forms. The Elements that reveal or "symbolize" this consciousness represent the inner logic underlying the appearance of created forms. They are common to the different aspects of the manifest world and express certain data about the creative modality. Such elements may thus serve as intermediaries between mankind and Divine thought of which the created world is an expression. This is why the Sacred lives through symbols, to which magical values are attributed, since they create the possibility of a link with the divine. In actual fact, such symbols must comply with certain basic data concerning the structure of the universe. If they are merely conventional, we enter the domain of the falsely Sacred. In fact, the permanence and universality of certain symbols, as well, their utilization in efficacious rites, means that they may be considered as precise interpretation of the processes of manifestation of the Creator's Mind as indications of the structures that influence the supernatural states of being that show through certain aspects of the created.

**Traditions of God**

Of all the animals, man alone speaks a language, other than his own. He communicates with the birds and beasts. He also delves with Gods, Spirits, and Ancestors. He has learnt the "language of God," the "ritual language." Ritual language is always a code, which points beyond that which cannot be expressed in normal human language. In its essential form, it is a fourfold structure, consisting of: (a) esoteric word, (b) gesture, (c) sound, and (d) everyday language of communication. Borrowing Sanskrit terms, these may be called *mantra, mudrā, dhvani* and *vyavahārikī*, respectively. Each has its own face, own significance.

THE MAORI OF NEWZEALAND CHANT

*From nothing the begetting*
*From nothing the increase*
*From nothing the abundance*
*The power of increasing*
*The living breath.*

THE CHINESE MYTH OF P'AN KU IS TYPICAL

The world was never finished until P'an Ku died. Only his death could perfect the universe. From his skull was shaped the dome of the Sky, and from his flesh was formed the soil of the fields; from his bones came the rocks, from his blood the rivers and the seas; from his hair came all vegetation. His breath was the wind, his voice made thunder; his right eye became the Moon; his left eye the Sun. From his saliva or sweat came rain. And from the vermin which covered his body came forth Mankind.

FROM THE KORAN

"It is God who hath given you the Earth as a sure foundation, and over it built-up the Heaven, and formed you, and made your Lord. Blessed then be God, the Lord of the Worlds!

"He is the Living One. No God is there but He. Call then upon Him and offer Him pure worship. Praise be the God, the Lord of the Worlds!

"Say: Verily I am forbidden to worship what ye call on besides God, after that the clear tokens have come to me from my Lord, and I am bidden to surrender myself to the Lord of the Worlds.

"He it is who created you of the dust, then of the germs of life, then of thick of blood, then brought you forth infants: then he letteth you reach your full strength and then become old men (but some of you die first), and reach the ordained term. And this that ye may haply understand.

"It is He who giveth life and death; and when He decreeth a thing, He only saith of it, 'Be,' and it is."

— Sura XI, The Believer: 66-70

FROM THE TESTAMENT MYTHS

In the beginning God created the Heavens and the Earth. The Earth was without form and void, and darkness was upon the face of the deep; and the Spirit of God was moving over the face of the waters.

> And God said, "Let there be light;" and there was light.
>
> And God saw that the light was good, and God separated the light from darkness, And God called the light day, and the darkness he called Night. And there was evening, one day.

And God said, "Let there be a firmament in the midst of the waters, and let it separate the waters from the waters." And God made the firmament and separated the waters which were under the firmament from the waters which were over and above the firmament. And it was so. And God called the firmament Heaven. And there was evening and there was morning, a second day.

And God said, "Let the waters under the heavens be gathered together into one place, and let the dry land appear." And it was so. (10) God called the dry land Earth, and the waters that were gathered together, he called Seas. And God saw it was good. (11) And God said, "Let the Earth put forth vegetation, plants yielding seeds, bearing fruit in which is their seed, each according to its kind, upon the Earth." And it was so. (12) The Earth brought forth vegetation, plants yielding seed according to their own kinds, and trees bearing fruit in which is their seed, each according to its kind. And God saw that it was good. (13) And there was evening and there was morning, a third day.

Lord God had taken from the Man, he made into a woman and brought her to the man. Then the man said,

*This at last is bone of my bones*
*and flesh of my flesh;*
*She shall be called Woman,*
*because she was taken out of Man.*

FROM VEDIC HYMN

*From the North and the South, the East and the West,*
*Let the light of God*
*direct on this village*
*sustenance, welfare, and ease.*
*May the power of God, grant us freedom from foes,*
*removing all fear, deflecting all wrath,*
*Below and above,*
*below and before,*
*Grant us freedom from enemies, O power of God* — *AV* vi, 40

NOW THE KHARIA PRIEST

*O ye Khunt! and Baghia Spirit*
*Today, I am offering sacrifices*
*Today, in your name, I am offering to you*
*Mahua, Bar, Fig — all these fruits,*
*I am worshipping you,*
*Do ye protect (our) bullocks, buffaloes,*
*Goats, Men, etc. in jungle and brushwood,*
*From Tigers and Bears.*

Here, the Vedic *ṛṣi* and the Tribal Priest, both try to overcome fear of nature, propitiating the divine being. The content and the code are the same; only the *vaikharī* language is different.

**The Islamic Code**

THE NAME OF GOD, THE MERCIFUL,
THE MOST COMPASSIONATE

The Islamic code is the name given to the principles and laws which God revealed and which He requires all Muslims to adhere to strictly in all their actions, whether in their relations with Him or in their dealings with mankind. The actions through which Muslims draw near to their Lord, recall His greatness, and show their trust in Him by their observance of His divine rules are known in Islam as *worship of God*. The actions through which Muslims uphold their interests and repel evils in themselves, between themselves and their neighbours, and between Muslims and non-Muslims, the actions through which they prevent maltreatment, preserve rights, fulfil the general good, and establish peace and security, are known in Islam as *dealings*. The great number of laws which make up the Islamic code are classified under these two headings — worship and dealings.

*Worship of God*

The worship of God is made up of prayers, fasting, payment of religious tax and pilgrimage. Basic to the worship of God is the acknowledgment of God's oneness and Muhammad's heavenly purpose in life, the cleansing of the heart and soul, the strict observance of obedience to God in all actions. This is the foundation; these are the pillars on which Islam is built. Therefore, the Prophet (may God bless him) has said, "Islam is put upon five principles — belief in the single God and in Muhammad as his Messenger, performance of prayers, payment of religious tax, keeping of the roza during the month Ramadan and pilgrimage to the Holy Mosque by whoever finds the way clear to do it."

*Prayer*

Prayer is a form of physical worship assigned to the Muslim five times a day at specified times. In prayer, he stands wherever he happens to be at the scheduled time and turns his face toward the Divine Mosque in Mecca. He begins his prayer by saying in a fairly loud voice, "God is the Most Great," praying reverently with profound intent to worship God. He then recites the Good Book's first *Surah,* along with a passage of the Quran which he has learned by heart, trying to understand its inner meaning. He then bows by bending until his back makes a straight horizontal line, holding his knees with his hands, and saying to himself as he bows, "Great God." Then he lifts his head, saying, "God the Most Great," and kneels down, touching his forhead to the floor, saying as he goes down, "God the Highest." He then lifts his head, saying "God the Most Great," and sits comfortably on his heels. Then he touches the floor with his forehead a second time. This process is called one kneeling.

There are five daily prayers. First is the morning prayer which the Muslim performs at the beginning of his day between the small hours of the morning and sunrise. It is made up of two kneelings, at the end of which the worshipper sits to salute his Lord, admitting His oneness and the mission of His Prophet in a manner which has been universally copied from Muhammad (may God bless him). He then salutes the right side and the left side with the words, "Peace be upon you together with God's blessings." The second prayer is the midday prayer which is performed from noon until halfway between noon and sundown. The afternoon prayer comes between mid-afternoon and sunset. Each of these prayers is made up of four kneelings. The early evening prayer has three kneelings and is offered between sunset and the vanishing of the twilight from the horizon. The late evening prayer is performed after the twilight disappears; it is the last prayer of the day when the Muslim welcomes the night, and is made up of four kneelings.

With these prayers, the Muslim thinks of his Lord five times during each day and night, appearing before his Lord repeatedly and saluting his name within his heart and soul, submitting himself to God, looking forward to his favour. Therefore he perseveres in obeying His commands.

The Muslim can perform these prayers anywhere — at the mosque, at home, in the field, at the factory, in the office — wherever he happens to be when the time falls due for prayer. He can pray alone, or he can pray with others standing in a line or lines arrayed closely in straight formation, like a highly disciplined military parade, behind a leader who is followed by the congregation in all that he does. Congregational prayer in Islam is the best form of prayer because it encourages acquaintanceship, intimacy, co-operation, joint entreaty, remembrance and cheerful submission to God, the Lord of all peoples.

Muslims are reminded of the time for prayer by the call to prayer which is given from the minaret of the mosque in the form taught by the Prophet, "God is Most Great, God is Most Great. I avow that there is no God other than Allāh. I avow that there is no God other than Allāh. I avow that there is no God other than Allāh. I declare openly that Muhammad is the Messenger of God. I declare openly that Mahammad is the Massenger of God. Welcome prayer. Welcome prayer. Welcome good fortune. Welcome good fortune. God is most Great. God is most Great. God is most Great. There is no God but Allāh."

Islam also has a weekly prayer, known as the Friday prayer because it is performed at noon on Friday. It is a congregational service with preaching before the prayer, which is made up of two kneelings. There are also two other prayers like the Friday prayer which are performed twice a year on the mornings of the two Islamic feasts, the first day following the month of Ramadan and the tenth day of the month of Dhulhaj. These two prayers are known in Islam as the prayers of the two feasts, Ramadan and al-Qurban.

In addition to the daily prayers, the Friday prayer, and the prayers of the two feasts, there is in Islam the funeral prayer, a religious ceremony expressing the Muslims' loyalty toward their dead. Muslims are required to prepare their dead for burial by cleaning the body and wrapping it from head to foot in unstitched cloth; the body is then placed on a bed and the mourners stand in line and, led by one of them, join in the prayer for the dead person. They repeat four times the phrase "God is Most Great" and recite together the preface to the Quran; then they ask God's blessing on the deceased. The body is later buried. According to Islam, the grave may be in the ground or on the surface level, but should not be elevated either for a member of the masses or for a prophet who has completed a heavenly mission.

**Reference**

*Islam, The Straight Path: Islam Interpreted by Muslims,* ed. by Kenneth W. Morgan, Motilal Banarsidass, Delhi.

# Part I
## Philosophy and Religion

# 1

## Homage to Mahatma Gandhi

*Baidyanath Saraswati*

M.K. GANDHI used to say —

> I love all mankind, as I love my own countrymen, because God dwells in the heart of every human being, and I aspire to realize the highest in life, through the service of humanity.
>
> I have not seen Him, neither have I known Him. I have made the world's faith in God, my own, and my faith is ineffaceable. I regard that faith, as amounting to experience.
>
> I can see that in the midst of death, life persists. Hence I gather, "God is Life." "Truth is Light." He is the "Supreme God."

The purer I try to become, the nearer to God I feel myself. The belief in God has to be based on "Faith" which transcends reason. God is not outside this earthly case of ours.

But, He is not God who merely satisfies the intellect; if he ever does.

God to be God must rule the heart, and transform it. He must express Himself, in every smallest act to His votary.

To me — God is Truth and Love; God is ethics and morality. God is fearlessness. God is the source of light and life, and yet He is the Supreme.

I know, too, that I shall never know God as *Brahman* — the unmanifest, the seed of all. It is by the sound that the soundless is revealed. The sound here is *oṁ* — the Word before the World. It is the First manifestation, the concentrated reality made Word — sound, content, form, matter, and spirit. God delights in the unstruck (*anāhata*) notes.

"Why I am a Hindu?" was the title of an article that Gandhiji wrote in 1927. He gave two main reasons for his attachment to the religion of his birth.

It was the "most tolerant of all religions." Its freedom from dogma gave the coterie "the largest scope for self-expression." Not being an exclusive religion it enabled the followers not merely to respect all the other religions, but . . . to admire and assimilate whatever may be good in the other faiths. Non-violence is common to all religions, but it has found the highest expression in Hinduism. Hinduism believes in the oneness not only of merely all human life but in the oneness of all other lives. God, Allāh, Rāma, Nārāyaṇa, Īśvara, Khudā were descriptions of the same being. Gandhi quoted the saint Narasimha — "The different shapes in which gold was beaten give rise to different names and forms; but ultimately it was all gold." "God's grace and revelation were not the monopoly of any race or nation; they descended equally upon all, who waited upon God. No religion was absolutely perfect, all were equally imperfect or more or less perfect." Gandhi told an American missionary in 1937:

> I . . . do not take as literally true the text that the Jesus is the only begotten son of God. God cannot be the exclusive Father and I cannot ascribe exclusive divinity to Jesus. He is as divine as Kṛṣṇa or Rāma, Mohammed or Zoroashtra. Similarly, I do not regard every word of the Veda or the Koran as inspired. The sum total of these books is certainly inspired, but I miss that inspiration in many of the things taken individually. The Bible is as much a book of religion with me as the *Gītā* and the Koran.

Albert Einstein, a great scientist, contemporary and admirer of Gandhi, wrote in 1934 that

> the more profound scientists were not without a religious feeling though it was different from the religiosity of the common man.
>
> But the scientist is possessed by the sense of universal causation. His religious feeling takes the form of a rapturous amazement at the harmony of the natural law which reveals an intelligence of such superiority that compared with it, all the systematic thinking and acting of human beings is an utterly insignificant reflection.

Einstein added that this feeling of the scientist was the guiding principle of life, and "in so far as he succeeds in keeping himself from the shackles of selfish desire, it is . . . akin to that which possessed the religious geniuses of all ages." Among these geniuses Einstein included Gandhi. Einstein considered that the moral qualities of its leading personalities "are perhaps of even greater significance for a generation, and for the course of history than purely intellectual accomplishments." His tributes to Gandhi paid in 1939 can hardly be improved upon:

> A leader of his people unsupported by any outward authority; a politician whose success rests not upon craft or the mastery of technical devices, but simply on the convincing power of his personality; a victorious fighter who has always scorned the use of force and inflexible consistency, who has devoted all his strength to the uplifting of his people and the betterment of their lot; a man who had confronted the brutality of Europe with the dignity of the simple human being and thus all times risen superior. Generations to come, it may be, will scarcely believe that such a one as this ever in flesh and blood walked upon this Earth.

Gandhi, like Gautama Buddha, did not try to escape the evident truth of human suffering through seeking mindless oblivion or neurotic distractions, nor did he choose to come to terms with it through compensatory spiritual ambition or conventional religious piety. Rejecting the route of cloistered monesticism, he pondered deeply and agonizingly upon the human condition, and sought to find the redemptive function and the therapeutic meaning of human misery. Translating his painful insights into daily acts of *tapas* — self-chosen spiritual exercises and the repeated re-enactments of lifelong meditation in the midst of fervent social activity — he came to see the need for a conditional rediscovery of the purpose of living by all those who reject the hypnosis of bourgeois society, with its sanctimonious hypocrisy and notorious "double standard for individual and public life." Gautama Buddha had taught his disciples in *saṅgha* that *bodhicitta,* the seed of enlightenment, may be found in the cleansed heart and controlled mind, and that it may be quickened by diligent practice of meditative altruism and honest self-examination of one's unconsicous tendencies and hidden motives. As stressed in the later Mahāyāna Schools of India, China and Tibet, *bodhicitta* can serve, like the Upaniṣadic *antaḥkaraṇa.*

Ramana Maharshi, one of the most venerated Indian saints of the twentieth century, is stated to have remarked that Gandhi "was a good man who had sacrificed his spiritual development by taking too huge burdens upon himself." Gandhi's signal service to Hinduism lay in his attempt to shift it from its individualistic moorings. He went so far as to say that the only way to find God was to "see Him in His Creation and be one with it." He did not know, he said, any religion apart from human activity; the spiritual law did not work in a vacuum but in the ordinary activities of life; religion which took no account of practical affairs and did not help to solve them was no religion. God, he once said, "can only appear to the poorest of the poor in the form of work." He told N.K. Bose, the anthropologist (who worked as his secretary for a few months in 1946-47), that a man was best represented not by the highest flight of thought which he reached at rare moments, but by the actual measure of the ideals of his daily life. C.F. Andrews, who studied Gandhi's life and thought closely, wrote to Romain Rolland that in Gandhi's inner life "it was the passion for others which is supreme." In another memorable phrase, Andrews called Gandhi, "a saint of action, rather than of contemplation." Another British friend of Gandhi, Horace Alexander, also observed how the Mahatma had deviated from the beaten path of Indian saints. "Gandhi was a mystic," Alexander wrote, "but he was a very matter-of-fact mystic; no dreamer of heavenly dreams, no visionary, who saw things unutterable when in a state of trance. When the inner voice spoke to Gandhi, it was only to tell him, what to do tomorrow — how to act more effectively to bring union of hearts between Hindus and Muslims, or how to hasten the downfall of untouchability."

It is said about Lord Buddha that he once fainted, because he had been fasting. At that time a woman came and placed a few drops of milk on his lips. Did the milk rouse his appetite? No, on the contrary, he realised God soon after.

The purport of this verse is that we should fast for self-purification. But Śāstras tell us that while fasting, we should wish with all our strength for freedom from desire. If, in addition, we also yearn to see God, then only our fasting will bear fruit. If we desire that our appetite should subside, it is in order that we may see God. When we are fasting our one desire should be to see God. Our appetites stand in the way, and so we must weaken their hold on us. After a person has seen God, it is all one to him whether he eats or does not eat. Vinoba told me a story about Caitanya, that a lump of sugar placed on his tongue remained there undissolved, like a stone.

Caitanya felt all the time that it was God's grace which sustained him and that if he should eat at all, it must be only that he may see God one day. To see Him, one should completely conquer one's appetites, and even the instinctive pleasure that one feels in objects of sense must subside. This verse provides key to such a state. To curb the appetites, we should stop eating, that is, deny our senses their food. When they have no occasion to function, they will be denied their food. If, after this, we take the next step and concentrate our attention on attaining self-realization, our instinctive pleasure in objects of sense will subside completely. The man who attains such a state will be in the same condition as Janaka.

Four or five hundred years ago, in Europe and Arabia, they attached great importance to mortification of the flesh. In the time of the Prophet, prayer, fasting and keeping awake at night, were considered essential for subduing the *nafar* (This is a very good word denoting the sense-organs collectively; it also means desire.)

Belief in one God is the cornerstone of all religions. But, I do not foresee a time when there would be only one religion on earth in practice. In theory, since there is one God, there can be only one religion. But in practice, no two persons I have known have had the same identical conception of God. Therefore, different religions will, perhaps, always be there.

I believe that all the great religions of the world are true more or less. I say "more or less" because I believe that everything the human hand touches is imperfect, by reason of the very fact that human beings are imperfect. Perfection is the exclusive attribute of God and it is indescribable, untranslatable. I do believe that it is possible for every human being to become perfect, even as God is perfect. It is necessary for us all to aspire after perfection, but when that blessed state is attaind, it becomes indescribable, indefinable. And, I, therefore, admit, in all humility, that even the Veda, the Koran and the Bible are imperfect words of God and, imperfect beings that we are, swayed to and fro by multitude of passions, it is impossible for us even to understand this word of God in its fullness. Three of the greatest teachers of the world — Buddha, Jesus and Muhammad — have left unimpeachable testimony, that they found illuminations through prayer and could not possibly live without it.

Gandhiji said, "God is that indefinable, something we all feel but which we do not know. To me God is Truth and Love, God is ethics and morality. God is fearlessness, God is the source of light and life, and yet he is above and beyond all these. God is conscience. He is even the atheism of the atheist. He transcends speech and reason. He is a personal God to those who need his personal touch. He is the purest essence — He simply is to those who have faith. He is long suffering. He is patient but he is also terrible. He is the greatest democrat the world knows. He is the greatest tyrant ever known. We are not, He alone is."

When God's grace descends on us, bringing us peace, all our suffering ends. Who can harm him, who is protected by Rāma? He on whom God showers His grace has all his sufferings destroyed. The intellect of a man whose *citta* has become calm and whose only thought is of God, stands secured and is protected against error. Śrī Kṛṣṇa now describes a condition, the opposite of this —

> *The undisciplined man has neither understanding nor devotion; for him who has no devotion there is no peace, and for him who has no peace when happiness.*

The meaning is that the man, who has not become one in God, who is not a *yogī* established in *samādhi*, lacks the faculty of intellect altogether. One who is unsteady has an intellect which is many-branched; of what good is such an intellect? It feels no devotion, it does not utter *Rāmāyaṇa.* He who lacks devotion and does not meditate on God, how can he attain peace? The man who is filled with devotion, sits in single-minded contemplation of God, but the other man who has no peace, how can he be happy?

By *gods* we may understand all living beings or God's sustaining energy. Gods are the invisible forces. So long as a person has someone in sight for whom he works, he is not engaged in service; real service consists in working for those whom one does not know personally. The *thirty-three crore* of gods belong to the world of imagination.

God is a great economist. He is omnipotent. We cannot refrain completely from storing things for future use. But God never stores, for he can destroy and create the universe with a mere thought. He wants us, therefore, to provide only for each day.

Gandhi prophesied that for *thirty years after his death,* his ideas would be largely forgotten, but that, generations later, the *tapas* of millions would bear fruit, and that out of his ashes "a *thousand Gandhis* will arise." Even though this is still an elusive hope, it is enormously encouraging that courageous pioneers have emerged from the host of the disillusioned who find the *world of today* too ghastly to contemplate, a world of mindless mass consumerism induced by the rising curve of shallow expectations, a world in which there is a widespread alienation of lonely individuals from disintegrating societies, of conscience from the intellect, of angry rebels from the agonies of the compassionate heart of important politicians from the global imperatives of radical changes and genuine co-existence among all nations and peoples, creeds and ideologies. Ragnarok, the end of the Gods and of the world, is the sole alternative in Nordic mythology to the rainbow bridge between Heaven and Earth, Bifrost, at which crossing many many camp at the boundary of a new land, a new frontier, a new settlement. Whether or not a New Jerusalem is attainable on Earth in the lifetime of the humanity of the present, there is much wisdom in Gandhi's own well-tested message in time of trial. In "One Step Enough for me," he said:

> When, thousands of years ago, the battle of Kurukṣetra was fought, the doubts which occurred to Arjuna were answered by Śrī Kṛṣṇa is the *Gītā;* but that battle of Kurukṣetra is going

> on, for ever within us; the Prince of Yogīs, Lord Kṛṣṇa, the universal *ātman* dwelling in the hearts of us all, will always be there to guide Arjuna, the human soul, and our Godworld impulses represented by the Pāṇḍavas will always triumph over the demonic impulses represented by the Kauravas. Till, however, victory is won, we should have faith and let the battle go on, and be patient meanwhile.

Those who cannot share this testament of faith, rooted in the spiritual convictions of antiquity concerning the periodic descent of *avatāra*s or Divine Redeemers, the immortality of the soul and the inexorable law of *karma,* the law of ethical causation and moral retribution, may yet actively respond to "the still, sad music of humanity." After all, even agnostics and atheists, socialists, humanists and communists, may share a *living faith* in the future of civilization and hold a truly open view of human nature, social solidarity and global progress. All alike may well ponder upon Mahatma Gandhi's life message. Towards the end of his pilgrimage on Earth, he delivered a deeply moving and tastable challenge to theophilanthropists everywhere:

> I will give you a *talisman.* Whenever you are in doubt, or when the self becomes too much with you, apply the following test. Recall the face of the poorest and weakest man whom you may have seen, and ask yourself if the step you contemplate is going to be of any use to him. Will he gain anything by it? Will it restore him to a control over his own life and destiny? In other words, will it lead to *swaraj* (self-rule) for the hungry and spiritually starving millions? Then you will find your doubts and yourself melting away.
>
> God is conscience.
> He is even the atheism of the atheist.
> He transcends speech and reasons.
> He is a personal God to those who need his touch.
> He is the purest essence.
> He simply is to those who have faith.

He is long suffering.
He is the patient, but
He is also terrible.
He is the greatest democrat the world knows.
He is the greatest tyrant ever known.
We are not, He alone is.
God is Truth.
Hindu scriptures are known as having one thousand names of God.
But these one thousand names of God are by no means exclusive.
We believe — and I think it is the Truth —
That God has as many names as there are creatures/and,
therefore, we also say that God is nameless,
and since we all consider Him formless,
and He speaks to us through many tongues.
We consider Him to be speechless, and so on,
And when I come to study Islam
I found that Islam too had many names for God.
I would say with those who say God is Love,
God is Love.
But deep down in me I use to say that
God may be God:
God is truth above all,
and since we also consider Him formless,
and He speaks to us through many tongues,
We consider Him to be speechless and so on.
I would say with those who say
God is Love, God is Love.
But deep down in me. I used to say
That God may be God.
God is truth above all.

My own experience has led me to the knowledge that the fullest life is impossible without an immovable belief in a living law in obedience to which the whole universe moves.

A man without that faith is like a drop thrown out of the ocean, bound to perish. — M.K. Gandhi

# 2

# God and His Kindreds
## An Upaniṣadic View

*R.C. Sharma*

BRAHMAN is the goal of Upaniṣadic thought and this has been analysed again and again in different ways. Its kindreds or manifestations have also been explained variedly, some being physically present or visible and others only subtle or invisible. This chapter endeavours to highlight a few passages of early and main Upaniṣads where this theme has been discussed more emphatically. It may also be pointed out that the Upaniṣads generally follow the Vedic tradition of deities when gods in nature, sky or heaven were meditated upon or worshipped through *yajña*s, and the other deities were yet to appear.

The opening hymn of *Īśāvāsya* informs that the whole world or universe is the abode of God and whatever one sees or realizes is His manifestation. So nothing is left out beyond His jurisdiction or gaze.[1] This dictum was slightly modified in the *Gītā* when the outstanding forms (*vibhūti*s) were considered as His representations.[2] At the same time, the Lord upholds the Upaniṣadic vision when in the concluding remarks

---

1. ईशावास्यमिदं सर्वं यत्किंच जगत्यां जगत्..... — *Īśa*. 1.
2. यद्यद् विभूति मत्सत्त्वं श्रीमदूर्जितमेव वा।
तत्तदेवावगच्छ त्वं मम तेजोंऽश सम्भवम्॥ — *Gītā*, X.41.

following immediately after the above statement, He states that "I sustain the entire world with a fragment of mine."[3]

Let us recollect the famous story of Satyakāma Jābāla in the *Chāndogya*.[4] When the boy Satyakāma was returning to the *āśrama* of his teacher Gautama, after multiplying four hundred cows into one thousand in the forest, he was revealed different aspects of *Brahman* by creatures or forms of nature. The bull explained the shining (*prakāśa*) as one-fourth aspect which is seen in the four directions.[5] From fire he grasped the second fourth part of *Brahman* which is infinite (*ananta*) to be realized an earth, horizon, sky and sea.[6] In the meantime, the swan appeared and this celebrated waterbird also revealed the third quarter part of *Brahman* which is the luminary (*jyotiṣmān*) aspect and stays in fire, sun, moon and lightning.[7] The last was another friend of Satyakāma, the diving bird and it also could not resist itself to highlight the remaining one-fourth part of *Brahman* which is to be realized through one's own faculties or senses such as ear, breath, eye and mind. This is known as the supporting element or the *Ādhāra Brahman*.[8] Thus, the four friends of Satyakāma revealed sixteen aspects of God through

---

3. विष्टभ्याहमिदं कृत्स्नमेकांशेन स्थितोजगत्॥ — Ibid., 42b.
4. *Chāndogya Upaniṣad*, IV. 4-9.
5. प्राची दिक्कला प्रतीची दिक्कला, दक्षिणा<br>दिक्कलोदीची दिक्कलैष वै सौम्य<br>चतुष्कलः पादो ब्रह्माणो प्रकाशवान्नाम — Ibid., IV.4.5.2.
6. पृथ्वी कलान्तरिक्षं कलाद्यौः कला<br>समुद्र, कलैष वै सौम्यः चतुष्कलः<br>पादो ब्रह्माणोऽनन्तवान्नाम — Ibid., IV.6.3.
7. अग्निः कला सूर्यः कला चन्द्रः कला विद्युत्कलैष<br>वै सौम्य चतुष्कलः पादो ब्रह्माणो ज्योतिष्मान्नाम — Ibid., IV.7.3.
8. प्राणः कला चक्षुः कला श्रोत्रं कला मनः कलैष वै<br>सौम्य चतुष्कला पादो ब्रह्मण आयतनवान्नाम — Ibid., IV.8.3.

four main divisions which may be summarized for the sake of convenience as under:

A. *Prakāśavān* (Shining) comprising four main directions — east, west, south and north.

B. *Anantavān* (Infinite) with another four parts, viz. earth, horizon, sky and sea.

C. *Jyotiṣmān* (Luminary) with four bright organs like fire, sun, moon and lightning.

D. *Ādhāra Brahman* (Supporting) with four abodes as ear, breath, eye and mind.

All these sixteen elements are called *kalās* hence the *Brahman* or God is also addressed as *Śoḍaśakalātmaka.* The Vedic or Upaniṣadic convention continued in a modified form in the Purāṇas when a complete incarnation like Kṛṣṇa is called Ṣoḍaśakalāvatāra.

Through the discourse of Sanatkumāra to Nārada in the *Chāndogya*[9] twenty-three ascending steps have been described and the last is *Brahman,* which has been conceived as Bhūmā. These manifestations or steps in sequence are — 1. Name (*nāma*), 2. Speech (*vāk*), 3. Mind (*manaḥ*), 4. Will (*saṅkalpa*), 5. Intelligence (*citta*), 6. Contemplation (*dhyāna*), 7. Proper Understanding (*jñāna*), 8. Strength (*bala*), 9. Food (*anna*), 10. Water (*jala*), 11. Fire (*teja*), 12. Ether (*ākāśa*), 13. Memory (*smaraṇa*), 14. Hope (*āśā*), 15. Vital breath (*prāṇa*), 16. Truth (*satya*), 17. Thought (*vijñāna*), 18. Personal understanding (*mati*), 19. Reverence (*śraddhā*), 20. Faith (*niṣṭhā*), 21. Creation (*kṛtī*), 22. Happiness (*sukha*) and last 23. God or *Brahman* titled as Bhūmā. *"yo vai bhūmā tatsukham . . . bhūmaiva sukham."*[10] Of these some are visible, some invisible and some to be

---

9. *Chāndogya,* VII.1–25.

10. Ibid., VII.23.1.

experienced. The ascending sequence of some may appear debatable as truth which is so important is surpassed by thought, etc.

The *Bṛhadāraṇyakopaniṣad* also sheds valuable light on God (*Brahman*) and its kindreds. Some of the episodes are related to the renowned Vedic sage Yājñavalkya. His debate in the assembly of king Janaka or Videha furnishes a remarkable evidence in this regard. When Vācaknavī Gārgī shot a volley of questions to Yājñavalkya, a large number of offsprings of God emerged in the debate and these serve as warf and woof (*otaprota*) of or for *Brahman*. These begin from water and continue to emerge till the stage of *Brahman*. All are interwoven water (*āp*) — wind (*vāyu*) — atmosphere (*antarikṣa*) — *gandharvaloka* — Sun (*ādityaloka*) — Moon (*candraloka*) — Stars (*nakṣatraloka*) — Gods (*devaloka*) — Heaven (*indraloka*) — Prajāpati — *Brahman*. When Gārgī wanted to know the stage beyond God, she was rebuked and declared as crazy, as God or *Brahman* is Ultimate.[11]

Gārgī was followed by Ārūṇi Uddālaka, another learned scholar of Vedic studies. He would not let Yājñavalkya take away one thousand decorated cows unless the latter proved his wisdom in the science of *brahma-jñāna* which was revealed to Kāpya Patañcala by a *gandharva* in the Madra country. When Yājñavalkya nodded his head in affirmation, Uddālaka was not satisfied and insisted on its proper citation. Yājñavalkya started with the first element wind or air (*vāyu*) which serves as string and in which all the limbs are woven like pearls in a thread.[12] Uddālaka agreed with the beginning but he wanted

11. *Bṛhadāraṇyakopaniṣad*, III.6.1.
12. ...तत्सूत्रं वायुना वै गौतम सूत्रेणायं च
लोकः परश्च लोकः सर्वाणि च भूतानि
सन्हब्धानि भवन्ति ... — Ibid., III.7.2.

to test the knowledge of Yājñavalkya and asked him to elaborate further. The main query was to know how God is to be realized in different elements.

Sage Yājñavalkya then elucidated the sacred and mystic knowledge in detail and His manifestations. The phenomenon begins from earth and culminates into *ātmā* which although lives, pervades and controls the elements, yet remains unseen. All these are the bodies or forms of *Brahman* but it remains unknown to them, hence known as *antaryāmī*.[13] After earth (*pṛthivī*) is water (*āp*), fire (*agni*), atmosphere (*antarikṣa*), wind (*vāyu*), ether (*divi*), sun (*āditya*), directions (*dik*), moon and stars (*candratāraka*), sky (*ākāśa*), darkness (*tama*), light (*teja*) and semen (*reta*). It sees but not seen, It listens but not listened, It ponders but not pondered (*manana*), It knows but not known, It is everlasting but never lasts.

Everything beyond it perishes.[14] Thus the above-stated elements of nature are the forms or bodies or abodes of God and to be accepted as His manifestations or kindreds although none of these is *brahmavid*, knower of God. This is really a riddle.

The *Kenopaniṣad* holds almost the same view when it declares that the faculties function through the power of *Brahman* and in reality these are just instruments, whether intelligence, vital breath, speech, ear or eye.[15] For example the eye sees through the power of *Brahman*, even then it is unable to see *Brahman* itself.[16] Sometimes, even gods forget about the

---

13. यः पृथिव्यां तिष्ठन् पृथिव्या अन्तरो यं पृथिवी
    न वेद यस्य पथिवीशरीरं य पृथ्वीमन्तरो यमत्येष
    त आत्मान्तर्याम्यमृतः — Ibid., III.7.3.
14. Ibid., III.7.4-14.
15. *Kenopaniṣad*, I.1.2.
16. यच्चक्षुषा न पश्यति येन चक्षूंणि पश्यति।
    तदेव ब्रह्म त्वं विद्धि नेदं यदिदमुपासते॥ — Ibid., I.1.6.

source of their energy and think themselves as supreme. Their pride was once shattered by *Brahman* who appeared before them in the form of a *yakṣa* to test their power which none of them could prove. Then they realized that the cause of the victory over demons is the strength of *Brahman* and not their own might.[17] The *Kaṭhopaniṣad* also confirms that the joys through faculties are experienced only by the grace of God.[18]

In response to queries raised by seven seekers of knowledge of *Brahman,* i.e. Sukeśa, Satyakāma, Śibi, Gārgya, Kauśalyā, Bhārgava and Kabandhi, the great sage Pippalāda said that several gods and divine elements which although powerful and important but all ultimately controlled by *Brahman.* Prajāpati created *prāṇa* (vital breath) and *rayi* (matter) which also represent Sūrya and Candra.[19] The other kindreds of God are sky, wind, fire, earth, speech, mind and ear.[20] But when each of these started their own supremacy, it was found that *prāṇa* (vital breath) is the most important creation of *Brahman* as in absence of this, the body starts disintegrating.[21] This has already been pointed out through the *Bṛhadāraṇyaka Upaniṣad* (III.7.2) that the *prāṇa* functions as thread (*sūtra*) in which all the limbs of body are woven. This breath has a number of brothers who are important children of God. These are *prāṇa* main — with its abode in mouth and nose, *samāna* — living in the centre of body and *apāna* — in the rectum. The same *prāṇa* when lives in multiple forms through veins, is called *vyāna* and when it stays in heart, it is known as *ātmā.*[22] In other

---

17. Ibid., III.1 and IV.1.
18. येन रूपं रसं गन्धं शब्दान्स्पर्शांश्च मैथुनान्।
    एतेनैव विजानाति किमत्र परिशिष्यते॥ एतद्वैतत्॥ — *Kaṭhopaniṣad,* II.1.3.
19. *Praśnopaniṣad,* I.1.4–5.
20. Ibid., II.2.1.
21. Ibid., II.2.4.
22. Ibid., III.3.5–6.

words, the *ātmā* manifests Itself in different forms of air (*vāyu*) and functions as the chief controller of body.

Answering to the query of Sukeśa Bhāradvāja about the *Ṣodaśakalāpuruṣa* (God with all sixteen components), Pippalāda explained that He (*Brahman*) realized the vital breath (*prāṇa*) as Its substitute and there were created reverence (*śraddhā*), sky (*khaṁ*), wind (*vāyu*), light (*jyoti*), water (*āp*), earth (*pṛthivī*), senses (*indriya*), mind (*mana*), food (*anna*), semen (*vīrya*), penance (*tapa*), hymns (*mantra*), deed (*karma*), worlds (*lokaḥ*) and name (*nāma*).[23]

Goddess Kālī who emerges in the Gupta period and probably first mentioned by Kālidāsa[24] is seen in her prototype in the *Muṇḍakopaniṣad* which actually desribes the flames of the Vedic fire looking darkish, terrific, swift, red smoke column, etc.[25] About the creation and its further progeny, this Upaniṣad maintains that the *prāṇa, mana,* all senses, wind, light, water, earth were born from *Brahman*.[26] The cosmic form of God has been visualized with fire being head, sun and moon as eyes, directions as ears, speech as Vedas, air as *prāṇa,* whole world as heart and the earth as feet.[27]

The *Aitareya Upaniṣad* informs, before the beginning of creation only *ātmā* (God) existed. He desired to create worlds and created first the upper worlds (*ambhaḥ*), then atmosphere (*maucī*), this world (*maram*), water (*āp*) and then the worlds below (*adhaḥ*).[28] He then desired to originate the guardian

---

23. Ibid., VI (स प्राणमसृजत् प्राणच्छ्रद्धां खं वायु).
24. *Kumārasambhavam,* IX.49.
25. काली कराली च मनोजवा च सुलोहिता या च सुधूम्रवर्णा।
    स्फुलिङ्गिनी विश्वरुची च देवी लेलायमाना इति सप्त जिव्हाः॥
    — *Muṇḍakopaniṣad,* I.2.4.
26. Ibid., II.1.3.
27. Ibid., II.1.4.
28. *Aitareyopaniṣad,* I.1.1–2

deities (*lokapālas*) and they emerged from water. The Man (Cosmic Person) also emerged from water[29] in the shape of "egg" from which different organs, senses and faculties emerged.

The *Taittirīyopaniṣad* presents almost the same view about God and His kindreds. Whether Vedas call it *asad* or *sad Brahman* always existed.[30] It desired to multiply and did *tapa* (acted) and created all this (world). Since the whole world is His creation, it is called *sukṛtam.*[31] For His fear wind moves, sun rises, fire, Indra and death run.[32] This scripture pronounces the importance of *annam* (food) as part of *Brahman* at several places and at one place, the *annam* itself has been called as *Brahman.*[33]

Thus the Upaniṣadic view is that God or *Brahman* or *ātmā* or *antaryāmī* is the Supreme and Ultimate and He is to be realized through His multiple forms. Many of these play vital roles in sustaining the world and are parts or His own kindreds. Some are seen and others are sto be experienced. God as per Upaniṣadic thought creates the basic elements which control the entire world and also the bodies of the living beings. But their energy is derived only from God.

---

29 Ibid., I.3.

30. *Taittirīyopaniṣad*, II.6.1.

31. तदात्मानं स्वयमकुरुत। तस्मात्तत्सुकृतमुच्यत इति। — Ibid., II.7.

32. भीष्माद्वातः पवते। भीषोदेति सूर्यः।
भीष्मादग्निश्चेन्द्रश्च। मृत्युर्धावति पञ्चम इति। — Ibid., II.8.

33. अन्नं ब्रह्मेति व्यजानात् III.2, अन्नं बहु कुर्वीत III.9, अहमन्नमहमन्नमहमन्नम्... III.10.

# 3

# God in Tibetan Thought

*H.H. Tenzin Gyatso*

TIBETANS divide the world according to the nature of the beings it contains and by this means there are six divisions:

***Gods*** — These include beings in the world of celestial forms and of formless spirits, and the six kinds of gods found in the sensual world.

***Demi-gods, or Titans*** — These are like gods in every respect except that they are mischievous.

***Human Beings***

***Yi-Dag, or Pretas***: Living spirits who are afflicted constantly with the miseries of hunger and thirst.

***Animals***

***Hells*** — There are different grades of hells, and the living beings in each of them are also of various nature, according to their past *karma*.

His Holiness Tenzin Gyatso, the 14th Dalai Lama of Tibet, has a number of principal identities. He is a Buddhist monk in the Order founded by Śākyamuni Buddha around 525 BCE and revitalized by Lama Tsong Khapa in CE 1400; hence, a spokesman for the ancient educational tradition of the Buddhists. He is a reincarnation of the Buddha Avalokiteśvara, the Mahāyāna Buddhist Archangel of Compassion, and especially the Savior of Tibetans, the king of Tibet. And, he is a Vajra

Master of the esoteric *Maṇḍala*s of the Unexcelled Yoga Tantras, especially of the *Kālacakra* (Wheel of Time); hence deeply and perhaps prophetically concerned with the positive evolution of all intelligent life in our sacred environment on this planet.

He was asked about "Wholeness" — The whole Man, the whole Person.

Q. Would you say that Buddha is Whole Man?

Ans. Yes — on the high level. Yes certainly. But when I speak of the good qualities of a human being, all that means our ordinary human being, on the human level. Buddha is already beyond the human level.

Q. If Buddha is beyond ordinary human nature, then some people might think of this as cold-hearted — some sort of superhuman, that does not care.

Ans. No, no, no, no. What we call Buddha as warm-hearted man developed infinitely, love perfected. And also infinite enlightened was — Oh yes.

Q. "Are human beings, as they are, in any way unfinished?"

Ans. In the spiritual sense.

Q. Yes, and in the evolutionary sense also, perhaps. Have they reached the fulfilment of their evolution, perfected their brain and heart and understanding or are they unfinished in that sense?

Ans. In that sense, I don't know. The human brain may develop or it may decrease. I am not at all sure.

Q. But isn't Buddha a being with a more developed brain?

Ans. But that's not natural evolution.

Q. Isn't it? It is not test-tube development!

Ans. I think, you see, without effort, that kind of evolution, we are speaking about I cannot take place. For example, first an animal goes on four legs, then on two legs, then it is easier to run around, yes? Now that is without effort, is'nt it?

Q. I don't think that it is without effort.

Ans. Not in the sense that, for example, those four-legged creatures need some effort to go on two legs — that kind of effort, yes. But I speak of evolution in the Buddhist sense: for example, in the primordial eon, beings do not depend on grosser food. Then they go down, and finally reach a ten-year life span. That period in the world, the human can reach. Then again another rise, and finally they reach the time of Maitreya's teaching. That we may call "evolution." And that without special effort.

Q. I see what you mean.

Ans. Simply as you see the seasons changing, there are cycles. We are still, you see, on the line of decline. . . .

Q. Unfortunately?

Ans. You can't say unfortunately. That is just the way it is.

Q. But, an individual who is reborn after an effort in his individual life — for example, one who creates the spirit of enlightenment, who conceives that higher mind — then he advances in evolution, even though he is in a world like this.

Ans. You see, the human level of mental development, of course, is not a finished one even in the ordinary sense, within our inner state, there are still many things to explore. This has nothing to do with religious ideology; this is spiritual. I think some part of the brain's capability may be fully utilized only through deep meditation. But meantime, there are certain things still to be explored in the ordinary way. So from that viewpoint, the human being is unfinished.

Q. Does Buddha have more brain, do you think, in His *uṣṇīṣa?*

Ans. It is not a question of that. The grosser consciousness depends heavily on particles of matter; so, it is the grosser level that has very much to do with the brain. The subtler consciousness is more independent. So, the innermost subtle consciousness does not depend so much on the brain. If it did, it could not exist without the brain; and you see, in the Buddha state, the grosser mind completely disappears. Luminance, radiance, imminence — the states of the subtle mind — all of these disappear in the clear light, the clear light of supreme innermost subtle consciousness.

Q. I understand your teaching to say that the Buddha nature is inherent in every person. There is also an expression, especially in Zen Buddhism, "effortless effort," which is often misunderstood to mean an inner passivity. What kind of active inner effort is necessary for the liberation of the whole person within?

Ans. This "effortless effort" is what is called the effortless striving. Right now, in the meditation of mental quiescence, in the nine states of mind, there is a state where striving must be abandoned; an effortless concentration is necessary at a certain stage. It is effortless; that means, your mind becomes very tranquil — with good qualities, with its character complete. At that moment, if you make effort, that disturbs the tranquillity. So, in order to maintain that pure tranquillity, the sort of effortless effort must be used. Of course, it is a kind of effort. You have to make at least a mental effort, "Now, I don't want to move effort." That means effort in order to have less disturbance of meditation.

Q. Is there a relationship with one's own suffering which is not usually understood?

Ans. In Christian teaching, suffering has some powerful meaning, doesn't it? for example, Jesus took the suffering himself. Now that, you see, was not in the ordinary sense, but something very meaningful. Now in Buddhist tradition, we have every right to avoid, to overcome suffering; but when the suffering actually happens, then, instead of being discouraged or mentally distressed, you simply utilize that occasion in such a way that it will minimize your mental disturbance, for a long run, you develop a certain kind of motivation, that will help you to gain more virtues.

Q. Your Holiness always say that suffering increases your inner strength.

Ans. That is right.

Q. But some people might think: well then, I should seek more suffering in order to become stronger.

Ans. This I don't mean.

Q. But voluntary suffering in a way, isn't that what it is. Don't *bodhisattvas* sometimes seek suffering on purpose?

Ans. O yes, they do. "I want to take on myself all the suffering of living beings." They directly enter into suffering that way. But in that case, you see, actually the suffering does not come.

Q. Ahh, Is that so? When they seek the suffering, they don't get any?

Ans. No, Never. The wishing for suffering makes the suffering disappear.

# 4

# God

*Uma Marina Vesci*

God is a difficult matter to be taken up as a discussable subject for many reasons. First because, God is the unreachable *par excellence,* but also because there are several ways to tackle the matter among which the ones concerning us here are the views of the scholars (from the *outside*) and those of the believers (from the *inside*). Both however are incomplete — the believers, because they take too much for granted and by connecting themselves directly with the object of their faith do not see some of the human origins in defining their "God" and in proposing their myths (visible to others from outside), while the scholars, though able to find the origins of the different religious constructions, are missing the inner involvement of the faithful followers and their inner emotions. Now, in this attempt here I shall try to balance the two points of view as far as possible.

Secondly, another difficulty arises from the fact that under the definition of what we are calling here God, many aspects of him/her/it come to the front. As the historians know, though the theologians refuse to acknowledge, the very idea of God has kept on changing along the ages, even inside the history of a single nation or of a single religion as such. And this goes on from the simplest feelings towards the surroundings of early habitats, to the highest sophisticated mystical experiences and philosophical definitions.

Since the position given to this subject matter in this sequence, Death, Life and its expansion through senses, suggests to look into God from his highest position, we shall turn to the concept directly, as worked out by the greater religions and spiritualities. Yet, the "reversal" order in descent direction appears to be harder than the ascending one. This vision of God is obviously held by those religions that, at a certain moment of their history, went through a big change brought about by the inspiration of some very high spiritual personalities. A few of them went even so far as to create new religions altogether — among the most important we can point out at the Jains, the Buddhists, the Zoroastrians, the Christians and the Muslims, while others simply inserted in their attitude toward the Divine a much higher spiritual value, like the Hindu sages, the Hebrew Prophets and the Greek philosophers. Except for the last two in the first list, which came rather late in history, all the others, including similar movements in China, took place from the seventh to the sixth century BCE. The aim of those reformers, or thinkers and spiritual mystics, was to open to human beings the possibility of meeting God face-to-face in a direct way, and not through rituals and priestly interventions. The end result of all this deep contribution of human Mind (at work through very special and gifted persons) has been a profound spiritualization of the very concept of God, actualized according to two different perspectives — the personal and the impersonal one. For some of such new spiritualities, in fact, God remained a Person but became totally transcendent, like the Yahveh of the Jews and the Ahura-Mazda of the Zoroastrians, and, in somehow a lower range the Zeus and Jupiter of the Greeks and Romans respectively. I say of a "lower range" because, though retaining their higher positions of chief or king of the other Gods, they were overpowered by an impersonal Entity called Ananke (Necessity) by the firsts and Fate by the seconds. For the others, God, or better the Godhead, became so high and out of reach that It lost even any perceivable form or even expression, and became a pure Spirit, or the Immobile First Mover at the origin of the Universe as such (Aristotle).

Among the Indians, beginning with a deeper immersion into the divine realm by some profound sages and thinkers, the concerned philosophy started following two main ways of representing God to themselves — the *sādhanā* and the *upāsanā*. For the followers of the first, the final aim is to nullify oneself in order to merge and disappear into the Absolute, even beyond the definition of God. From the point of view of the *upāsanā* (devotion), such a path is again split into two branches — the *nirguṇa* and the *saguṇa.* According to the first, God is absolute and without any form (*guṇa*) and therefore totally detached, and above everything; for the other He is with form and, as such, not only is in contact with the worlds, but he is their creator. As such He is reachable by his devotees and by people in general through prayers, rituals and reciprocal love, in the Supreme God, who lovely receives them into his bosom. In the *Bhagavad-Gītā,* Kṛṣṇa presents himself in both these features. In some places He declares himself to be *saguṇa,* being the Creator deeply involved with the form and matter He loves as such; but later in the text He rebukes as "fools" those who dare to call Him *saguṇa,* while He is *nirguṇa* at all effects (*Bhagavad-Gītā* where the actual words used are *vyakta* and *avyakta* respectively, which practically stand for the same meaning).

The *nirguṇa* way is obviously difficult, since it requires long strenuous exercises, submission of mind and body till reaching the total oblivion of oneself, therefore it is limited to a few well determined persons. The *saguṇa* way, on the contrary, is relatively easier, and therefore has a much larger quantity of followers. I said "relatively" because even here the obstacles and difficulties may be as strong for the one who is seriously involved on the way. Yet *saguṇa upāsanā,* if no longer seen only in its mystical engagement for the devotees, may also be roughly translated as common religion for the people, where the object of worship is not only the highest possible God, but also his many different and minor representatives. In polytheistic religions the members of the different pantheons are many, and cover a vast range of personalities even on hierarchical scale. Many gods and goddesses are related to various natural aspects, as Wind, Sacred Trees, Waters, Mountains, etc. or to some constellations or single star or planet; or even as patrons and teachers of various technical works, like agriculture (as introducers of wheat seed like Demeter in ancient Greece, for instance), or metallic extraction and fusion (like *Vulcanus* in Latin, *Ephestos* in Greece, *Twarst* in Vedic India, etc.) or as *Agni* in India who, as Fire in his cosmic as well as earthly aspects, taught men very useful technicalities about the use of normal fire (for cooking, warming, melting metals and similar ones), as well as infuses in them the awe and fear of fiery calamities both natural and man-produced.

From what has been said up to now, we can sum up this short enquiry about such a high and vast subject, by considering that it may be possible that the atheistic scholarly surmise that God is after all a product of human Mind, is not totally incorrect. As we have seen, the reaching of the idea of an Absolute Entity (either personal or impersonal; either in contact with the worlds as Creator, or totally transcended the earthly level) is but the mystical "discovery" or rendering of highly enhanced sages and philosophers, who rather experienced such an almighty power more than developed it as an idea. Common people, however were since the beginnings attracted by *saguṇa* deities, visible and representable in given forms as statues, paintings or even symbols (like a few coins for Lakṣmī, in Hinduism) so that they could even be sheltered in proper temples or shrines.

There are also other kinds of worshipped items whose attraction goes back to the prehistoric times like the mentioned Sacred Tree, Ponds, Rivers, Mountains, or, on another level, some personifications of technical devices and skills, like Viśvakarmā worshipped by the skilled workers and labourers all over India, by communist trade unions as well. As it can be seen, the most ancient forms of God are more persistent to these very days among all sorts of people.

# 5

# Radiance of God

*S.N. Tewari*

THE truth of the matter is: there is only the radiance of God in the world, and everyone is the image of God (Swami Shri Muktanandji). It is similar to the shadow of the tree.

So let us explore and reflect on how we can see the reflection of our ownself in God. (Ibid.)

With an open mind, we know that tiger delivers tiger, snake a snake, sheep a sheep and dog a dog and so on. Similarly why God can't do so of his own? That is why with selfless mercy (*ahaitukī kṛpā*) he has created human being in this beautiful universe.

सर्वो ममायं विभव इत्येवं परिजानतः विश्वात्मनो विकल्पानां प्रसरेऽपि महेशता ॥

*sarvo mamāyaṁ vibhava ityevaṁ parijānataḥ viśvātmano vikalpānāṁ prasare'pi maheśatā.*

(यह विश्व शिव की वाटिका है, सैर करने के लिए)

As is of his own, but with some object. The object is: let the human being know through his "birth" what relation he has with God as well as who is God?

One has to obtain some techniques for it. As such, this technique is entirely based on *guru*. Find and gratify the *guru*.

एवं गुरुपदं श्रेष्ठं देवानामपि दुर्लभम् ।
हाहाहूहूगणैश्चैव गन्धर्वैश्च प्रपूज्यते ॥25 ॥
ध्रुवं तेषां च सर्वेषां नास्ति तत्त्वं गुरोः परम् ।
आसनं शयनं वस्त्रं भूषणं वाहनादिकम् ॥26 ॥ ▷ गुरु-गीता

*evaṁ gurupadaṁ śreṣṭhaṁ devānāmapi durlabham* ।
*hāhāhūhūgaṇaiśraiva gandharvaiśca prapūjyate* ॥

*dhruvaṁ teṣāṁ ca sarveṣāṁ nāsti tattvaṁ guroḥ param* ।
*āsanaṁ śayanaṁ vastraṁ bhūṣaṇaṁ vāhanādikam* ॥

The human being is *jīvātmā*. Means *triguṇātmaka*. So *jīvātmā* is part of *paramātmā* in the form of *ātmā*. A man adorns his physical body with clothes and ornaments and gives it exercise to keep it healthy. Similarly, he must take care of his inner spiritual body and develop its beauty to that potency from where he can realize the similarity of God. "Develop" means cleanness of inner-self, as we are with clothes. But how can it be? That can be; through chanting of *mantra-japa*, *svādhyāya*, etc. the mind automatically becomes active and vigorous; the heart towards purity and peace. Anxieties vanish gradually. The *sādhaka* is absorbed in love and contentment inside. The image of God shines henceforth.

Inner radiance starts to reform the following:

1. *Buddhi* — It is a property of every normal human being. Though sometimes it lies in the form of *jaḍa*, *duṣṭa*, *ahitakara*, *buddhihīna*, *vācāla*, etc.

2. *Subuddhi* — After reformation of *buddhi*. Better than *buddhi*.

3. *Viveka* — Superb(uttama) । "संशय मिटा विवेक कराया । भवसागर से पार लंघाया । अमर प्रदीप जलाकर कर दी । निशा दूर इस तन की । भेदों बीच अभेद बताया । आवागमन विमुक्त कराया । धन्य हुए हम पाकर धारा । ब्रह्मज्ञान निर्झर की । (Grace of Guru)

4. *Ahaṁkāra* (Ego) — This brings the man totally on the

top as well as in the bottom.

खेत में बोये बीज कुछ उगते हैं कुछ नहीं। जो नहीं उगते हैं उनके ऊपर कंकड या पत्थर है। कोई दवाब है जिसके कारण नहीं उग पाते हैं। ऐसा ही अहंकार है।

5. *Citta* (Pin-point) — ऐसे ही जिसका चित्त किसी बोझ से दबा है, वह न तो उदास और न ही हँस सकता है और न तो ईमानदारी से रो सकता है। अतः यह पवित्र रखने हेतु है। ध्यान करके चित्त को स्थिर या स्वाध्याय से अपने आत्मबल को जगाया जा सकता है तब चित्त बाहर- भीतर के विकारों से प्रभावित नहीं होगा। चित्त-पूजन होना चाहिए। यह महानतम् सम्पत्ति है। साधारण मत समझें। चित्त से कर्मफल प्राप्त होता है।

6. आत्म-दर्शन — साधक की उसकी योग्यता और रुचि के आधार पर शक्ति (चित्ति) उसकी उससे साधना कराती है। प्रेम-भक्ति से रस आता है, लेकिन प्रेम में ज्ञान नहीं हो तो काम विकार आने का भय रहता है और ज्ञान में प्रेम नहीं होगा तो ज्ञान शुष्क रह जायेगा। ज्ञान और प्रेम के साथ योग नहीं होगा तो सामर्थ्य नहीं आयेगा। ज्ञान और प्रेम हो साथ में ध्यान योग हो तो साधक का सर्वांगीण विकास होने लगता है, और आत्म-दर्शन की ओर अग्रसर हो जाता है।

— गुरु-गीता-115

कुण्डलिनी योग की साधना भीतर से प्रेम जगाती है, योग भी स्वतः करवाती है। और साधक को सद्‌गुरु तत्त्व के ज्ञान की तरफ ले जाती है, क्योंकि साधना करने से मति/बुद्धि सूक्ष्म होती है और सूक्ष्म मति, ज्ञान को शीघ्र ही अपना लेती है। इस तरह प्रत्येक जीवात्मा में अद्‌भुत सामर्थ्य छिपा हुआ है। कहने का तात्पर्य है कि "Faith earns Faith." जैसे ही ईश्वर को जीवात्मा का विश्वास लगने लगता है वैसे ही ईश्वर उस विश्वास के प्रति अपना विश्वास जगा देता है। इसीलिए —

This can be exemplified by a professional physician/surgeon — "I treat, He cures." A fracture patient requires immobilization through plaster. Rest of calcification of bone is left to the mercy of God. God is kind enough to heal the fracture and the patient comes back to his previous normal condition. This is "faith earns faith," meaning a relationship with God. That is the potentiality of an individual which was explored only by faith in human being that he is similar to God.

जीवात्मा, शरीर सम्बन्ध न देखने पर भी, माँ के कहने पर ही विश्वास कर लेती है कि अमुक पुरुष मेरा पिता है, क्योंकि माँ कहती है, परन्तु जानते हुए भी हम जिसकी संतान हैं उस पर विश्वास नहीं कर पाते हैं कि हमारा भी उसी तरह उनसे सम्बन्ध है। ग्रन्थों के कहने के पश्चात् भी। धिक्कार है। हमसे तो अच्छा है माँ के कहने पर जीवात्मा का अन्धविश्वास कर लेना। That is why we are not aware of His Kindred.

शोषणं पापपङ्कस्य दीपनं ज्ञानतेजसाम्।
गुरुपादोदकं सम्यक् संसारार्णवतारकम्॥१३॥

अज्ञानमूलहरणं जन्मकर्मनिवारणम्।
ज्ञानवैराग्यसिद्ध्यर्थं गुरुपादोदकं पिबेत्॥ १४ ॥ — गुरु-गीता

*śoṣaṇaṁ pāpapaṅkasya dīpanaṁ jñānatejasām* ।
*gurupādodakaṁ samyak saṁsārārṇavatārkam* ॥

*ajñānamūlaharaṇaṁ janmakarmanivāraṇam* ।
*jñānavairāgyasiddhayartha gurupādodakaṁ pibet* ॥

To destroy ignorance, the cause of rebirth and to dry up the mire of one's sin and to ignite the light of knowledge by which one can cross the ocean of the world, one has to seek a *guru* and sip the water of His feet (*caraṇāmṛta*).

काशीक्षेत्रं तन्निवासो जाह्नवी चरणोदकम्।
गुरुर्विश्वेश्वरः साक्षात् तारकं ब्रह्म निश्चितम्॥16॥ — गुरु-गीता

*Kāśīkṣetraṁ tannivāso Jahnavī caraṇodakam* ।
*gururvīśveśvaraḥ sākṣāt tārakaṁ brahma niścitam* ॥

His dwelling is the sacred Kāśī. *Caraṇāmṛta* is river Gaṅgā. The *guru* himself is Kāśī Viśvanātha Bhagavān, granting *mokṣa* (salvation).

The syllable *gu* is darkness and syllable *ru* is said to be light. Ignorance of darkness is swallowed by the light — (*Guru-Gīta* 23)

गुरुर्ब्रह्मा गुरुर्विष्णु गुरुर्देवो महेश्वरः ।
गुरुरेव परब्रह्म तस्मै श्रीगुरवे नमः ॥32 ॥

त्वं पिता त्वं च मे माता त्वं बंधुस्त्वं च देवता ।
संसारप्रतिबोधार्थं तस्मै श्रीगुरवे नमः ॥35 ॥ — गुरु-गीता

*gururbrahmā gururviṣṇu gururdevo maheśvaraḥ* ।
*gurureva parabrahma tasmai śrīgurave namaḥ* ॥

*tvaṁ pitā tvaṁ ca me mātā tvaṁ bandhustvaṁ ca devatā* ।
*saṁsāra pratibodhārtha tasmai śrī gurave namaḥ* ॥

Is it not His kindred? Yes, Yes, Yes.

Śrī Guru is Śiva without three eyes. He is Viṣṇu without four arms. He is Brahmā without four faces. Is it not His classical kindred?

It means merely one has to practise regularly by obtaining *guru-kṛpā* by which he becomes capable enough as an aspirant for self realization. This is a must to know the Kindred of God.

गुरुर्बुद्धयात्मनो नान्यत् सत्यं सत्यं न संशयः ।
तल्लाभार्थं प्रयत्नस्तु कर्तव्यो हि मनीषिभिः ॥9 ॥

*gururbuddhayātmano nānyat satyaṁ satyaṁ na saṁśayaḥ* ।
*tallābhārtha prayatnastu kartavyo hi manīṣibhiḥ* ॥

Every wise man must try to obtain *guru.*

गूढविद्या जगन्माया देहे चाज्ञानसंभवा ।
उदयः यत्प्रकाशेन गुरुशब्देन कथ्यते ॥10 ॥ — गुरु-गीता

*gūḍhavidyā jaganmāyā dehe cājñānasaṁbhava* ।
*udayaḥ yatprakāśena guruśabdena kathyate* ॥

He by whose light true knowledge arises is known by the word *guru.*

Ignorance resides in the body and vanishes after *śaktipatha.*

It is very difficult to obtain this true knowledge even in three worlds. *Brahman* is nothing other than *guru*. This is the absolute truth.

दुर्लभं त्रिषु लोकेषु तच्छृणुष्व वदाम्यहम् ।
गुरुं विना ब्रह्म नान्यत् सत्यं सत्यं वरानने ॥15 ॥ — गुरु-गीता

*durlabhaṁ triṣu lokeṣu tacchṛṇuṣva vadāmyaham* ।
*guruṁ vinā brahma nānyat satyaṁ satyaṁ varānane* ॥

That is why to sing the glory of the *guru*'s name is to sing the glory of God Śiva (*Guru-Gītā*, 54).

No sooner self-realization is attained, the very moment the soul is united with God and proclaims "*ahaṁ brahmāsmi*" ।
Then only:

ॐ पूर्णमदः पूर्णमिदं पूर्णात् पूर्णमुदच्यते ।
पूर्णस्य पूर्णमादाय पूर्णमेवावशिष्यते ॥

*oṁ pūrṇamadaḥ pūrṇamidaṁ pūrṇāt pūrṇamudacyate* ।
*pūrṇasya pūrṇāmādāya pūrṇamevāvaśiṣyate* ॥

As such, one should infuse himself with divine power (*citi śakti*). That can be done by the grace of *guru* only (*śaktipatha*) and through meditation.

इस प्रकार पुण्यात्मा स्वयं ही महान् बनती है और दूसरों को भी महान् बनाती है ।

(Be great and make others even greater)

अङ्गुष्ठमात्रपुरुषं ध्यायतश्चिन्मयं हृदि ।
तत्र स्फुरति भावो यः शृणु तं कथयाभ्यहम् ॥115 ॥ — गुरु-गीता

*aṅguṣṭhamātrapuruṣaṁ dhyāyataścinmayaṁ hṛdi* ।
*tatra sphurati bhāvo yaḥ śṛṇu taṁ kathayābhyaham* ॥

Meditate on the thumb-sized person in the heart, who is consciousness.

स्वयं तथाविधो भूत्वा स्थातव्यं यत्रकुत्रचित् ।
कीटभ्रमरवत्तत्र ध्यानं भवति तादृशम् ॥118 ॥ —गुरु-गीता

*svayaṁ tathāvidho bhūtvā sthātavyaṁ yatrakutracit* ।
*kīṭabhramaravattatra dhyānaṁ bhavati tādṛśam* ॥

After being aware that he himself is like *Brahman* one may live anywhere. *"ahaṁ brahmāsmi,"* Now no kindred is required.

समुद्रे च यथा तोयं क्षीरे क्षीरं घृते घृतम् ।
भिन्ने कुम्भे यथाकाशस्तथात्मा परमात्मनि ॥162 ॥ — गुरु-गीता

*samudre ca yathā torya kṣīre kṣīraṁ ghṛte ghṛtam* ।
*bhinne kumbhe yathākāśastathātmā paramātmani* ॥

Water merges in the ocean, milk in milk, ghee in ghee and when a pot is broken the individual soul merges in the universal soul (God — Supreme Being). एक बूँद सागर में मिल गई, जिन्होंने मन मार लिया।

In this way the realized soul is merged in the highest soul. Both worldly enjoyment and liberations come to him. Goddess Sarasvatī dwells on the tip of the tongue (*Guru-Gītā*-165).

His kindness dispels sufferings, promotes health, wealth and increases knowledge, strength and fame and leads one to the realization of self. What more?

# 6

# Supreme God and its Lesser Denominations

*K.N. Sahay*

THE topic of this chapter is so comprehensive, full of mysticism, and unending that we can't explain many things. Many people may write volumes so easily — without final conclusions. God is so myriad and elusive that it can't stick within a purview of rules. So, apart from quoting some scholars, religionists and mystics, we would concentrate on those areas within which directly or indirectly and in our day-to-day life, we come across the "reflections" and "indications" of the God working through various activities. In fact, there are a few problems — faith, vanity, fickleness, ordeals and controversies — all relating to God. Initially, the divinity was "abstract" — formless, i.e. *niḥakṣara Brahman,* omnipotent and omnipresent. Later, It willed to look after the next denomination of the Power–Creator who was *Akṣara Brahman,* and it gradually started creating going down to the lesser denominations and corresponding facets — "positive" to "negative," "abstract" to "gross." Eventually, it went on multiplying into diverse types of things and ideas, from which emerged a large range of models under multiple circumstances — logics and counter–logics — with which many people are likely to get confused. In fact, there are "muddles of models" in this regard. Hence we don't mainly concentrate on the philosophical or metaphysical paradigms, but on those which are based on my spiritual interactions and experiences. It may be a personal approach with applied implications, but I am sure, a number of others who are enquirers, disturbed or need tips, may consider them to be relevant.

**What is God?**

God is a Superhuman Being or Spirit, being worshipped over nature, different walks of life, and human fortunes. It may have an image, anthropomorphic animals or other objects believed as divine, or symbolized as a god or deity. In Christianity and other monotheistic religions God is "the creator and ruler of the universe; the Supreme Being" (R.E. Allen's *The Concise Oxford Dictionary of Current English*, Oxford University Press, Bombay, 1990, p. 506).

In Hindi, *bhagavān* (भगवान्) has the adjective like being glorious, divine, to be adorned; worshipful, the Supreme Being and especially equated with Viṣṇu-Kṛṣṇa. It is the title of venerated deity (R.S. McGregor, *The Oxford Hindi-English Dictionary*, Oxford Press, Delhi, 1997, p. 756). There is another Hindi connotation of God, i.e. *Īśvara* (ईश्वर) who is the "lord, master, ruler, king" and has supremacy, divine and almighty power (ibid., p. 110).

The "Supreme God" is the "Supreme Soul," i.e. *paramātmā* and is also variously known as "Supreme Being," "Supreme Consciousness," "Universal Consciousness," "Infinite Spirit" and the like. In many different societies, the Supreme power has lesser denominations and is known with different norms. The original title was given as "God and its kindred." The present author suggested a scientific term like "Unexplored Supreme Factor" (USF).

Mystics tell that three fourth of the cosmic space (*tri-pād*) is *amṛta* (nectar) — full of "pure consciousness" and serves as the foundation of creation. It is associated with *Niḥakṣara Brahman* (Supreme Being without attribute), differently known as *skambha* or *parama puruṣa*. One-fourth of the cosmic space (*eka-pāda*) has *Akṣara Brahman* under *Akṣara maṇḍala*. It has "primordial nature" which symbolizes *māyā* (illusory power) or *paramāṇus* (atoms). The spontaneous will (*ekṣan*) of *Niḥakṣara Brahman*, produces *Akṣara Brahman* who creates and conducts (*calāvanahāra*) the universe under the *eka-pāda* of the space.

*Prakṛti* is in the "even state" of *sattva, tamas* and *rajas*. But as soon as tremor starts in the *paramāṇus* with the *Akṣara Brahman*, the creation starts. The five Brāhmanic and ten *anahad* sounds, three lights (*jyoti*), eight spiritual centres in the body (*aṣṭa cakra*), seven *prāṇas* (vital breaths), *iḍā, piṅgalā, suṣumnā* nerves, and all the visible phenomena of the *piṇḍa* and *brahmāṇḍa* come under *prakṛti*. Just as pots are made out of clay and ornaments out of gold, similarly, the whole universe is created out of the distortions (*vikṛti*) of the *prakṛti* (permutation and combination of its three components mentioned above in different proportions). So long as there is motion in the *paramāṇu* the creation works but as soon as it stops the creation gets annihilated (*pralaya*). Creation and annihilation both are the characteristics of the *prakṛti* (Maharshi Sadafal Dev, 1978; Sahay, 1999: 226-27).

It may be noted that the concept of God and deities varied in importance in Pre-Vedic, Post-Vedic or some other historical periods: Paśupati, Lord Indra and natural deities may be mentioned. Some geographical areas may also vary in importance. There is still another important point that people coming from a particular religious group, associate with other religions, particularly religious personalities, saints, shrines, or marginal norms connected with Sāī Bābā, Niẓāmuddin Auliā, Moinuddin Chisti of Ajmer, Our Lady of Bandra at Mumbai, Our Lady of Health at Vailankanni in south India and a number of others.

The Unmanifest Supreme God generates positive feelings and vibrations, and the people who have the proper wavelength, catch it accordingly through conscience just like "radio signals." Incidentally, *yoga-sādhanā* and electronic gadgets like computer have marked similarity — some people scientifically even call the God as "Super (*parama*) Computer." The God has His own reflections. *Gītā* in chapter 10, *śloka* 41 tells —

> यद्यद्विभूतिमत्सत्त्वं श्रीमदूर्जितमेव वा ।
> तत्तदेवावगच्छ त्वं मम तेजोंऽशसम्भवम् ॥
>
> *yadyadvibhūtimatsattvaṁ śrīmadurjitameva vā* ।
> *tattadevāvagccha tvaṁ mama tejoṁ 'śasambhavam* ॥
>
> Whatever is glorious, good, beautiful, and mighty, understand thou that to go forth a fragment of My Splendour.

Still there are some people who do not believe in "God" as such, but concentrate on "hard work" which is "worship," force and inspirations coming from the Unmanifest Supreme factor itself. "Gītā teaches *karma-yoga*." One has to "work through *yoga* (concentration). In such concentration in action (*karma-yoga*), there is no consciousness of the lower ego present. The consciousness that I am doing this and that is never present when one works through *yoga*" (Vivekananda, 1970: 81). *Gītā* in chapter II, *śloka* 47 tells —

> कर्मण्येवाधिकारस्ते मा फलेषु कदाचन ।
> मा कर्मफलहेतुर्भूर्मा ते सङ्गोऽस्त्वकर्मणि ॥
>
> *karmaṇyevādhikāraste mā phaleṣu kadācana* ।
> *mā karmaphalaheturbhūrmā te saṅgo 'stvakarmaṇi* ॥
>
> Thy business is with the action only, never with its fruits; so let not the fruit of action be thy motive, nor be thou to inaction attached.

The Christians believe in the name of *the Father* and of *the Son*, and of *the Holy Spirit* — who are three different dimensions of the same God. During the Mass with a congregation, the celebrant speaks — "The grace of our Lord Jesus Christ and the love of God and the fellowship of the Holy Spirit be with you all."

It won't be out of place to mention a few relevant stanzas of Bible —

> In the beginning was the Word, and the Word was with God, and the Word was God. — St. John/1 : 1

> In the beginning God created the heaven and the earth. And the earth was without form, and void; and darkness *was* upon the face of the deep. And the Spirit of God moved upon the face of the waters. And God said, let there be light: and there was light. — Genesis/1-3

The Muslims call God as Allāh who is the "unmanifest Supreme Being" and he has many other similar attributes. The Ahmadia Movement (N.D., 49-51) talks about 103 attributes of God. It tells — these attributes "are either expressly mentioned in the Quran or are deducible from Quranic verses. A consideration of these attributes helps to visualize the plan of the spiritual universe, which the Quran puts forward that God created the universe, and for the development and enlightenment of the human soul, God has revealed the 'Law of *Shari'at*' (sacred law)" (ibid., 1).

Hindus have one thousand adjectives or attributes, and the implications of God as given in a scripture (*Viṣṇu Sahasranāma*).

### God and Mystic Writings are Secret

The God or *parama sattā* is enigma and the Veda tells that it is unable to explain Him. One cannot conceive or formulate the God, and *ṛṣis* tell the last word — *neti, neti* (unending).

There are a number of writings of Hindu saints, references of Vedas, Upaniṣads, *Gītā*, *Rāmāyaṇa* and other sacred scriptures like Quran, Bible or others, which refer to mysticism.

> Mysticism involves a *sacred* and *secret* meaning hidden from the eyes of the ordinary person, and is only revealed to a spiritually enlightened mind. It also seeks or attains direct intercourse or communion with *God* which elevates religious feeling to ecstasy. — Kirkpetrick, 1983 : 838

Kabīr tells that "the goal of a mystic is really inexpressible in human language. It is beyond both the finite and infinite":

> हद्द चलई सो माणवा । वेहद चलई सो साध ।
> हद्द वेहद्द दोउ तजइ ताकइ मता अगाध ॥

> *hadda calaī so māṇavā, vehada calaī so sādha* ।
> *hadda vehadda dou tajai tākai matā agādha* ॥

The mystics like Maharshi Sadafal Dev (1978) as referred earlier, say, there are two eternal entities in the Universe — (1) *Niḥakṣara Brahman*, and (2) *Akṣara Brahman*. Incidentally, there are four other eternal entities — (3) *jīva* (living being — creature or individual soul), (4) *sadguru* or *choṇavanahāra* (who relieves a soul from the bondage of life and death), (5) *prakṛti*, and (6) *kāla* (time). The first four entities are in purely conscious form and animate, the fifth is inanimate, while the sixth is neither of the two categories (1.i.8).

Divine writings or verses are generally concealed and secret — have underlying meanings. Scholars, religionists and mystics interpret the texts differently, but the mystics always interpret it more properly. "Sacred," "secret" and "mysticism" always go together.

In Urdu language, poems — *śāyarī*, *g͟hazala*, and *kawwālī* have mostly double meanings — secular or romantic, and spiritual. The main purpose is to communicate with the readers, listeners and appropriate persons. It needs wavelength.

Goswāmī Tulsīdās refers in one of the relevant stanzas —

उलटा नाम जपत जग जाना, वाल्मीकि भए ब्रह्म समाना ।

*ulatā nāma japata jaga jānā, vālmīki bhae brahma samānā* ।

The sage Vālmīki recited the reverse *nāma*, name of God — at the moment "Rāma" — and became united with the *Brahman*.

The usual meaning is that, the sage Vālmīki while reciting the reverse name of *Rāma*, i.e. *marā* (मरा), became united with *Brahman*. But the real meaning is that the *surati* (consciousness) of the commoners usually go down to the worldly things. If they could reverse and ascend vertically to the higher spiritual dimension of God, will become united with the *Brahman*.

*Atharvaveda* (9.9.20) refers to a relevant *śloka* —

द्वा सुपर्णा सयुजा सखाया समानं वृक्षं परिषस्व जाते ।
तयोरन्यः पिप्पलं स्वाद्वत्यन श्नन्नन्यो अभिजाक शीति ॥

*dvā suparṇā sayujā sakhāyā samānaṁ vṛkṣaṁ pariṣasva jāte* ।
*tayoranyaḥ pippalaṁ svādvatyana śnannanyo abhijāka śīti* ॥

There are two birds that are friends and are perching on the same tree. One of them eats the fruit while the other does not eat the fruit, but just looks at it.

But the underlying meaning of the *śloka* is that the *ātmā* (soul) and the *paramātmā* (Supreme soul) both are present within the human body. The *jīva* (soul) enjoys the *karma* (deeds), while the *paramātmā* is indifferent, detached, and witnesses it.

Kabīr tells —

जल में कुंभ कुंभ में जल सहै, बाहर भीतर पानी ।
फूटा कुंभ जल जलहिं समाना, यह तत कहेहुं गियानी ॥

*jala meṅ kuṁbha kuṁbha meṅ jala hai, bāhara bhītara pānī* ।
*phūṭā kuṁbha jala jalahiṅ samānā, yaha tata kahehuṅ giyānī* ॥

There is water-pot containing water and the pot is again within water. As soon as the pot is broken, the water becomes all the same. The seeker must think of the implications and ponder over it.

The *santas* who are connected with *sādhanā* (spiritual practice) and *yoga* talk of a number of things and experiences which are highly mystic. Kabīr tells —

बिन चंदा उजियारी दरसै, जंह-तंह हंसा नजर परै।
दसवें द्वारे तारी लागी, अलख पुरुष जाको ध्यान धरैं॥

*bina candā ujiyārī darasai, jahaṁ tahaṁ haṁsā najara parai* ।
*dasaveṁ dvāre tārī lāgī, alakha puruṣa jāko dhyāna dharain* ॥

Some of the couplets of Kabīr are *ulaṭabāsī*s (incoherent verses). They are as follows —

कबीर दास की उलटी बानी, बरसे कम्बल भीगे पानी।
*kabīra dāsa kī ulaṭī bānī, barase kambal bhīge pānī* ।

The first verse of *R̥gveda* (1.1.1) tells —

अग्नि मीळे पुरोहितं यज्ञस्य देवमृत्विजम्। होतारं रत्नधातमम्॥
*agni miḷe purohitaṁ yajñasya devamr̥tvijam,*
*hotāraṁ ratnadhātamam* ॥

The simple meaning is —

"मैं अग्नि की उपासना करता हूँ। यह प्रकाशमान देवता, पुरोहित और ऋत्विक है। वह सबका स्वामी है।" यह अग्नि की बड़ी महिमा है।

(I worship fire that is the deity and is effulgent. There is a priest and assisting materials, which are shining and helpful. The priest officiates it and he is the lord.)

The mystic connected with *brahmavidyā* like Maharshi Sadaful Dev (1951) interprets it differently —

मैं (यज्ञस्य) ज्ञानयज्ञ के (देवम्) प्रकाशक परमदेव (अग्नि) शब्द प्रकाश स्वरूप परब्रह्म को तथा (रत्न धातमम्) ज्ञान रत्न को धारण करने वाले नित्य अनादि सद्गुरु को एवं (पुरोहितं) ज्ञानयज्ञ को कराने वाले पुरोहित चाहने वाले सद्गुरु को एवं (ऋत्विजं) सर्व पदार्थों को प्रकाशित करने वाली ब्रह्मविद्या को और (होतारं) ज्ञानयज्ञ करने वाला आत्मा (मीळे) को नमस्कार, स्तुति करता हूँ।

The summary tells that the supreme deity — fire who is

> shining and contains the sacred wisdom of the *sadguru* who communicates illuminating *brahmavidyā* to the souls. They are being greeted and eulogized.

Coming to the early Christianity (King James Version, 1816) it had an esoteric character something akin to the mysteries of Eleusis. Its origin spoke of secret doctrines, which were taught and also initiated. Christianity seems to have developed the spiritual techniques of "link-up" with the highest Supreme Being as reflected in several passages of the Bible, specially the book of Revelation (Apocalypse). However, the common Christians hardly interpret it properly and it is similar to Indian mysticism. The term "spirit" is frequently used in the Bible to describe the character of the man who has "entered the kingdom of God and has the "Holy Spirit" as the vital determining principle of his life." Some of them may be referred as below —

> The light of the body is the eye: if therefore thine eye be single, thy whole body shall be full of light. — Mathew: 6.22
>
> That which is born of the flesh is flesh; and that which is born of the Spirit is spirit. — St. John: 3.6
>
> Behold, I stand at the door, and knock: if any man hear my voice, and open the door, I will come into him, and will sup with him, and he with me. — Revelation: 3.20
>
> And they shall see his face; and his name *shall be* in their foreheads. And there shall be no night there; and they need no candle, neither light of the sun; for the Lord God giveth them light; and they shall reign for ever.
>
> — Revelation, 22 : 4-5

## Communication with God

When one has belief in God, the religious practice leads to communicate with Him like repetition in a low tone of an incantation of the name of the deity, counting silently the beads of a rosary, muttered prayer, meditation on the name of a deity, different types of worship, or the performance of religious observances.

The *ṛṣis*, saints and sages were the pioneers of the method of the glory of the *Gāyatrī mantra.*

> This method produces not only spiritual progress of the soul, but also physical, mental, social and emotional progress of an individual as well. . . . This *mantra* is very powerful. It transforms any individual who repeats it with faith into a person of purity, strength, vitality and wisdom. In fact, it helps a man to become a *Brahman* in the real sense. It is only a person who attains *brahma-jñāna* or knowledge of God or *Brahman* who can be called a real *Brahman* . . . *Gāyatrī mantra* invokes Universal Divine Mother Gāyatrī Devī.
>
> — Nambiar, 1983: 1-3.

The Mother Gāyatrī is also known as Aditi Devī in the Vedas. *Symbolically,* Gāyatrī Devī is "five-faced and seated on a lotus flower." It is the Universal Divine Mother, who has complete control over nature, which includes the five elements — earth or solid, water or liquid, fire or light or gas, air or oxygen and ether or atomic and subatomic matter. People accept this Mother as God and worship Nature, its powers and wonders (ibid.: 3).

The root of the lotus plant is in mud. It implies that the life begins in ignorance or inertia, i.e. *tamas.* When the stem of the lotus comes up over the water, it indicates, *rajas,* which is full of activities. Once it goes above the surface of water, it becomes beautiful and lovable, it indicates *sattva* or purity. All living beings exist in this universe under the influence of these three *guṇa*s or qualities.

The *mantra* and the meaning

> Introduces one to knowledge of God or *brahma-jñāna* so as to become a real brāhmaṇa. Here a person sees God as Mother as well as Father in one glorious form. This is called *ekam sat vipra bahudhā vadanti,* truth is only one, men of wisdom explain it differently.
>
> — *Ṛgveda*

The *Gāyatrī mantra* beholds the form of Divine Mother Gāyatrī at *tripuṭī* — the space between two eyebrows. — Ibid.: 4-5

The *Gāyatrī mantra* is followed as below :–

*oṁ bhūr bhuvaḥ svaḥ, tat savitur vareṇyam* ।
*bhargo devasya dhīmahi dhiyo yo naḥ pracodayāt* ॥

In repeating this *mantra,* God is praised by uttering His first nine names. It is the worship of the God. The meaning of the *mantra* follows —

> Let us meditate on God and His glorious attributes, which is the basis of everything in this universe as its creator, who is fit to be worshipped as omnipresent, omnipotent, omniscient and self-existent conscious being, who removes all ignorance and impurities from the mind and purifies and sharpens our intellect. May God enlighten our intellect.
> — Ibid.: 1-9

**Deifying a God in Temple**

Initially, God had no form. But in course of time people installed images of the deities, or some ancient images (*Śivaliṅga*s) — which appeared on their own, and which were believed to be manifestations of God by devotees. It starts a convention; the images go on reinforcing religious surroundings, and automatically become a tradition. It cannot alter norms, beliefs get cumulated, infused and become functional. Repeated prayers — rituals, beliefs and consecration of a symbol become a reality. With that mindset, as the ether is charged with supernatural powers or forces from different sources, "specific power" as conceived or inspired by the mortals get automatically infused within the symbol. In turn, the powers respond reciprocally on mental and spiritual levels, through dreams, miracles, supernatural happenings or the like.

Besides established temples, there are temporary religious *paṇḍāla*s, of *Durgā-Pūjā, Sarasvatī Pūjā, Kālī Mā Pūjā* and the like. The images, brought from their makers or modellers, are consecrated and worshipped through a series of rituals, followed by *mantra-pāṭha* and festivity. The images are made as per the traditional specifications, get-ups and decorations. During the occasions of *pūjā*, clay modellers make the images on a mass scale quite in advance. If you look at the clay images and the props, which are still in the making process and incomplete, it looks somewhat philosophically like the process of creation — abstract (idea) to materialization. It comes to the mind that the images are without a "gender." After the completed images are brought to a *paṇḍāla*, they are duly consecrated with religious piety, are revered, and with prostrations to the deity, offerings, prayers and rituals officiated by the priest are worshipped by devotees, followed by music of sorts and excitement for a number of days. But on the last day pervades "a sense of melancholy" as the images are ritually seen off and taken for immersion in rivers or ponds — even though slogans of the presiding deity and some sort of music still continue for some time. When the image is thrown in the water, some persons "trample" over "it" to submerge it quickly — "it" here means the deity which was earlier considered to be highly sacred and revered.

The sacred images "without gender," and trampling during immersion, symbolize that the manifestation of the deity is not the real form — they are just an imagination and tradition. These things look very dramatic. The reality is "ephemeral," a "supernatural force," "unmanifest" (*nirākāra*), and people impute it in the form of an image (*sākāra*). It is relative and we should not make value judgement, or argue on it.

Apart from the traditional context, there are cases in which a person, for whom somebody or a group of people have deep respect is followed by offering of incense before a photograph of the person, becomes deified. Here we may refer to George Simmel (J. Yinger, 1970, *The Scientific Study of Religion*) who tells that religion "comes out of the non-religious things." It is the heightening and abstracting from the particular content of certain human relations like exaltation, devotion and fervency. It is the highest development of faith, which becomes corporate.

Several years ago a family had fans of the erstwhile actress, Meena Kumari and they worshipped her as a "Goddess." The "Goddess Meena Kumari" reciprocally responded through dreams, and whenever the family had any problem, helped to guide them and give prosperity. Similarly, it has been told that the citizens of Kolkata, who were great fans of Amitabh Bachchan, built a "temple" in his name. Rajnikant and Khushboo (actress), who also are very popular in south India, were said to have such temples of their names. At the moment I don't have the details, but the way such temples have been built, it might follow the rituals and beliefs — may be for restricted people only.

## God Loves Man

On the worldly parlance there are three aspects of "time" (*kāla*) — "present," "past" and "future" — and the business of life works accordingly. But on a mystic level, one goes "vertically" on the subtle level and the three aspects of tisme get mixed up and united. It goes beyond the usual concept of time and works transcendentally. The commoners don't have this awareness. They get lost in the maze of logic, which has serious limitations. One has to go into the higher dimension to appreciate truth. We may refer to an example.

Under the scorching heat of sun, on a hot summer noon, when earth was burning like a frying pan and one couldn't dare to walk a short distance, a man stood for some time under the shade of a tree waiting for a rickshaw but finding none, got distressed. He prayed to God to send a conveyance, so that he could safely go back home. Within about fifteen minutes of saying the prayer, a rickshaw appeared in sight.

He heaved a sigh of relief, and thanked God for responding to his prayer. It is not an exceptional situation. Such things happen frequently with a man, who believes in the glory of the all-pervading Lord, but hardly strains to know how it happens.

It is significant to analyse the event a bit rationally, and appreciate the implications. When the man prayed for conveyance, it *did appear* on the scene within minutes (present). But it didn't mean that the rikshaw materialized all of a sudden — "out of nothing." The rikshawala must have left on a particular route nearly two hours ago (past) picking up and dropping a few passengers on the way, and finally approaching nearer to the man. When the last passenger was dropped, the "Providence" put the vacant rickshaw in the man's sight by "responding to the prayer." Is it not that the Lord knew the prayer just in advance, "inspired" the man to pray (past) as per His divine will, so that the devotees need for help could be met accordingly?

The God plans transcendentally that the person could "confirm his faith" that "the Lord exists and accedes to his request." A devotee may get tips that are likely to transform his life (future). Those people, who are non-sensitive, miss the "indications" and grope in the dark.

There is another situation in which God loves man. A devout person went to Badrīnātha and Kedāranātha in the Himalayas on pilgrimage. When he reached Rishikesh, it was known that there was landslide on the route, and the journey was delayed for three-four days. The enthusiasm was dampened and he wanted to go back, but there was "some force" which didn't allow it. In this state of mind, a problem haunted him. He was alone and there were all types of strangers. He worried as to how to secure his valuable things, when he goes for bathing, etc. Incidentally, he saw a yellow robed mendicant who also was alone, handicapped and searching for a suitable companion. One of his legs was amputated and he used a "wooden leg." It was "God's appropriate answer to the question" which perturbed him for some time — and the two worked as the ideal company for each other till they came back from the Himalayas.

Old people and religionists suggest that one should always recite the God's name to enhance "spiritual merits" (*puṇya*). People do it, or not depending upon the mood. But there is still another situation. When God loves a person the "sacred name" automatically appears in his mind like *anāhat nāda* (unstruck sound), and continues for hours together without interfering in the usual chore of life. It is a "special grace of God."

**The God and its Denominations**

Theology has different categories of religion and belief system like Supreme Being without attribute (*Niḥakṣara Brahman*), Supreme Being with attribute (*Akṣara Brahman*), Monotheism, Monolatory, Polytheism, Animism, and worship of demons, ghosts or spirits. However, each of the categories may not be exclusive or strictly in evolutionary sequence. In a particular culture, monotheism may go side by side with animism, or animism may have a high God. Among the tribes of Chhotanagpur, people in spite of their belief in gods, deities, spirits and magic, believe in Sing-bonga, Bedo Gosāin and Dharmeśa — the pervading Supreme Being and also symbolized as "Sun" (Prasad, 1961: 283).

The God and its various lesser denominations are ten, which cover the basic categories from top to the lowest, though some overlapping may not be ruled out depending on the perception and the background. It is also because when we talk about supernatural things and belief, one can't stress over an arithmetical formula. It is bound to be flexible — of course with certain indications and priorities. They are — (1) Supreme

Power or Consciousness (unmanifest), (2) Supreme Power (manifest) — the Creator God, (3) Three manifestations of the Creator — (Trinity) i.e. three dimensions of Lord Brahmā (creator), Lord Viṣṇu (nourisher), and Mahādeva (destroyer), (4) Several gods or deities of special liking and intense attachment, i.e. *Iṣṭadeva* (tutelary God) — generally believed to be the "Supreme Being," (5) Incarnations, Prophets, Self-realized souls, (6) Power-cult (higher or lower), (7) Semi-Divine — a personality who helps to elevate people, (8) Forces of Nature, (9) Ancestral Spirit, and (10) Lower Spirits, Ghosts, Demons who are malevolent.

The God and its denominations have been shown in Table 1, which have three horizontal columns — (A) Dominant Spiritual/Religious/Magical/or other Practices, (B) Explicit Goals usually attributed to the Practices, and (C) Main Supernatural Experiences or *anubhūtis* (perception).

The details of content in different columns are self-explanatory. The power-cult has two sub-categories — higher manifestations, i.e. up to Creator God 2, or lower grading down to 10.

Still another relevant point may be further elaborated. As *Taittirīya Upaniṣad* tells, the soul in man (tiny soul) is screened by five covering bodies known as *pañca kośa* or "five sheaths." The first of them is the sheath of "Bliss" (*ānanda*) known as *ānandmaya kośa* (cosmic body). The second is the manifestation of "Intelligence" (*buddhi*) that determines what is truth. This is the sheath of *jñāna* and is known as *jñānamaya* or *vijñānamaya kośa* (bauddhic body). The third is the sheath of "Mind" (*manas*) composed of the organs of senses and is called *manomaya kośa* (astral body). The fourth is the sheath of "Energy" or life-force (*prāṇa*) composed of the organs of action and this is called as *prāṇamaya kośa* (ethereal body). The fifth and the last sheath is that of "Gross-matter" which is born out of, and gets nourishment through, *anna* (food) and is called *annamaya kośa*

**Table 1**
**Denominations of God, Its Manifestations and Corresponding Facets**

| Headings | A | B | C |
|---|---|---|---|
| *Various Manifestations of God and the Term of References* | *Dominant Spiritual/Religious/ Magical or Other Practices* | *Explicit Goals Usually Attributed to the Practices* | *Main Supernatural, Other Experiences or Anubhūtis (Perception)* |
| 1. Supreme Consciousness/ All-Pervading and Unmanifest/Impersonal *Supreme Power* (*niḥakṣara Brahman*) | Complete Functional knowledge of the Highest Science of *Consciousness* (*brahma-vidyā* through the medium of a highly Realized Soul (*sadguru*) | Unity with God and freedom from the *bondage of life and death cycle*, self-realization and seeking of truth | *Cetana samādhi*, Perfect Unity with God, *Suśman Pravāha*, Arousal of Mystic Serpent-Power (*kuṇḍalinī*), merging of mind in its root-cause, opening of Tenth-door, Experience of Unity in diversity, Eternal Bliss, Complete detachment, Perfect Spiritual |
| | or | | |
| 2. Supreme Power/Manifest and the Creator God (*Akṣara* | Knowledge of partial aspects with marginal experience | | |

| | | | |
|---|---|---|---|
| *Brahman*) It is *nirākāra* up to this point. | | | wisdom, Guidance of higher spiritual knowledge of *sadguru*, associated with *ānandmaya kośa* |
| 3. Three Manifestations of the Creator God — Trinity — with different dimensions of Lord Brahmā (creator), Lord Viṣṇu, (nourisher) and Lord Mahādeva (destroyer). It starts *sākāra* from this point. | Puritanism, Penance, Prayer, Rituals, Offerings, Abstinence, Recitation of Sacred Texts, in company of Realized souls, *mudrās*, *haṭhyoga*, *brahmāṇḍī* and *piṇḍīya sādhanās* relating to five *brahmāṇḍī* and ten *anāhat* sounds with or without the guidance of Religious Preceptor, Presence or absence of Idol-Worship, Pilgrimage, *aṣṭāṅga yoga* | Subduing of Ego, Devotion to and grace of a deity, Security and/or fulfilment of partly mundane desires and prosperity, divine protection using supernatural powers, if any, for helping others | Devotion, partial peace of mind, Concentration, Spiritual wisdom and detachment, Visions, Mystic dreams, Divine guidance, Spiritual powers, Associated with *ānandmaya kośa*, *jñānmaya kośa*, *manomaya kośa* |
| 4. Several Gods or Deities of special liking and intense attachment with *Iṣṭadeva* | | | |

| | | | | |
|---|---|---|---|---|
| (Tutelary God) — generally believed to be the "Supreme Power"<br><br>5. Incarnation/Prophet/Messengers of God/self-realized Soul/Embodiments of God | | | | |
| | Higher | Up to no. 2 or 1 | Up to no. 2 or 1 | Up to no. 2 or 1 |
| 6. Power-Cult | Lower down to Lowest | Spiritual *sādhanā* relating to *brahmāṇḍī* sounds and *piṇḍa*, Eight *cakras*, *pañcakośas*, *mudrās*, *dhyāna*, Pilgrimage, to Black and/or White Magic with or without the guidance of a Preceptor, Intoxication, Bloody sacrifices on the lower side | Prosperity, success in life, hankering after supernatural powers and control over the forces of nature, for one's own gain and to help others for the sake of one's own name and fame, supernatural protection | Inflation of Ego, Sense of control over events and supernatural powers, attachment to things, visions, Fear and Tension, Devotion in some cases, Experience of Mystic light, *anāhat* and *brahmāṇḍī* sounds Mystic dreams, Associated with *manomaya* or *prāṇamaya kośas* |

| | | | |
|---|---|---|---|
| 7. Semi-Divine, Divine Attendant | Fetishism, Magico-Religious Ritualism, Offering and/or Sacrifices | To acquire specific Supernatural powers or fulfil mundane desires | Achievement of specific Supernatural power subservient to devotion or not Mystic dreams, Visions, Associated with *manomaya* or *prāṇamaya kośa* |
| 8. Forces of Nature including animal and plant world possessing human characteristics but not human in origin | Attitude of fear, Reverence followed by worship, offerings and/or sacrifices | To save themselves from their wrath and gain favour so that life could make it easier and prosperous | Emotional, economic and other securities, Mystic dreams, Visions, Associated with *prāṇamaya kośa* and *annamaya kośa* |
| 9. Ancestral Spirit | Magical and Religious rituals, offerings and Bloody sacrifices | Prosperity and success in life | Sense of Ancestral protection and security, Mystic dreams, visions, Associated with *prāṇamaya kośa* and *ānnamaya kośa* |

| 10. Lower Spirit, Ghost or Demons which are Malevolent | Fetishism and Black Magic under the guidance of Magicians, Witch-Doctors, Superstitions, Taboos, Bloody sacrifice | Prosperity, Vanity, Ventilation of Negative feelings | Fear, Tension and wish fulfilment, Purposeful dreams, Visions, Associated with *annamaya kośa* |
|---|---|---|---|

(physical body). This is the outermost physical body of man (Giri, 1972: 14-16). It is in course of spiritual practice, that a practitioner "pulls" his consciousness upward from one sheath to the other starting from the *annamaya kośa* till it reaches the *ānandmaya kośa*, or even beyond — depending upon the nature of his spiritual practice of course added by the spiritual power of his spiritual preceptor. In the final stage, the pure soul gets united with the Supreme soul (Sahay, 1998: 84-85). The positions associated with the different *kośa*s have been tentatively shown in different columns of the Table. The practitioner may evolve rapidly if he gets proper inspiration, and the position of different *kośa*s may vary.

Following is a figure in which a person, i.e. *Ego*, refers to ten different denominations of God showing three corresponding facets — the Dominant spiritual/religious/ magical or other practices; Expected goals; and Main experiences or *anubhūti*s.

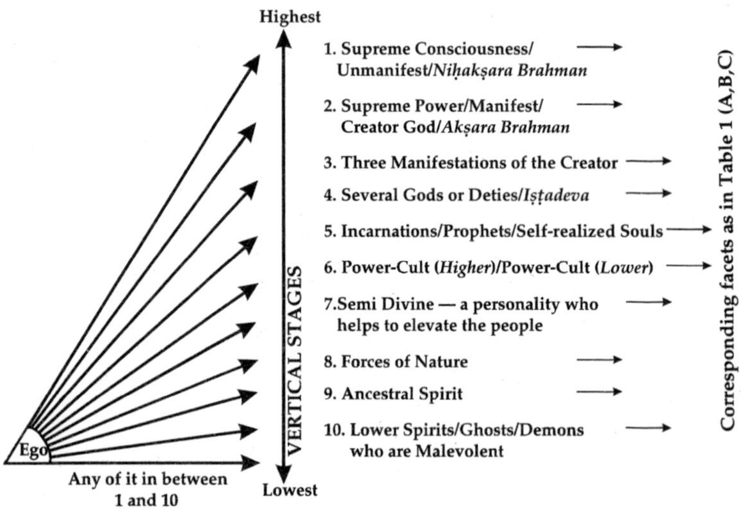


Figure 1 : Term of References of Different Denominations of God and Corresponding Facets

**Sadguru — "Above the God"**

Of the whole universe, God is considered to be the "Supreme Being." But it is interesting that in certain aspects, another entity — *sadguru* goes beyond. A *guru* is a teacher or preceptor, who gives all types of mundane knowledge and ethics. But when it comes to *sadguru,* he not only gives important worldly and ethical teachings but spiritual and mystic knowledge also which leads the disciple (*śiṣya*) to the *parama sattā, sāra śabda* or the *Brahman.* The *sadguru* is important as he guides the disciple in such a manner that the latter gets *united* (*yoga*) with God. Hence, the *sadguru* is more important than God Himself.

A *sadguru* has been equated with the *Brahman.* The glory of the *sadguru* is eternal and pervasive, and only he can lead to the God who is again eternal and pervasive. Kabīr tells —

> सतगुरु की महिमा अनंत, अनंत किया उपकार ।
> लोचन अनंत उघाड़िया, अनंत दिखावण हार ॥

> *sataguru kī mahimā anańta, anańta kiyā upakāra* ।
> *Locana anańta ughāṛiyā anańta dikhāvaṇa hāra* ॥

Further, Kabīr refers to four relevant couplets about the greatness of the *guru* (*sadguru*). The first one tells that a *bhṛṅga* (a type of insect) is like a *guru* and as soon as it comes in contact with another insect, the latter also becomes like the *bhṛṅga* —

> गुरु को कीजै दण्डवत, कोटि कोटि परनाम ।
> कीट न जाने भृंग को, गुरु करले आप समान ॥

> *guru ko kījai daṇḍavata, koṭi koṭi paranāma* ।
> *kīṭa na jāne bhṛṅga ko, guru karale āpa samāna* ॥

The second one tells that if the *guru* and Govinda (God) are together, the disciple must bow down to the guru first, as it is he who had showed the disciple the path to the God. Kabīr tells —

गुरु गोविन्द दोउ खड़े, काको लागु पांय ।
बलिहारी गुरु आपनो, गोविन्द दियो बताय ॥
*guru govinda dou khaṛe, kako lāgu pāṅya* ।
*balihārī guru āpano, govinda diyo batāya* ॥

The third one says that Brahmā, *deva*s, men, sages and the deities got tired of searching for God and salvation, and so you must bow down and serve the *guru* —

जेहि खोजत ब्रह्मा थके, सुर नर मुनि अरु देव ।
कहैं कबीर सुन साधवा, करूं सतगुरु की सेव ॥

*jehi khojata brahmā thake, sura nara muni aru deva* ।
*kahaiṅ kabīra suna sādhavā karūṅ sataguru kī seva* ॥

The fourth one tells that when the *deva*s, men, sages and even Brahmā, Viṣṇu and Mahādeva could never get satisfied or complete without receiving the mystic initiation from the *satguru* (*sadguru*), then what to talk about the ordinary people? Kabīr tells —

बिन सतगुरु उपदेश, सुर नर मुनि नहिं निस्तरे ।
ब्रह्मा विष्णु महेश, और सकल जिव को गिनै ॥

*bina sataguru upadeśa, sura nara muni nahiṅ nistare* ।
*brahmā viṣṇu maheśa, aura sakala jiva ko ginai* ॥

## Arguments about God, Spirituality and Spiritual Evolution

The God is omnipotent and pervasive with different dimensions. Many people communicate with the God with specific path, which is convenient — the family or group socialized with, and other emerging factors, for them.

There are different types of thinking about God and different ways of achieving Him leading to different arguments. But it is futile — if you feel convinced that different people with different spiritual calibres (status) are placed on different ladders. Such a perspective implies "spiritual evolution" proceeded under the "fruits and effect and incarnations" system. Under this background, different dimensions of God — denomination or the kindred, deities or even malevolent forces — with varying limitations, degrees of positive or negative attributes — contribute significant factors.

A person lives in a room with specific sofa, chairs, tables, curtains, carpet, flower-vase, fan, fluorescent lamps, television and the like. If another person is outside the room, he gets another setting — lawn, garden chairs, plants with flowers, compound, gate, vapour light. If still another person is outside the compound, another perspective may be witnessed — a road, shops, lamppost, telephone wires, people moving, vehicles, road crossings or a temple. These three persons placed with different settings or backgrounds, would observe different scenes. If they compare their notes, their details won't tally. Still whatever they saw would be perfect and there won't be any scope for arguments.

We may change another perspective more meaningfully. If you imagine that three different persons start ascending a mountain at different gaps, the details of cartography, sceneries and the feelings may be different, depending on the varying heights and surroundings. They would have different stages and can't argue about the altered backdrops.

That is why, a dimension of the Supreme Being and its different denominations — and devotees associated with it, can't have common arguments. They are placed on different "spiritual ladders." You can just appreciate their experiences, but can't argue.

There may be another relevant point. The world has many negative factors like jealousy, hatred, insult, cruelty and violence, and, by and large, people are subjected to such passions. It is difficult to control these passions, but by doing it, people get satisfied and relaxed. The "negative pool," which is a powerful force, tries people to "misguide them" so that they could get distracted from the spiritual point of view.

*Kaṭhopaniṣad* (Nikhilananda, 1949) tells that there are *śreya* and *preya* paths in life. Those who are intelligent and knowledgeable by analysing the pros and cons of these two paths, will prefer to choose the first one — the excellent path of true welfare, *śreya,* than the second path of worldly pleasures, *preya.* But, with poor intelligence people choose and adopt only the second path of *preya* from the viewpoint of fulfilling their worldly desires and lusts. It is significant that the two paths are "highly relative" and "opposed." Any of the two persons deeply involved with it, may consider the other to be "inferior" or "useless" — the two terms of references depending upon the "spiritual" and "worldly" life respectively. The relevant *śloka* (1.2.2) —

श्रेयश्च प्रेयश्च मनुष्यमेतः तौ सम्परीत्य विविनक्ति धीरः ।
श्रेयो हि धीरोऽभि प्रेयसो वृणीते प्रेयो मन्दो योगक्षेमाद्वृणीते ॥

*śreyaśca preyaśca manuṣyametaḥ tau samparītya vivinakti dhīraḥ* ।
*śreyo hi dhīro 'bhi preyaso vṛṇīte preyo mando yogakṣemādvṛṇīte* ॥

If a person gets involved in worldly things — unless "he does a thing without motive" (*Gītā*) — the malevolent forces "feel happy" as they are working exactly as they wish as per the person's *prārabdha.* People who have spiritual attributes and close communion with God, get elevated, control themselves and don't harm others. A person should develop a "philosophy of life" that whatever happens him, "good" or "bad," on the higher level (indirectly) it is the God Himself who is responsible.

There is co-ordination of *prārabdha* of a person, which works through specific situations in which persons while interacting get insulted or harmed. So, *apparently* nobody harms or helps others. It is the *prārabdha,* which works through a person. So, you must have this awareness — whatever harm you do to others, your negative deeds are credited to your "account."

So you should "swallow a *bitter medicine*" everyday. Of the other prayers, "ask God to help everybody — even those who try to harm you." It may be difficult, but if you are convinced about it and cultivate the habit, some of your bad deeds would be neutralized and transformed.

It may be noted that a person has a *two-tier life.* The "worldly life" works with mundane norms and values. But, there is another "spiritual life." Both are equally important. Both aspects have close interactions. In case there is a disease or a number of worldly problems, and in spite of remedies, solutions do not work, people ponder over it and take recourse to spiritualism. Spiritualism is "a way of life." It is not like a "business — give and take." Normally, it works when one has a spiritual way of life since early age.

## God Doesn't Interfere with Human Prārabdha

If you believe in the process of "fruits of action" (*karamaphala*), God doesn't interfere with the *prārabdha* (destiny) of a person. It takes its own course except miracles, which are rare, and comes under the special grace of God, which nobody could claim. A devotee narrated an event from an old volume of the religious magazine *Kalyāṇa* (Geeta Press, Gorakhpur). It is narrated as follows —

> A poor but old deeply devout Hindu was going on a pilgrimage on foot to Purī (Orissa) for a sacred audience with the Lord Jagannātha Jī. When he had covered most of the distance, he got severely ill — cholera or diarrhoea — and his clothes got soiled. He became unconscious. In the course of his illness for two dsays, when he regained consciousness he saw a "handsome boy" of nearly ten years

> of age, cleaning his dirty clothes and nursing him. As he was so weak and disorganized, he couldn't talk properly, and frequently fainted. When he felt better, he asked — "Who are you?" Why are you cleaning my dirty clothes and helping me?" The boy smilingly said — "I am the Lord Jagannātha Himself, for whose sacred audience you are going." The traveller was flabbergasted, but after a few seconds questioned — "In case you think that you are my Lord, how is it that I got ill during the course of my pilgrimage and why should you clean my dirty clothes? You could have easily transported me to your *dhāma*?" The "divine boy" responded and this was very important. He said — "Even though I am the Lord, you have to suffer your own part of *prārabdha.* I cannot interfere. Yes! As you love me, and vice versa, I tried my level best to help you and mitigate your sufferings. . . ." The "divine boy" disappeared, the traveller became all right and reached the destination.

There is another famous instance of Lord Kṛṣṇa. During *Tretā-yuga* (Giri, 1990: 3-24) Lord Rāma had killed Vāli, which many people thought was not justified — they called it as "perfidious." At the time of death, Vāli asked Lord Rāma — "Why are you killing me by siding my brother Sugrīva." Lord Rāma tried to justify his act, but still He told Vāli that in future when *Dvāpara-yuga* comes — "I shall get incarnation in the form of Lord Kṛṣṇa and you would be born as "hunter. You would avenge and compensate your death." As was the destiny, towards the end of Lord Kṛṣṇa's life when the hunter shot an arrow at His heel, he became thoroughly disturbed and got a guilty feeling. He didn't have this awareness that he was avenging Lord Rāma in *Tretā-yuga.* Lord Kṛṣṇa, while dying, told the hunter not to be grieved as He reminded the Vāli's episode of *Tretā-yuga* saying that now the circle was complete.

**Prārabdha versus the God's Grace**

It is a fact that even though God never remits the *prārabdha* of a person, but if a devotee has close communication with God, God bestows His grace and can give certain concessions. God gives two things to a person — (a) creates a set of situations under which a person has to work — good and bad, followed by the momentum of his *prārabdha* — and (b) *jñāna* (awareness of wisdom) so that when the person is in trouble, he endures it easily and if there is happiness, he expresses gratitude to the God. The *jñāna* gives "neutral situation" and the person becomes elevated.

When the wisdom dawns upon a person, he gets closer communication with God. If there is any bad *prārabdha,* God gives alternatives to him, so that the suffering may be the "minimum" — depending upon the proportion of intensity of communication. But he "doesn't have the awareness of the intensity of sufferings." We may refer to an example.

If there is an accident in which a person falls down from a building, he gets multiple fractures and is put in plasters — two hands, one leg and bandage on the head. He becomes bedridden for about six months without moving his body and natural calls are attended on the bed itself. The other alternative is that the person falls down in such a manner that he was injured and plastered, but somehow hops and goes to the lavoratory. In the third alternative, the person falls exactly over a moving-truck full of straw. Miraculously he escaped grievous injury except bruises and cramps. He limped for a week and then after preliminary check up, became all right.

There was another example in which an old and devout person, full of academic activities, when he got serious urinary problem for about three years — he was mostly on catheter which was troublesome, or at times he felt miserable. He had to move to different areas on an all-India level for treatments, but he never felt disheartened and got tremendous energy, creativity and religious-spiritual inspirations. Rather, he got awfully stuck with reasearch and writing work, and within this period, contributed some major significant publications. People hardly imagine that he had serious ailments.

There is still another example — mystic and rare, in which a person undergoes nightmarish experiences like trouncing, scourging, maiming and slaughtering.

### "Auspicious" and "Inauspicious" both under God's Purview

Under the worldly management, "auspicious" and "inauspicious" both come under God's purview. If people think that God only leads to "auspicious things," it is just lopsided thinking. In fact, God manages "good" and "bad" things as well in the whole world. It is interesting that people talk only about "auspicious things," and in case somebody refers to bad things, they would immediately react — "Talk only auspicious things" (*śubha-śubha bolo*).

A man has a "soul" (*ātmā*) and the Lord is the "supreme soul" (*parmātmā*). Similarly, there are *aṇu ātmā* (tiny soul) and *vibhu ātmā* (Universal Soul). Both are deeply connected and complementary — even though many people don't have the awareness. Just as the *paramātmā* has "positive" and "negative" aspects, the *ātmā* also correspondingly has the same propensities — it is another thing that negative tendencies become more easily manifest, and one had to struggle and develop positive attributes very carefully.

We may also note that in the universe, there are two "pools" — positive and negative. If you do good things, you get connected with the "positive pool" and feel inspired and encouraged to do more good things. But if it is bad, similarly it gets attached with "negative pool" and gradually goes down to the worst. So, when somebody asks not to talk inauspicious things, it means that one should avoid negative things and concentrate on positive things only. A person doing negative or positive things eventually gets connected with the universal pool accordingly and it influences his life.

The countenance (*vigraha*) or disposition of the God and lesser denominations (*sākāra*) may reflect "compassion" and "protection," or alternatively — "fear" and "threat." The first is naturally "reassuring" for devotees. The second one, viz. Pañcamukhī Hanumān, Goddess Kālī, Mahādeva, etc. depicts specific mythological contexts. The purpose is to invoke fear in the devotees to be cautious that he should not go against the traditional or established norms. The devotees mostly concentrate on the first type, because it is homely and convenient. For the second, devotees have to conform to "complicated norms" and unless they do it strictly and fulfil certain conditions, there may be some sort of risk or harm. It may refer to Tāntric worship. Another example may be the *Chaṭha Parva* (Sun worship) where devotees of Bihar worship the sun with grace and greater sanctity — so much so that, even if a child does a mistake even unwittingly, the worshipper thrashes him.

Hindu religion has nine *graha*s (planetary influence). In fact, there are nine planets (Sun, Moon, Mercury, Rāhu, Ketu, Mars, Jupiter, Saturn and Venus). Basically, they are considered to be "neutral," but if planetary position in a person's horoscope (*kuṇḍalī*) is *favourable* or otherwise, effects would change accordingly.

Many people think that Rahu, Ketu, Saturn and also Mars are considered to be the *pāpa graha,* which generally eclipse the life of a person and make it disastrous. Saturn is considered to be the "king" of *graha*s and "harms," or some time "helps" accordingly. However, many people fear these planets. The nine *graha*s direct the destiny of a person (*daivika, daihika, bhautika*) — accidents, illness, litigation, jail term, politics, influence of spirits, other negative forces as in column 10 in Table 1, other obstacles and the like — whether he has awareness about the *graha*s powers or not. In general, many people who are young, ignore or disbelieve such things. But when such persons become older and get into trouble, they start believing in astrologers, *paṇḍita*s or others.

It is believed that God "delegates" powers to the *graha*s and they work on their own. They are autonomous and God never interferes in their working. But in certain positions, they make a person pauper or give plenty of wealth and property. However, it works on a higher level — remotely having a bearing on the "fruits and effect" and *prārabdha* system.

### Determinants of Triguṇas

An awareness of the individual consciousness in man is formless; it is immortal, it does not die and is continuous. But it is mixed up with sense awareness, body awareness and mind awareness (Satyananda Saraswati, 1974: 39-40). A study of spirituality requires the understanding of the ancient Indian concept of *triguṇa — sāttvika, rājasika* and *tāmasika*, the three basic attributes or innate dispositions of man. It will help to understand the "spiritual-calibre" of culture.

Caraka (Bhattacharya, 1937: 614) elaborates the several mental types bearing the three basic elements of *guṇa*s. According to *Bhagavad-Gītā*, it is the nature of the innate faith, the types of worship and sacrifice, religiosity, austerity, penance, gift and charity a man makes, and the type of food he relishes that determines the character of the people. Elaborating this innate faith of man *Bhagavad-Gītā* (17.2) talks about the three kinds — *sāttvika, rājasika* and *tāmasika*:

त्रिविधा भवति श्रद्धा देहिनां सा स्वभावजा ।
सात्त्विकी राजसी चैव तामसी चेति तां शृणु ॥

*trividhā bhavati śraddhā dehināṁ sā svabhāvajā* ।
*sāttvikī rājasī caiva tāmasī ceti tāṁ śṛṇu* ॥

While elaborating the nature of faith in man and different mental constitutions, *Bhagavad-Gītā* (17.3) says —

सत्त्वानुरूपा सर्वस्य श्रद्धा भवति भारत ।
श्रद्धामयोऽयं पुरुषो यो यच्छ्रद्धः स एव सः ॥

*sattvānurūpā sarvasya śraddhā bhavati bhārata* ।
*śraddhāmayo 'yaṁ puruṣo yo yacchraddhaḥ sa eva saḥ* ॥

The faith of all men conforms to their mental constitution, Arjuna. This man consists of faith, whatever the nature of his faith, he is verily that.

It has been found that a man's nature conforms to the kind of actions he performs. Generally, it may be *sāttvika, rājasika* or *tāmasika*. And as nature (*guṇa*s or modes of *prakṛti*) is embedded in the mind, his frame of mind is believed to reflect his nature (Goyandka, 1978: 693).

Elaborating the religious inclinations and worship, *Bhagavad-Gītā* (17.4) says —

यजन्ते सात्त्विका देवान्यक्षरक्षांसि राजसाः ।
प्रेतान्भूतगणांश्चान्ये यजन्ते तामसा जनाः ॥

*yajante sāttvika devānyakṣarakṣāṁsi rājasāḥ* ।
*pretānbhūtagaṇāṁścānye yajante tāmasā janāḥ* ॥

Men of a *sāttvika* disposition worship gods; those of a *rājasika* temperament worship demi-gods and demons; while others, who are men of a *tāmasika* disposition, worship the spirit of the dead and groups of ghosts.

It is a fact that a person has different types of *guṇa*s — each of them is changing very frequently and different attributes are influencing him. The *sāttvika guṇa* is decisive and the person involved in spiritualism struggles to eliminate *rājasika* and *tāmasika* qualities, and develop the *sāttvika* attributes so much so that in course of time he becomes elevated. He goes through the rigorous *yoga-sādhanā*, of course with the guidance of a capable preceptor (*sadguru*) and gets into the "mystic dimension," gradually "uniting with the God" — if not in the present life, at least in other lives to come.

**Abstract-Gross-Abstract**

In different societies, while talking about genesis, people tell that God created things — *abstract* to *gross* — society, economy, technology, beliefs, rituals and the likes. If it comes to spirituality, it reverses — *gross* to *abstract*.

Maharshi Sadaful Ji (1978) while talking about self-realization tells that originally the human soul was in its purest form known as *haṁsa śarīra, haṁsa deha* or *kaivalya śarīra*. Being in its purest conscious form, it was in union with the Supreme Conscious Power. But then it suffered from the illusion of *aham brahmāsmi* (I am the *Brahman*) and as a result of this Ego, and under the influence of the strong illusory Power (*māyā*), it had a gradual downward devolution — it passed through the four other stages like *mahākāraṇa śarīra, kāraṇa śarīra, sūkṣma śarīra,* and *sthūla śarīra*. The last one coincides with the physical plane of human existence. This process had gradually changed human beings from *subtle* to *gross* conditions.

Against the background, starting from the bottom, i.e. from the gross state of being, spiritualism refers to a process of gradually acquiring the various subtle states one after the other till one attains the *haṁsa śarīra*. Maharshi expressed it in the following verse —

झीन आय झीना चलो, मन व त्याग संयोग ।
क्रमशः सूक्ष्म हो रहो, अग्र गमन गति योग ॥

*jhīna āya jhīnā calo, mana va tyāga saṁyoga* ।
*kramaśaḥ sūkṣma ho raho, agra gamana gati yoga* ॥

You have come from a "subtle state" and you have to return to it. You gradually become subtler by disassociating yourself from the mind and marching ahead through the technique of *yoga*. — Sahay, 1998: 85-86

## Action-Reaction and Quick or Deferred Mechanism

There are certain aspects in which spirituality, mysticism, science and new physics have parallels (D.S. Kothari, 1983: 29-45; Talbot, 1981; Harold Sherman, 1958: 13, 21; Sheila Ostrander and Lynn Schroeder, 1970; Fritjof Capra, 1975). "Fruits and effect" (*karmaphala* of the individual) has basic "action-reaction mechanism" in Hindu society and this concept is eternal. In a scientific experiment, whenever a "matter" or "situation" is placed for anlaysis, we get a result — quickly or within a reasonable time. But in human life, if there is similar action, the response may be deeply delayed or get lost — perhaps "taken over to the next life."

It is the "faith" (*āsthā*) of a person which counts. But under the present situation of the worst enduring conditions of life, faith changes as the Kali-yuga (Giri, 1990: 3-24) is passing through. It makes an important variable factor. Many people strongly feel that "the God has skipped functioning." One or two generations ago, by and large people were sincere, peaceful, had higher values and deep faith. In case there were cases of injustice, offences, exploitation, privileges denied, murder, theft, etc. — it was felt that it would be retributed, and faith would be vindicated much to their satisfaction.

In the same old context, barring such aspects of injustice, people didn't have full awareness and worked in the same rut. "Awareness" is an important thing and has its own mechanism. Awareness follows a "desire" for something. It makes "action" and it starts functioning. Whether God responds — helps quickly, within a reasonable time, defers, or just ignores — come under the ambit of *prārabdha*. It may be because, the conception of "time" of the mortals in present life and that of the creator, are "relative." They work differently. A human being expects retribution within a short time but for the creator it works conveniently over a number of births (incarnations). However, within the present lifetime it has the bearing of faith. Naturally, if the creator plans the "housekeeping" in its own way on a cosmic level, humans cannot conceive it properly and get all types of frustrations — unless they are *jñānī*s and have proper tuning with the God.

Here it may not be out of place to refer to an Urdu *śa'ir* (verse):

लम्हों ने ख़ता की थी, सदियों ने सजा पाई।

*lamhoṅ ne khatā kī thī, sadiyoṅ ne sajā pāī* ।

A person who makes a mistake for a moment, he gets punishment for centuries.

### Whether God Ignores "Mass Accidents"?

Very often, there are serious accidents connected with plane, train or buses and hundreds or thousands of people die or are injured. It is shocking. Those who are relatives, friends, or even strangers when they know about it become sensitive. Some of the tragic accidents haunt people for some time and they just wonder why such group come from the same family, or others of different areas, countries, economic status, languages, ethnic groups, men, women, children — travel together and die in an accident on the same spot. A person or persons dying in accidents on road, in an epidemic, flood, or earthquake — constitute a somewhat usual phenomena; though it is tumultuous it is understandable. But the categories of other accidents as said above are still more tragic, baffling and one looks to God for the real explanation. How is it that different types of people with diverse backgrounds and situations, come together on the same spot and die in the accident — are all of them sinners?

To explain the phenomena, you have to look into mysticism — particularly "transcendentalism." *Jīva*s (individual or creature) work through the "life-death cycle" with varying backgrounds from different births. God manages everything eternally. The conception of "time" (*kāla*) on worldly level is relative and different from the time of Lord Viṣṇu or the Trinity (Viṣṇu, Brahmā and Mahādeva) in celestial dimension. There is a general legend that "one day of the Lord Viṣṇu" equals a number of thousands or lakhs of years (Giri, 1990: 3-24). One could very well imagine that when a genuine spiritualist or saint attains *saṃādhi* — prolonged meditation or its culmination in the state of unity with the Universal Consciousness — forgets awareness of a sense of time (*kāla*). The deities like Lord Viṣṇu and Mahādeva also, as per myths, go into *samādhi*. As such, reckoning of time of the normal humans would be different from that of the deities.

In worldly chore of life also, for persons who are deeply involved with fascinating and creative work "time shrinks very fast" — as opposed to those who are idle or disturbed. The cosmonauts on inter-planetary level, or those who travel in a fast jet-plane on long journey, have similar feelings.

In context with Lord Viṣṇu and human's time perspectives, if man lives sixty-five years on an average, Lord's time would just be a smallest particle. That is why, some people remark that apparently from the Lord's point of view, "He plays with humans, just as small children play with toys and enjoys," but the purpose is very serious.

As such, it is no wonder that various individuals (*Jīva*) pass through several reincarnations coming from different places, economic, religious, social, linguistic status or other backgrounds. The creator has a grand cosmic planning by uniting the "present, past and future" transcendentally, and covers the *prārabdhas* (destiny) of deeds of individuals in different previous rebirths — working out relevant "account of credits and balance" with great precision. When the appointed place and time coincide together, the creator locates, collects such different individuals conveniently, and puts in a plane, train or bus and the accident is created. Those people, who don't have the awareness about the cosmic planning, get bewildered.

**Epilogue**

1. God who is the Unmanifest Supreme Power has created a number of lesser denominations and vertically they go down from "abstract" to "gross" (conception and connected aspects), benevolent to malevolent — down to the spirits, ghosts and the like. Of the various such spiritual forces or God's kindreds, I have tried to categorize basic ten forces as given in Table 1. When we talk about the purpose of life, one has to go back vertically to the abstract level through spirituality and mysticism so that the person finally gets "united" with God.

2. God and the devotees have close dichotomy. God wants to love and help His devotees, and the devotees also want to respond accordingly. But the intervening factor — "fruits and effect" mechanism comes in between the two. It is the "illusion," or *māyā* which doesn't want that the *ātmā* should go in the path of God and unite with *paramātmā*. So, it creates a series of problems. Going down, involved with wordly life on horizontal level, implies "separation" from God. On His own side God repeatedly tries to give certain "indications," but people forget them and say that God should mercifully give a tip and transform them.

3. People conceive the Supreme Being as "unmanifest" and "Universal consciousness." *Gāyatrī mantra* is highly sacred and is an important *śloka* frequently used by *ṛṣis*, saints, spiritualists, religionists and *paṇḍitas*. But though this *Gāyatrī mantra* is addressed to the "Lord, Father of the Universe," at the same time it symbolizes

the "Five-faced Mother Goddess sitting on a Lotus flower," with control over the five elements — worshipping in complete surrender to Her by mentally repeating the *mantra.*

4. God is sacred and secret. It is mystic, transcendental and the people try to communicate with God in their own way. A number of verses refer to His mystic dimensions and *anubhūtis*. In certain aspects, a *sadguru* has greater importance than God, and it is he who guides the person to reach God. The *sadguru* goes up vertically through *yoga sādhanā,* and the person (*ātmā*) in course of time by concentrating on *sāttvika* attributes becomes "pure consciousness" and unites with the God (*paramātmā*) who also is the "pure consciousness."

5. Many people argue about God, but they don't have the agreement because different people stand on different "spiritual ladders," and the terms of reference and perception about God must be different. So, one could just compare notes and appreciate them. Life is two-tiered — "mundane" and "spiritual" — and both have close interactions. God just gives "indications" or "codes." You have to "uncode" them. You can understand them quickly if you have cultivated *sāttvika* attributes. An individual has a "tiny soul," which is a part of the "Universal Soul." Both of them are deeply related. The Universal Soul is full of consciousness. But the individual is combined with three qualities — *tāmasika, rājasika* and *sāttvika.* In case the person gets elevated, eliminates *tāmasika* and *rājasika* qualities and becomes full consciousness, "pure soul" (*santa śarīra*), immediately he unites with God.

6. God does not interfere with the *prārabdha* of a person. But if one has close "communication with God," certainly, He showers His grace and indicates the

better alternatives. Suffering would be there, but one won't have the real awareness.

7. God manages all types of things — "auspicious" as well as "inauspicious," "positive" and "negative." One should understand this and hence be neutral. Those, which are inauspicious, have bearing with *graha*s — especially *pāpa graha*s that affect the people, all working under the "fruit-effect scheme." God Himself "delegates" the *graha*s and *inauspicious forces* under the cosmic planning.

8. The mortals face to two serious dilemmas. Firstly, it is not sure whether a person doing "good deeds" would be rewarded, ignored, deferred or lost. On the other hand, it has been generally seen that the person doing "wrong things" looks "prosperous." Secondly, there are some persons who meet with some accident. People tell that "this accident was *minor*. It could have been more serious, but the God helped and a major accident was averted." People wonder whether the "minor accident was really the grace of God and He should be thanked," or this mishap was a "routine matter."

9. Everyday in life has a scheme of development — physical development in age, language, social norms, etiquettes, education and the like. Unless one develops or changes, he will become stagnant. So is the case with religion. Everybody practices his own religion, but in the religion itself there are different dimensions or layers — routine, more involved, puritanical, highly ceremonious, etc. But there is a certain aspect which gets evolved, the main essence of religion. It helps the people irrespective of differences to cultivate good characteristics like honesty, humanity, morality, kindness, purity from *sākāra* to *nirākāra*, self-realization, quest for truth and spirituality. Symbolically, if you

want to start a car, it doesn't move unless you press a lever by which the "car really moves." Sticking to religious rituals or recitations of *pāṭha,* etc. are not enough, unless you really help the people — who are poor and in adversity. If it is done, certainly, it will have a real religious development.

10. It is the "faith" in God, which is functional followed by "conviction," deep love and feelings for others — which are most important. It supersedes the "formal aspects of religion" to which people by and large have acquiescence. There are a few people, however, who have guts and do not flock together. They chart out their own things with firm faith in the Supreme Power. They conceive it positively and believe that there is ether throughout and the Supreme Being animates everywhere. In case you conceive any type of form, it will get materialized.

11. Before one elevates and communicates with the God, he should neutralize the negative forces that influence people. Jealousy, insult, hatred, cruelty, and violence are some of these forces which people unwittingly direct towards others by weaving their own bad *prārabdha.* But if you know the mechanism, you may pray to God and convey your positive vibrations to every body — even to those who have bad feelings for you. And your *prārabdha* would be minimized and you become closer to God.

12. People believe that basically God is unmanifest and the worldly things you see are just "illusions" and different from truth. However, the feelings (*bhāvanā*) and vibrations (*spandana*) of love, kindness, mercy, compassion and similar positive attributes — which are just abstract, are eternal and constitute the "basic

materials of creation." It is these attributes which get abstracted from different types of social relations, interactions and activities. It is these unique seminal things which have reflections from God.

## References


Ahmadia Movement (Head), n.d. "Characteristics of Quranic Teachings," *The Nazir Dawat-o-Tabligh Sadar*, Anjuman Ahmadiyya, Qadian.

Allen, R.E., 1990, *The Concise Oxford Dictionary of Current English*, Bombay: Oxford University Press.

*The Bhagvat or the song Divine* (with Sansksrit Text and English tr.), Gorakhpur: Gita Press, 1964.

Bhattacarya, Haridas, 1937, *The Cultural Heritage of India*, vol. III, The Philosophies, Calcutta: The Ramkrishna Mission Institute of Culture.

Capra, Fritijof, 1975, *The Tao of Physics*, Collins: Fontana.

Giri, Swami Sri Yukteshwar, *The Holy Science*, Los Angeles: Self Realization Fellowship.

Goyanka, Jayadayal, 1978, *Śrīmad Bhagavad-Gītā*, Gorakhpur: Gita Press.

King James, 1816, *The Holy Bible*, Old and New Testaments (King James Version), New Delhi: American Bible Society.

Kothari, D.S., 1983, *Atom and Self*, Meganath Saha Medical Lecture 1978, Bombay: Bharatiya Vidya Bhavan.

McGregor R.S., 1997, *The Oxford Hindi-English Dictionary*, Delhi: Oxford University Press.

Nambiar, A.K. Krishna, 1983, *The Glory of the Gāyatrī Mantra*, Delhi: Spiritual India Publishing House.

Nikhilananda, Swami, 1949, *The Upaniṣads* (*Kaṭha Upaniṣad*), vol. I, New York: Bonanza Books.

Ostrander, Sheila and Lynn Schroeder, 1970, *P.S.I. Psychic Discoveries Behind the Iron Curtain*, London: ABACUS.

Prasad, N., 1961, *Land and People of Tribal Bihar*, Ranchi: Bihar Tribal Research Institute.

Sadafal Dev, Maharshi, 1951, *Ṛgveda-Brahmavidyā-Bhaṣya* (Hindi), Pakri, Ballia: Mukti Pustakalaya.

——, 1951, *Atharvaveda-Brahmavidyā-Bhaṣya* (Hindi), Pakri, Ballia: Mukti Pustakalaya.

——, 1978, *Svarveda-Bhaṣya* (Hindi), Part I, Gadwar, Ballia: Adhyatmik Yantryalaya, Sadguru Sandesh Karyalaya.

Sahay, K.N., 1998, *Spiritual Anthropology*? (The Spiritual Dimension of Man), New Delhi: Commonwealth Publishers.

——, 1999, *Beyond the Thousand Petalled Lotus and the Science of Consciousness*, New Delhi: Commonwealth Publishers.

Saraswati, Satyananda, 1974, *Yoga: From Shore to Shore,* Mnger: Bihar School of Yoga.

Sherman, Harold, 1958, *How to Use The Power of Prayer,* New Delhi: A Premier Book.

Talbot, Michael, 1981, *Mysticism and the New Physics,* A Bantam Book.

Vivekananda, Swami, 1970, *Thoughts of The Gītā,* Calcutta: Advaita Ashrama.

# 7

# God in Different Religions

*B.D. Tripathi*

THE nature and function of God differs in different religions. In spite of the numerous views on God, there is unanimity about him on certain points. Let us start with the Vedic God.

Vedic God (*Īśvara, Bhagavān, Brahman*) is the creator of the entire existence. Whatever, wherever, whenever there exists anything, it is due to the will of God. In the beginning, only He was there. Then He wanted to multiply and became multiple. He moved from unity to diversity. He binds the entire diversity with His presence. God is present in the minutest constituent of the existence, and the entire existence as a unit is encompassed by Him. He encompasses the whole creation and yet transcends it.[1] For God, there is no division in time. He stands stretched between the polarities of time and yet remains to be stretched further. He is beginningless, endless. He is eternal. He is omnipresent, omnipotent and omniscient.

From God's navel arose the sky; from His head arose heaven; from his feet arose the earth; from his ears arose the directions. Moon arose from the mind of God. From his eyes arose the sun. From his nostrils arose air and life (*prāṇa*). From

---

1. *Yajurveda*, Puruṣa-Sūkta, 31.1.

His mouth arose fire. Brāhmaṇa arose from His face. From His arms arose Rājanya; from His thighs arose vaiśyas and from his feet arose śūdras.[2]

According to *Īśopaniṣad,* God is full of all attributes, yet He is beyond all attributes. God moves through space, yet He does not move. He is far, yet he is near. He is within all, yet He is without all.[3] In the allied Vedic literature, God is laden with several physical attributes. He comes nearer to man. He feels concerned to rejuvenate the degenerated social order. According to the *Gītā,* He reincarnates. He punishes the evil-doers and rewards the virtuous ones.

There is no unity of view in respect of the nature and function of God among the commentators of the Vedic and allied literature. There are monists and dualists. Monists believe that there is no essential difference between *Brahman* and *jīva.* In the eyes of monist philosophers, *jīva* minus ignorance is just *Brahman.* There is apparent multiplicity in the creation. The entire multiplicity is reducible to the single principle of *Brahman.* Multiplicity is illusion. Unity is verity. Multiplicity is based on ignorance. Unity is based on knowledge. In monism, there is no dualism, no deity, no worshipper. In dualism, devotion is *must* for the attainment of man's unity with the ultimate reality.

In the Vedic and allied literature, there is detailed description of hell-heaven, sin-virtue, bondage-freedom, life after death, rebirth of soul and many such others. These concepts are interwoven in the entire Vedic text. Vedic faith is said to be polytheistic which in fact is not. One and the same supreme deity is conceived in many forms. All deities are reducible to one supreme deity. Thus Vedic faith preaches henotheism, which is a modified form of monotheism.

---

2. Ibid., 31.13, 12, 11.
3. *Īśopaniṣad,* 5.

In Zoroastrian faith, God (Ahura Mazda, i.e. wise lord) created the entire existence, sky, water, earth, vegetable, animal, and man at six stages. At the first stage, sky was created and the last creation of the Lord was man. The four mid-category creations are water, earth, vegetable and animal. Above and beyond all deities stands the Lord of the entire creation, Ahura Mazda. With the view to look after the affairs of the creation, particularly man, Ahura Mazda created Zarathushtra (Zoroaster).

In Zoroastrianism, virtue and vice, good and evil are seen as interlaced dyads. The idea of inseparable dyad of virtue and vice has been explained with the help of an analogy. Ahura Mazda has two sons who are twins. These are Serpenta Mainyu and Angra Mainyu (Ahriman). Serpenta Mainyu symbolizes all that is positive, good and virtuous in the social life, truth (*āśā*), benevolent thoughts, words and deeds. Angra Mainyu symbolizes all that is negative, bad and non-virtuous in human life, lie (*druj*), malevolent thoughts, words and deeds.

At the time of birth, both the Mainyus are just identical twins, with no difference between them. Later, one of the two chooses truth (*āśā*) and becomes Serpenta Mainyu and the other chooses lie (*druj*) and becomes Angra Mainyu. Thus ultimate source of both — good and bad, right and wrong is Ahura Mazda. Both *āśā* and *druj* are external elements and both inhere in the supreme deity.

According to Avesta, the Zoroastrian scripture, after death the soul is awarded, rewarded or gets punishment in proportion to his good and bad deeds. If a soul's good acts outweigh bad acts, he is rewarded a blissful life in the heaven (Anagra Raocha, a place full of infinite light). If on the other hand, soul's sins outweigh his virtues, he is sent to hell, a place of perpetual torture. If, however, soul's good and bad acts match equally, he is sent to Hamistagan. This is a region of void. Here there is neither pleasure nor pain, neither joy nor agony.

Like Vedic faith, Zoroastrianism is a henotheistic religion. Here faith is put in one supreme deity. Along with Him, there are other subordinate deities. In Zoroastrianism, Ahura Mazda is the supreme deity, but along with Him the two Mainyus and other nature-gods such as sun, moon, stars, goddess of learning called *deva*s are also worshipped.

Buddhism does not believe in eternalism, neither in the sphere of immanent nor in the transcendent. As such, it does not possess Supreme deity in the usual sense of the word. Buddhism does not believe in anything eternal, constant, static, changeless and immutable. Buddhism assumes eternity as illusion and ignorance. This very assumption of this faith logically repudiates the idea of something which is eternal, constant and changeless that is God. In other words, the existence of Supreme deity and soul is incongruous with the key assumption of Buddhism.

Buddhistic philosophy pleads for the mid-path (*madhyama mārga*). Mid-path posits that on the one side, nothing is purely eternal and constant and on the other, nothing is purely ephemeral, perishable and mortal. To explain the idea behind this, the analogy of a burning lamp is cited. The flame of the burning lamp appears as constant. But, this appearance is an illusion and not a verity. An outgoing flame in the burning lamp is continuously replaced by incoming flames without any temporal gap. This arouses the illusion of continuity in a constantly changing phenomenon. Like a burning lamp, change is occurring every moment, everywhere but due to the obsession of constancy, man fails to form the real image of the phenomenon.

Buddhism may be divided between two paths, trunk and branch. The trunk part is the original Buddhism. It consists in the pre-sectarian and pre-philosophical belief system of Buddhism. Lord Buddha regarded certain queries beyond explanation (*avyākṛta*). The query in respect of existence or non-existence of God and soul comes in this category. After trunk, Buddhism was split into two sects, i.e. Theravāda and Mahāsāṅghika. The original idea was marginalized. Along with the marginalized trunk belief system, new and high-sounding philosophical structures sprouted. Buddhistic philosophy ranged from Sarvāstivāda (pantheism) to Śūnyavāda (nihilism). The simple belief system preached by Lord Buddha lost its direction. The new belief system that grew in the name of Buddhism just negated the original belief system. Later philosophers raised Lord Buddha himself to the status of God, sitting in the heaven under the name of Amitabha. Even after full extinction (*parinirvāṇa*), he is believed to incarnate to teach the principle of *nirvāṇa* to the suffering mankind.

Though essentially an agnostic faith, Buddhism continues to be a major religion of the world. This is because it puts faith in other attributes of religion such as life after death, rebirth, doctrine of *karman* and so on. Buddhism preaches *nirvāṇa,* which in some measure is equivalent to *kaivalya* (onliness) of Jainism and *mokṣa* of the Vedic faith. Buddhism subscribes to the doctrine of rebirth in spite of the fact that it voices full-throated repudiation of the entity of the soul. In Jātaka stories, there are myths of several previous births of Lord Buddha, as an apostle of peace and compassion. Also Buddhism talks of deities. One of such deities is Māra (Cupid) which dissuaded Siddhārtha Gautama from pursuing the right path. In spite of weak ontology, social ramifications of Buddhism are very strong. Buddhism though weak at the root, is very sound and powerful at the top. Buddhism rose against the reckless slaughter of innocent animals in the name of *yajñas* and raised the public psyche against it. Later, Vedic philosphers such as Śaṅkarācārya and Kumārila Bhaṭṭa, however, revive the Vedic faith to its original glory but the practice of killing animals in the name of *yajñas* was buried forever. Buddhism is put in the category of non-Vedic or heterodox system of philosophy, as it does not put faith in the authority of Vedas and challenges the same on several key issues.

Jainism is a dualistic religion. Jain ontology believes in two mutually exclusive and irreducible substances called *jīva* and *ajīva*. Potentially, *jīva* is equipped with enormous possibility of self-optimization, self-actualization and self-maximization. But the *ajīva* elements impede him from growing up. They flow towards the *jīva* and bind him from all sides. *ajīva* elements fall in five sub-categories which are as follows: (i) *Pudgala* — All tangible items which can be perceived through senses come in this category; (ii) *Dharma* — it is an element which creates motion. (iii) *Adharma* — It is an element which provides rest for objects. *Dharma* and *adharma* jointly create a sate of balance or equilibrium which is a must for smooth functioning of the physical world. (iv) *Kāla* (Time) — This element is responsible for change in the system of things. *Kāla* is assumed to be devoid of entity. (v) *Ākāśa* — It acts as the shelter for all that exist.

Out of two broad categories of substance, *jīva* possesses consciousness and all the *ajīva* elements are assumed to be devoid of consciousness.

*Pudgalas* have the primordial tendency to flow towards the *jīva*. In Jain terminology, this is called *āsrava* (inflow). The inanimate *pudgalas* bind *jīva*. This is called *bandha* (bondage). *Kaivalya*-aspirant *jīva* must get rid of the *pudgalas* which fill him up. For this, he has to check the inflow of *pudgalas*. The first step in moving towards the goal of *kaivalya* consists in checking the inflow of the *pudgalas* towards the *jīva*. The process of checking the inflow of *pudgalas* is called *saṁvara*. The second step consists in eliminating the already deposited *pudgalas*. This step is called *nirjarā* (elimination). The final step after *nirjarā* is *kaivalya*, when the *jīva* gets rid of all the *pudgalas* and attains the sstate of onliness (*kaivalya*). At this stage, *jīva* transcends the birth and death cycle and becomes *arhat* or *tīrthaṁkara*. *Arhat* is equivalent to God. It is believed that after attaining the high position of *arhat* or *tīrthaṁkara*, the *jīva* transcends all limits of self-culture and sits motionlessly on the *siddhaśilā* (the abode of highest virtue). In the Jain creation myth, it is believed that the world is *eternal*. Man's suffering is due to his interlinkage with the *pudgalas*. Like Buddhist faith, Jainism challenges the authority of Vedas and as such it is put in the heterodox category of philosophy by the followers of the Vedic faith. As Jainism does not believe in any Supreme Creator, it is branded as an atheistic faith like Buddhism by the adherents of the Vedic faith. Except non-belief in the Supreme Deity (God), Jainisim has all the key-attributes of Hindu religion, namely, after-life, other world, rebirth, doctrine of *karman* and several others.

Under the Jain ontology, theism or monotheism is not possible. Attributes of God cannot be imputed on *jīva*, as it has the vulnerability of attracting *pudgalas* towards himself. *jīva* cannot be God because of his plurality attribute. By definition God transcends all plurality. He is believed to be one and the only one.

Let it be mentioned here that Jain ontology is very close to Sāṁkhya philosophy. Jain *jīva* has all the attributes of Sāṁkhya *puruṣa*. Like *puruṣa*, *jīva* possesses the attribute of consciousness. Also *jīvas* are many like *puruṣa*. *ajīva* of Jain ontology is just *prakṛti* of Sāṁkhya. Both are inert and inanimate. Like *prakṛti*, *ajīva* elements particularly *pudgalas*, have a tendency to attract *jīva* (*puruṣa*).

Judaism is the religion of the Jews. It was founded by Lord Moses. The supreme deity of this religion is Yahveh (also called Jehovah). Yahveh revealed this faith to the most pious member of the "chosen people" on the earth. He revealed to him the secret of divinity along with the codes of proper conduct. Yahveh gave Moses the do's and don'ts of social life in the form of Ten Commandments. Judaism is a monotheistic religion opposed to idolatry at least in principle if not in practice. Judaic God is just and merciful. He is the perfect one. He created the world in six days and went on to rest on the seventh day (*sabbath*). Judaic God is highly demanding as well as exceedingly forgiving. Judaic God Jehovah on occasions becomes vindictive and revengeful.

Torah is God's will revealed to Moses. It is believed that Torah existed before the creation as God's guide for creation. Torah is the most precious possession of God. As people of Israel (Jews) accept Torah as their guideline of action, they are so close and dear to Jehovah.

Jews are highly possessive of their God. They believe that their God is exclusively their own and nobody else's. In return, Yahveh is very much involved in the affairs of Jews. When Jews commit sin, Yahveh patiently waits for them to repent and expiate and helps them to do so sometimes by punishing them to remind them of their responsibility. Being "chosen people" of Yahveh, Jews possess Torah. But this does not exempt them from the demand of righteousness. As Yahveh has a special love for Jews, they bear more responsibility before Him. When misfortune befalls Jews, they believe that their dear Lord has punished them for their misdeeds. Jews always remain confident of Yahveh's rule. They await God's favour and blessing.

Jews believe in the continued existence of soul after the physical death of man. After death, the soul is taken from the body for preliminary judgement and purification to Yahveh. Then, it is rejoined to its purified body. Wicked are utterly destroyed under Yahveh's judgement. Less culpable receive limited term of expiatory punishment. Yahveh rewards the righteous ones. The Judaic word for soul is *ruah* or *nefesh*.

Christianity is a faith of love, affection and compassion. This faith came into being after Christ (Messiah) who himself was not a Christian but a Jew. Jesus Christ played the same role in respect of Judaism which Lord Buddha played in respect of Vedic religion. Like Vedic religion, animals were sacrificed for the propitiation of Yahveh, the Judaic God. Jesus rose against this practice and condemned it vehemently. Often, he freed the animals herded for sacrifice. He rose against certain other practices prevalent in Judaic faith which he believed arrested the flow of love among human beings. He flouted the *sabbath* rule. Jesus offended Jews psyche by his deeds. This ultimately culminated in his crucifixion. Disclaiming his rumoured Judaic prophethood he declared, "Not that I have come to replace Lord Moses, but that I have come to mend him." Mending Lord Moses was the limited mission of Jesus. But his crucifixion transformed the whole scenario. Later, the event of resurrection metamorphosed him into a charismatic figure. Jesus became Christ. He became a craze for the masses. In the beginning, a sect sprouted after him which later grew into the size of ecclesia and ultimately into a world religion.

Christians believe in the trinity. Trinity consists of God (Holy), Holy Spirit (holy ghost) and the Son (Jesus Christ). God is the supreme deity of this faith. Holy spirit is a mid-point between God and the son. It is the holy spirit through which the son is linked to God. God is purely transcendent. Holy spirit is a derivation from God. The son symbolizes the man. Virgin Mary is believed to have conceived from the holy spirit.

Christian God is very much involved in human affairs. He is very kind, benevolent, merciful and compassionate. He is never vindictive like Yahveh. Christianity believes in the after-life and the other world. After death, the soul is judged for the evil and virtuous deeds by God. Man is punished for his misdeeds and rewarded for his good acts on the day of judgement.

Islam is the third in order in the chain of Semitic religions. The word Islam is derived from the word *Aslam* which means to surrender to God. Islam, therefore, means the act of surrender to God.

According to Islam, Allāh has the following attributes.

(i) He is one and the unique and that Mohammed is His Rasūla (Messenger or Prophet). There is no deity other than Allāh which deserves to be worshipped by men. He neither begets nor is He begotten.

(ii) He is eternal.

(iii) Nothing precedes God. He created the world and all that is in it. He did not create things from pre-existing matter. He created the world *ex nihilo.*

(iv) God is unlike all created things. He is neither body, nor substance. He has no spatial limit or position.

At another place, a different description of God is available. According to this description, God is seated on a throne on the seventh sheath of the sky. His figure is man-like.

(v) Quran is the word of God spoken and written by man.

(vi) God's will is supreme. He controls all mundane events.

(vii) God (Allāh) will judge all human beings on the last day after the dead arise from their respective graves. In His judgement, God will reward the virtuous and will punish the sinners. With the help of a balance, God will weigh good and bad acts of people. Virtuous will be sent to heaven (*jannata* or *bihista*) and sinners to hell (*dozakh*).

(viii) Mohammed and other prophets will be permitted to intercede with Allāh for sinful members of their community.

(ix) Paradise and hell exists eternally.

(x) Islam believes in the continuity of soul (*rūha*) after death. Soul of man remains attached to the body till the day of judgement (*qayāmata*). In spite of the belief in the continued existence of soul after death, Islam does not believe in rebirth.

(xi) Islam also does not believe in the descendence of divinity in the human world. Instead of descending to the world in human form and figure, Allāh manages the human affairs through his mediators called angels, Rasūlas and Pag͟hambaras.

(xii) God will be seen by *Momins* (Believers) in the paradise.

(xiii) In the series of prophets from Abraham to Mohammed, Mohammed is the last one.

In the Islamic faith, God (K͟hudā or Allāh) is believed to be absolutely transcendent. As opposed to Allāh, man (*bandā*) is immanent. The implication of this dualism is that there cannot be direct contact between K͟hudā (god) and *bandā* (man). Allāh does not manage the affairs of the world directly; He forces his will on man through his angels (*faristā*) like Gabriel. He transmits His will to the human mortals through his angels to His Rasūlas, *nabī* or *Pag͟hambaras* (Prophet or Messenger). So Allāh talks to common man through his angels and prophets.

In the Islamic faith, man is expected to devote himself to Allāh. He is bound to follow the fivefold duties.

(i) Full faith in the oneness of Allāh. This is called *tauhīd*.

(ii) Five time namāẓa everyday.

(iii) *Roẓā* (Fast) in the month of Ramadan.

(iv) Distributing specified part of one's income among the poor (*ẓaquāt*).

(v) Haja (Pilgrimage to Mecca) at least once in a lifetime.

In the Islamic pantheon, though only the supreme deity (Allāh) is worshipped. Yet in addition to Him there are other astral beings who are either benevolent or malevolent. Gabriel, for example, is a benevolent angel. But evil astral beings like Satan are also there. Such evil forces misguide man and abet him to commit sins. Sometimes, such evil spirits misguide benevolent angels like Gabriel. Let it be mentioned here that the concept of Satan is common in all the three Semitic religions namely Judaism, Christianity and Islam.

Taoism is a religion which flourished in China in the pre-Christian era and continues to be a live force even today. This religion was founded by Lao-tzu, a great saint of China. The most prestigious possession of this religion is Tao which is quite close to Upaniṣadic *Brahman*. It is believed that Tao precedes everything including *Shang-ti* (God) and *Tien-ti* (Lord of Heaven). Tao stands beyond the reach of human senses. It is invisible. The phenomenal or the visible world (*Yu*) emerges from nothing (*Wu*). Tao lies even beyond *Wu*. *Yu* is the manifested form of Tao. Tao is essentially formless, limitless and nameless; it is eternal and boundless.

Tao rests on two forces *Yin* and *Yang*. These two forces though mutually antithetical and laden with opposite attributes, are complementary in temperament, constitution and orientation. They are female and male respectively. It is these two forces which maintain order and balance in nature. Whereas *Yin* is shady, cold, passive, feminine, *Yang* is luminous, warm, active and masculine. Further, *Yin* is receptive, consolidative, contractive and negative female energy. As opposed to this, *Yang* is extensive, productive, expansive and positive male energy. It is the interaction between the *Yin* and the *Yang* that produces multiplicity and diversity in the world. None of the two forces solely goes by its native attributes. *Yin*, in some measure, contains the attributes of *Yang*. Similarly, *Yang* latently contains *Yin* attributes.

In Taoism, cosmos is believed to have come into being in the course of interaction between *Yin* and *Yang*. Cosmos is an integration of time and space. Cosmos emerges from chaos. Cosmos is a dynamic process; it is not a static structure. Each and every item of the cosmos from the smallest to the largest contains spirit. No matter in the cosmos is devoid of spirituality. According to Chuang-tzu's interpretation of Taoism, Tao symbolizes totality of existence. Tao embraces everything, all creatures, vegetables and inorganic physical objects. All forms of beings and life are encompassed by Tao. Tao is the constant process of change. Once man knows Tao as it is and goes along with the process of change without resisting or passing judgement on it, he can never be harassed or tormented by the conventional ways of thought. He welcomes poverty as well as prosperity. He rejoices sickness as well as health. He rejoices life as well as death. All these are the parts of Tao. According to Chuang-tzu, Tao has self-contradictory attributes like the Supreme deity of the Upaniṣads. In Chuang-tzu's eyes as and when a searcher knows the secrets of Tao, he is established in the state of actionlessness (*Wu-Wei*).

Capra highlights the secret of Tao, *Yin* and *Yang* in the following words:

> The Chinese philosophers saw reality whose ultimate essence they called Tao, as a process of continual flow and change. In their view, all phenomena we observe, participate in this cosmic process and are thus intrinsically dynamic. The principal characteristic of the Tao is the cyclical nature of its ceaseless motion; all developments in nature, those in the physical world as well as those in the psychological and social realms show cyclical patterns. The Chinese gave this idea of cyclical pattern a definite structure by introducing the polar opposites of *Yin* and *Yang*, the two poles that set the limits for the cycle of change.[4]

---

4. Fritjof Capra, *The Turning Point*, London: Flamingo, 1983, p. 17.

Adherents of Taoism believe in the continuity of soul after death. It is believed that there are two shades of soul — immanent and transcendent. Immanent soul called *P'o* comes into being as life of a human individual being. After *P'o* is enshrined in the body, the transcendent soul called *hun* emerges. *Hun* is a transcendental vital force which manifests itself in the form of consciousness and intelligence. *P'o* is a physical force. It is expressed in bodily strength and movement. *P'o* and *hun* jointly constitute the psychosomatic personality of the individual. After physical death, *hun* migrates to the heaven (*Tien*) along with *P'o*. Later, *P'o* returns to the earth. In the event of an accidental death, *Hun* and *P'o* become ghosts and act maliciously. Another term for *Hun* is *Ling-hun.*

Confucianism de-emphasizes divinity and primarily concerns itself with the problems of man and society. How to evolve an ethical and responsible society was the major concern of Confucianism. Confucius taught people to be superior men (*Chun-tzu*). Superior man has ethical sensitivity and wisdom. He wanted to raise the ethical level of his fellow beings. He wanted the Chinese society to be ethically transformed. Confucius was against the practice of exorcism and divination which was very common in the Chinese society. Worship of ancestral spirit and countless deities was prevalent in the society. Confucius advised his followers to desist from such a worship. Confucius did not concern himself with deities and life after death. Life on the earth was more important for him. The supreme deity in Confucianism is called *Chai-Chi.*

Confucius wanted to usher a model society on the earth. According to him only superior man can materialize such a society on the earth. He contrasted superior man with inferior man. Whereas the superior man understands righteousness, inferior man understands only profit and self-interest. Superior man of Confucius is possessed of several virtues, the greatest virtue being *Gen* (benevolence). *Gen* also means humanism.

Man of *Gen* is a man of boundless virtue. Confucius preached to his disciples to live a life of harmony and equilibrium (*Chung*), a life between the two extremes of indulgence and austerity.

Let us see what Capra says about Confucianism:

> Confucianism derives its name from Kung Fu Tzu or Confucius, a highly influential teacher with a large number of students, who saw his main function as transmitting the ancient cultural heritage to his disciples. In doing so, however, he went beyond simple transmission of knowledge for he interpreted the traditional ideas according to his own moral concepts. His teachings were based on the so-called six classics, ancient books of philosophical thought, rituals, poetry, music and history which represented the spiritual and cultural heritage of the holy sages of China's past. He was neither the author, commentator nor even the editor of any of the classics. His own ideas became known through the Confucian Analects, a collection of aphorisms which was compiled by some of his disciples.[5]

Capra further says:

> Confucianism was a philosophy of social organization, of common sense and practical knowledge. It provided Chinese society with a system of education and with strict coventions of social etiquette. One of its main purposes was to form an ethical basis for the traditional Chinese family system with its complex structure and its ritual of ancestral worship.[6]

Shintoism, the native religion of Japan has evolved from tradition; it has no formal founder. The word Shinto means the path that links man to *Kami*, the supreme deity of this

---

5. Fritjof Capra, *The Tao of Physics : An Exploration of the Parallels between Modern Physics and Eastern Mysticism*, London: Flamingo, 1991, pp. 114-15.

6. Ibid., p. 114.

religion. *Kami* is believed to be a supernatural and awe-inspiring supreme deity that creates and maintains everything.

Shinto cosmology demarcates the cosmos vertically as well as horizontally. Vertically speaking, cosmos consists of the following three blocks:

(i) Uppermost block (*Taka manohara*): It is the block which is occupied by the supreme deity called *Kami.*

(ii) Middle block (*Nakat sukuni*): This block is occupied by man.

(iii) Underworld block (*Yomi*): This block is occupied by the spirit of the dead.

Horizontally speaking, the cosmos consists of two blocks:

(i) Phenomenal world: This block is occupied by mankind

(ii) Perpetual land (*Tokoyo*): This block exists at the edge of phenomenal world.

Shintoism is pre-eminently this-worldly religion. As such here *Taka manohara* and *Tokoyo* are not glorified as heaven is glorified in other religions of the world. In Shintoism human beings are believed to be the son of *Kami.* Man depends on the mercy of *Kami.*

After a brief discussion of the ten world religions, let us move to some local and tribal religions. Let us examine the nature and functions of supreme deity (God) in these religions.

A survey reports that there are roughly four thousand languages in the world. I think the number of the tribal and local religions must not be less than this figure. Out of the four thousand local and tribal religions, a short description of some religions is given below.

In South Africa, there is a tribe called Tswana. The Supreme deity of Tswana is Modimo. Modimo (God) is the ultimate source and the root of all existence. For Tswana tribals, Modimo is everything; He is mother; He is father; He is light; He is darknesss; He is life; He is death; He is benevolent; He is malevolent. Malevolent Modimo is called Selo (monster). Selo possesses dangerous power and damages man's interest if displeased. Along with Modimo, Tswana tribals worship ancestral spirits which they call Bodimo. Direct contact of man with Modimo is not possible. Bodimos act as intermediaries between the man and Modimo (God). If man wants any favour from Modimo, he must first approach Bodimo. Bodimo prays on behalf of the man concerned to Modimo and on the request of Bodimo, Modimo grants favour to the man in question. Bodimo nourishes paternal attitude towards the living members of his tribe.

Vanuatu tribe of Australia professes a religion where there is no supreme deity. They believe in a spiritual being called Natmas. Vanuatus worship moon along with Natmas. In their community gatherings, Vanuatus pray, sing, dance, and make food offerings to the moon on the wooden altar along with Natmas. In the Vanuatu's language, the equivalent word for the moon is *Sina*. Vanuatus believe that moon is the wife of sun. Sometimes, human sacrifices are made to propitiate Natmas.

Yakut tribe of southern Siberia worships *Lurungaiyy Toion* as the supreme deity. He is the lord of creative spirit. In the Yakut language, spirits are called *liyys*. Relationship between Yakut and their supreme deity is very personal. The lord of creation resides on the uppermost sky, the ninth sheath. On this region, snow white grass grows. Yakuts believe in the continued existence of soul (*Kut*) after death. Also Yakuts believe in black spirits which damage man's interest if displeased.

Members of the Yoruba tribe believe that a virtuous man becomes semi-deity (*Orisa*) and lives in the heaven after his death. According to Yoruba myth, there was a king. He was very virtuous and loved by his subjects. After death, he became the god of thunder called Sango. Along with thunder god, he is also worshipped as *Orisa*. The supreme deity of Yoruba is *Ase*.

John Pemberton has portrayed Yoruba world-view in the following words:

> The world-view of the Yoruba is a monistic one. The universe of their experience is pervaded by *Ase*, a divine energy in the process of generation and regeneration. Ase is without any particular signification, yet invests all things and all persons and, as the warrant for all creative activity, opposes chaos and the loss of meaning in human experience. Thus, for Yoruba, the universe is one, and it is amenable for articulation in terms of an elaborate cosmology, to critical reflection and to innovative speculation.[7]

After studying several tribal religions, Long found that belief in reincarnation (rebirth) is common among almost all of them. In Long's own words,

> The belief in re-birth in one form or the other is found in tribal or non-literate cultures all over the world. . . . For the Australian Aborigines, it is axiomatic that spirits of human beings are periodically incarnated in animal or plant forms or even in such inanimate entities as water, fire and wind or the sun, the moon and the stars. This belief is based on the presupposition that the soul is separable from the body and from any other physical object it may inhabit. By virtue of its capacity to survive independently of a physical abode, for at least a brief time, the soul possesses the capacity to travel from body to body and to inhabit a variety of forms ranging from stones and insects to animal and human beings.[8]

---

7. John Pemberton III, "Yoruba Religion" in the *Encyclopaedia of Religion*, New York, Macmillan Publishing Company, 1987, vol. XV, p. 538.
8. J. Bruce Long, "Re-incarnation" in the *Encyclopaedia of Religion*, New York, Macmillan Publishing Company, 1987, vol. XII, pp. 265-66.

## Religions Classified

World religions may be classified into two broad categories, Theocentric and Homocentric. In the first category come Hinduism, Zoroastrianism, Judaism, Christianity, Islam, Taoism and Shintoism. In the second category come the twin non-Vedic religions of India, Jainism and Buddhism. Confucianism is a mid-category. No doubt, it is a Theocentric religion but it lays high emphasis on social-moral order.

Let us now discuss the nature and function of God in the Theocentric religions. Hinduism arose from the soil of Vedic religion. Vedic literature starts from Saṁhitās, the collection of Vedic *ṛcā*s. Vedic literature encompasses a vast textual space within its fold such as the Upaniṣads, the sixth orthodox system of philosophy, the epics — *Rāmāyaṇa* and *Mahābhārata* — Smṛtis, Purāṇas and several others.

In the *Yajurveda Saṁhitā,* there is Puruṣa-Sūkta, a collection of 22 hymns composed by a *ṛṣi,* Nārāyaṇa Puruṣa. The deity of the *sūkta* is *puruṣa* or *Brahman* or God. In this *sūkta,* there is a detailed description of the Virāṭa Puruṣa (God). Following is the textual theme of the Puruṣa-Sūkta:

> God has innumerable heads, innumerable eyes and feet. He encompasses the entire cosmos and yet exceeds the same. God's greatness goes beyond verbal description. The entire creation is only one-fourth of His being. Three-fourth of His divine being lies in the space. The cosmos arose from God. He is the creator of the Vedas. He created the four *varṇa*s from different parts of his body. From his mind arose the moon; from his eyes arose the Sun; from His nostrils arose the air and the breath (*prāṇa*); from His mouth arose the fire; from His navel arose the space; from His head arose the *dyuloka;* from His feet arose the earth; from His ears arose the ten directions. Thus, He created the innumerable *loka*s.

> On the earth, first of all, He created water. God's consort is Lakṣmī.[9]

In the Upaniṣadic terminology, God is called *Brahman*. Following is the description of *Brahman* in the *Īśopaniṣad*:

> *Brahman* is complete in itself. Also the world is complete in itself as it has arisen from the *Brahman* which is complete in all respects. If a full unit is deducted from another full unit, the remnant is also complete or full unit.[10] Whatever there is in the cosmos, it is all permeated by the ultimate reality.[11] *Brahman* is full of contradictory attributes. It moves; it does not move. It is far away, yet it is very close. It is inside everything, yet it is outside everything.[12]

*Kenopaniṣad* describes *Brahman* in the following manner:

> *Brahman* is the ear of ears, mind of minds, speech of speeches, breath of breaths and eye of the eyes.[13] *Brahman* lies beyond the reach of senses. Human speech is unable to verbalize *Brahman* as it is ineffable. Behind the power of speech lies the power of *Brahman*. *Brahman* lies far beyond the reach of human mind. Mind derives its power from *Brahman*. *Brahman* lies beyond the visual power of man. In fact, eyes derive their perceptual power from *Brahman*. *Brahman* lies beyond the reach of ears. Ears derive their power of audition from *Brahman*. Even life derives its power of continuity from *Brahman*.[14]

*Kaṭhopaniṣad* describes *Brahman* in the following manner:

> Creative power of *puruṣa* (*Brahman*) is called *māyā*. *Māyā* is superior to the *jīva*. *Puruṣa* is superior to *māyā* but there is

9. *Yajurveda*, Puruṣa-Sūkta.
10. *Īśopaniṣad*, *Śāntipāṭha*.
11. Ibid., 1.
12. Ibid., 5.
13. *Kenopaniṣad*, 1.2.
14. Ibid., 1.38.

nothing superior to *puruṣa*.[15] *Brahman* permeates through every particle of the creation: it cannot however be identified. Only those equipped with subtle perceptual power can identify it.[16] All the human senses are extra-oriented; they cannot look within. There are, however, some who can look within through deep meditation.[17] Human body with eleven doors is the abode of *Brahman*.[18] *Brahman* is omnipresent. It is present in Vasu. It is present in the guest of the householder. It is sacred fire as well as oblation. It is present in the *yajña*-performer (Hotā). It is present in all human beings. It is present in deities as well as in ancestors. It is present in the sky, *ṛta*. It is present in all creatures.[19] *Brahman* regulates the breath in the human body. It remains in the body even after man is no more.[20] When the entire creation is dissolved, it is *Brahman* that remains. Everything depends on *Brahman*. The *Brahman* permeates in all creatures such as fire, air, and sun. *Brahman* is present in everything invisibly. It is spread over from micro to macro. *Brahman* is the ultimate source of all consciousness.[21] *Brahman* lies behind the light of the sun, moon and the stars.[22] *Brahman* is similar to an inverted banyan tree whose roots lie in the remotest space and whose branches are spread earthward. The entire creation is appended to such a *Brahman* tree. The entire creation arises from *Brahman* in the emergence phase. In the dissolution phase, the entire creation is ceded into *Brahman*. Every creature obeys the command of *Brahman*. The sun, the fire, the air, the death all move as commanded by *Brahman*.[23]

---

15. *Kaṭhopaniṣad*, 1.3.11.
16. Ibid., 1.3.12.
17. Ibid., 2.1.1.
18. Ibid., 2.2.1.
19. Ibid., 2.2.2.
20. Ibid., 2.2.3-4.
21. Ibid., 2.2.9-13.
22. Ibid., 2.2.14-15.
23. Ibid., 2.3.1-3.

> *Brahman* is beyond the reach of mind and speech. *Brahman* cannot be visually perceived.[24]

*Muṇḍakopaniṣad* describes *Brahman* in the following manner:

> Like spider *Brahman* creates the cosmos from its own being. The creation emerges from the immutable *Brahman* as hair grows on the human body.[25] *Brahman* is transcendent and formless; it does not incarnate. *Brahman* is devoid of life-force (*prāṇa*). *Brahman* is devoid of mind and senses. *Brahman* is all white (*śubhra*). *Brahman* lies beyond everything. From *Brahman* arise life-force (*prāṇa*), mind, five senses, sky, air, fire, water and earth. *Brahman* holds the entire cosmos.[26] Fire is the forehead of *Brahman*. The sun and the moon are the eyes of *Brahman*. Directions are the ears of *Brahman*. Vedas are the phonetic expression of *Brahman*. Air is the life-force of *Brahman*. Cosmos is the heart of *Brahman*. Earth is the feet of *Brahman*. *Brahman* is the conscience of all living beings.[27] In the front, in the rear, in all directions, upward, downward, everywhere there is *Brahman*.[28] Human body is like a tree. On this tree live two friendly birds, one *Brahman* and the other *jīva* in the same body-nest. Out of the two friendly birds, the *jīva*-bird is fully involved in tasting the fruit of the tree. As opposed to this, the *Brahman* bird is totally unattached, uninvolved with the whole affair. The *jīva*-bird turns oblivious of his bosom friend (*Brahman*) though He is so close to him. This oblivion costs dearly to the *jīva*-bird; he becomes wretched and helpless. His sufferings and grief evaporate the moment he realizes the supreme power of his bosom friend lying by his side.[29] *Brahman* is bigger than the biggest and smaller than the

---

24. Ibid., 2.3., 12.
25. *Muṇḍakopaniṣad*, 1.1.7, 9.
26. Ibid., 2.1.2, 3.
27. Ibid., 2.1.4.
28. Ibid., 2.2.11.
29. Ibid., 3.1.1, 2.

smallest. *Brahman* is not a subject of visual perception. He is farthest as well as nearest to the *jīva*.[30] Awareness of *Brahman* is possible neither through learned exposition nor through intelligence. Awareness of *Brahman* is also not possible through deep learning. *Brahman* reveals itself to the person of its choice.[31] *Jīvas* of weak temperament fail to evolve *Brahman*-consciousness. They too who are proud of their penance cannot evolve *Brahman*-conciousness. Those free from such vices and weaknesses can evolve *Brahman*-consciousness.[32]

*Māṇḍūkya Upaniṣad* describes *Brahman* in the following manner:

> All that is, is nothing but *Brahman*. The *ātman* is *Brahman*. So the *ātman* is four-footed.[33] *Brahman* is full of contradictory attributes. *Brahman* is devoid of all *prajñā* (intuitive knowledge). *Brahman* is full of *prajñā*. *Brahman* cannot be perceived through senses. *Brahman* cannot be conceptualized. *Brahman* cannot be clasped. *Brahman* is *praṇava*.[34]

*Aitareya* and *Taittirīya* Upaniṣads describe *Brahman* in the following manner:

> In the beginning, only *Brahman* was existing, nothing else. *Brahman* resolved to create the *lokas*. Later, *Brahman* created the *lokas*.[35] In the beginning, it was non-being (*asat*) everywhere. Being (*sat*) arose from the non-being. Later, God created his own being.[36]

---

30. Ibid., 3.1.7, 8.
31. Ibid., 3.2.4.
32. Ibid., 3.2.4.
33. *Māṇḍūkyopaniṣad*, 2.
34. Ibid., 7, 8.
35. *Aitareya Upaniṣasd*, 1.1.1, 2.
36. *Taittirīya Upaniṣad*, 2.7.1.

*Śvetāśvatara Upaniṣad* describes *Brahman* in the following words:

> In the piece of dry wood, fire is not visible, though fire is very much there. Similarly, *Brahman* is not perceptible through senses, yet *Brahman* is there everywhere in the imperceptible form.[37] Nothing exists beyond *Brahman*. Nothing is bigger and smaller than *Brahman*. *Brahman* holds the entire creation. Everything arises from *Brahman*. Everything dissolves in *Brahman*. *Brahman* has mouths facing all directions. *Brahman* has countless heads and necks. *Brahman* lies in the heart of all creatures, biggest as well as the smallest. *Brahman* is omnipresent.[38] *Brahman*'s hands and feet are everywhere. Eyes, heads and mouths of *Brahman* are everywhere. *Brahman* shines everywhere. *Brahman* encompasses the entire creation.[39] Though devoid of feet, *Brahman* moves very fast. *Brahman* visualizes and hears though it possesses no eyes, no ears. *Brahman* knows everything knowable, though nobody knows *Brahman*. Such is the greatness of *Brahman*. *Brahman* is bigger than the biggest and smaller than the smallest. *Brahman* lives in the body of all creatures.[40] *Brahman* can be caught neither from upside nor from downside, nor from middle side. Nothing is like *Brahman*. *Brahman* is formless.[41] *Brahman* has no work; *Brahman* has no senses like living creatures. What to say of anything bigger than *Brahman*, there is nothing which equals *Brahman*. Ṛṣis portray the transcendental power called *Brahman* in different ways. *Brahman* lies hidden in its own creation like a spider which hides itself in the web. *Brahman* permeates through the entire creation. *Brahman* is the conscience of all living creatures. *Brahman* is the master of

37. *Śvetāśvatara Upaniṣad*. 1.13.
38. Ibid., 3.9, 11.
39. Ibid., 3.16.
40. Ibid., 3.19, 20.
41. Ibid., 4.19.

> *karma*. *Brahman* is the shelter of all creatures. *Brahman* is also the sole witness of all that happens. *Brahman* stands beyond all attributes. *Brahman* is the sole holder of consciousness.[42]

*Bṛhadāraṇyaka Upaniṣad* describes *Brahman* in the following manner:

> In the beginning there was nothing. Everything was covered with death.[43] In the beginning, only *ātman* was there in the form of *puruṣa*. He saw only himself and nothing else. So, he called himself "I am (*ahamasmi*)."[44] He felt lonely and wanted the second. He divided himself into two parts and two became husband and wife.[45] *Brahman* is the only perceiver.[46] This *ātman* is *Brahman*.[47] In the beginning only *Brahman* was there. *Brahman* knew that the knower is *Brahman*.[48] *Brahman* is dualistic in constitution, tangible-intangible, mortal-immortal, static-dynamic. All existing things are ephemeral.[49] Here, there is not plurality, no multiplicity.[50] *Brahman* is imperishable (*akṣara*). *Brahman* is neither thick nor thin, neither small nor big, neither red nor white, neither solid nor liquid, neither shadow nor darkness, neither air nor space. *Brahman* is none of these: taste, odour, eyes, ears, tongue, mind, fire, vital elements, inside, outside. *Brahman* does not eat nor can *Brahman* be eaten.[51] *Brahman* cannot be perceived though *Brahman* perceives everything. *Brahman*

---

42. Ibid., 6.8, 10, 11.
43. *Bṛhadāraṇyaka Upaniṣad*, 1.2.1.
44. Ibid., 1.4.1.
45. Ibid., 1.4.3.
46. Ibid., 3.8.11.
47. Ibid., 2.5.19.
48. Ibid., 1.4.10.
49. Ibid., 2.3.1.
50. Ibid., 4.4.19.
51. Ibid., 3.8.8.

> cannot be heard though *Brahman* hears everything. *Brahman* transcends mind, yet *Brahman* thinks. *Brahman* is unknowable, yet *Brahman* knows each and everyone. There is no visualizer other than *Brahman*. There is no hearer, no thinker, and no knower other than *Brahman*.[52] The *ātman* is *Brahman*.[53]

*Chāndogya Upaniṣad* describes *Brahman* in the following manner:

> That (*Brahman*) thou art (*tat tvam asi*).[54] In the beginning, there was only one element. It was all alone without any second. Also it was unmanifested. From this primal element, manifestation (*sat*) arose.[55] All that exist is *Brahman*.[56] *Ātman* is sinless, ageless, deathless, sorrowless, hungerless, thirstless.[57]

*Yoga Darśana* describes God in the following manner:

> God (*Īśvara*) is a *puruṣa* of distinct category. He is beyond the five pains (ignorance, goodwill, ill-will, *asmitā*, *abhniveśa*). He is beyond action and action-chain, *sañcita prārabdha* and *kriyamāṇa*. He is beyond birth, age and *bhoga* (*āśaya*).[58]

*Sāṁkhya Darśana* talks about God and the related matter in the following way:

> In the event of God's existence being disproved.[59] God is extremely subtle. Empiricially His existence is not ascertainable.[60] There is no mediation by God in conjoining

52. Ibid., 3.8.11.
53. Ibid., 4.4.5.
54. *Chāndogya Upaniṣad*, 6.8.16.
55. Ibid., 6.2.1.
56. Ibid., 3.14.1.
57. Ibid., 8.7.1.
58. *Yoga Darśana*, 1.24.
59. *Sāṁkhya Darśana*, 1.92.
60. Ibid., 1.109.

*karma* and the fruit of the *karma*. There is unmediated link between the two.[61] The ultimate base has no further base. Therefore, the ultimate base stands all by itself.[62]

*Brahma-Sūtra* describes *Brahman* in the following manner:

> *Brahman* is the ultimate source of all creation. In the dissolution phase, all creation reverts to its source.[63] *Brahman* has two types of power, transcendent (*parā*) and immanent (*aparā*). *Parā* is related to the animate creature. *Aparā* is related to the inanimate objects.[64] *Brahman* is identical to its powers, transcendent and immanent, yet it is different from both of them.[65] *Brahman* starts creation with the help of its transcendent and immanent power. In the dissolution phase, the entire creation is sucked by the Supreme Being.[66] *Brahman* is both attributeful as well as attributeless. *Brahman* is dualistic in constitution.[67] *jīva* is immortal. Death and birth come to be associated with him when he is encased in the body.[68]

*Manu-Smṛti* describes the origin of cosmos in the following manner:

> In the beginning, everywhere there was darkness. From the darkness emerged *Bhagavān*. He manifested Himself. He then created the five elements of the tangible cosmos. He put seed in the water with a view to creating life. The seed became golden egg. From this egg, emerged Brahmā. On behalf of *Bhagavān* (*Īśvara*) Brahmā initiated the process of creation.[69]

61. Ibid., 5.2.
62. Ibid., 1.67.
63. *Brahma-Sūtra*, 1.1.2.
64. Ibid., 3.2.28.
65. Ibid., 2.1.22.
66. Ibid., 2.1.17.
67. Ibid., 3.2.11-26.
68. Ibid., 2.3.16-18.
69. *Manu-Smṛti*, 1.5-9.

Now, let us see what the *Gītā* says on God (*Īśvara*), *ātman* and allied issues:

> Body is perishable but the *ātman* is eternal.[70] *Ātman* is neither born nor does it die. *Ātman* is birthless, eternal. *Ātman* does not perish with the death of body.[71] God is birth-transcendent, eternal, lord of living beings, yet He incarnates Himself as and when *dharma* suffers erosion and degeneration. He does so in every age with the sole objective of rejuvenating and re-establishing *dharma*. He protects the virtuous and punishes the wrong-doers.[72] God has created the four *varṇas* according to the attributes and *karma* of the people. The creator of *varṇas* must be deemed as non-doer and eternal.[73] God is not involved in action, nor is He interested in the fruit of action.[74] Nothing is beyond God. In God, everything is embedded as thread runs through the flowers of the garland.[75] God is the light which lightens the sun and the moon.[76] God is the seed of all living beings.[77] God remains hidden under the thick veil of *māyā*. Those who pierce the veil, have the glimpse of God.[78] God is essentially non-manifested (*avyakta*). He transcends all alterations, variations and transformations. Ignorant people, however, believe Him to be manifested.[79] God is not visible to all and sundry. He lies behind the thick veil of His *yoga māyā*. God, in fact, transcends birth process and stands

70. *Gītā*, 2.8.
71. Ibid., 2.20.
72. Ibid., 4.7-8.
73. Ibid., 4.13.
74. Ibid., 4.14.
75. Ibid., 7.7.
76. Ibid., 7.8.
77. Ibid., 7.10.
78. Ibid., 7.14.
79. Ibid., 7.24.

beyond all changes.[80] *Brahman* is immutable (*avyaya*).[81] After a *jīva* realizes God, he transcends the chain of birth and death.[82] In the creation-phase, manifestation comes into being from the state of non-manifestation. In the dissolution phase, the manifested cosmos reverts to its non-manifestation. Manifestation phase symbolizes day and dissolution phase symbolizes night. The dual process of day and night operates continually.[83] God, who transcends everything, continues to exist even after the entire creation stands dissolved.[84] The entire creation is permeated by God. All creatures are held by God but godhood lies even beyond the creation limits.[85] God is like space. Creatures are like air. Space encompasses the air. So God encompasses the whole creation.[86] All creation is sucked by God in the end of the *kalpa*. In the subsequent *kalpa* the same is created once again.[87] Under God's instructions, the *prakṛti* weaves the entire animate and the inanimate world. Thus the creation continues to go on.[88] The ignorant people believe God as confined to the human body, who, in fact, is the Lord of the entire creation.[89] God is everything. He is *kratu* (*yajña*), *svadhā*, medicine, *mantra*, *ghṛta*, fire, oblation and the entire ritual of the *havana*. He is the holder of the enitre creation. He is also father, mother, grandfather, *praṇava* and the three Vedas. He is the ultimate cause of creation, dissolution, composition and decomposition. He is the immutable and ultimate. God

---

80. Ibid., 7.25.
81. Ibid., 8.3.
82. Ibid., 8.16.
83. Ibid., 8.18-19.
84. Ibid., 8.20.
85. Ibid., 9.4.
86. Ibid., 9.6.
87. Ibid., 9.7.
88. Ibid., 9.10.
89. Ibid., 9.11.

shines through the sun. God rains through the clouds. He is both life as well as death. He is truth as well as untruth.[90] God looks after those who singularly devote themselves to God.[91] *Ṛṣi*s and *deva*s do not know about the origin of God as it is God who has brought them into being. God is the supreme cause of the entire creation. Everything owes its origin to God.[92] There is no end of God's expansion. God is the beginning, mid and the end point of creation.[93] God is the ultimate source of all creatures. He is the creator of the animate as well as the inanimate.[94] God holds the entire creation by one of His manifested powers.[95] God's hands and feet are omnipresent. So are His eyes, heads, mouth and ears. He encompasses the whole creation and sits over it. He relishes the cognition objects of all senses though He has no senses. He feeds all creatures, yet He is not involved in it. He relishes all items of consumption, though He carries no attributes. Himself He is inside as well as outside of all creatures. He is mobile as well as immobile. He is incomprehensible because of His subtleness. He is very close, yet He is far far away. Though God is essentially indivisible, He appears as divided at the manifestation plane. He holds the entire creation; He creates it and also He demolishes it. God dwells in the hearts of all creatures.[96] In the procreation phase, nature plays a mother's role and *Brahman* plays a father's role.[97] The cosmos is like the eternal *pīpala* tree, set in the reverse position. The roots of the creation tree lie in the sky. The branches of the tree are stretched

---

90. Ibid., 9.16-19.
91. Ibid., 9.22.
92. Ibid., 10.6, 8.
93. Ibid., 10.19, 20.
94. Ibid., 10.39.
95. Ibid., 10.42.
96. Ibid., 13.13-17.
97. Ibid., 14.4.

> below. Vedas are the leaves of the creation tree.[98] The energy that makes the sun burn; the energy that makes the moon shine; the energy that makes the fire burn is actually God's.[99] God feeds all creatures.[100]

The above quotes from Vedic texts to the *Gītā* are direct translations from the origional hymns and the verses. As such they are free from the hermeneutical biases. Due to hermeneutical biases, sometimes new meanings are imposed on the scriptural text from the commentator's side. A macroscopic look over the texts ranging from the Vedic Saṁhitās to the *Gītā* reveals that while in the pre-*Gītā* scriptural text, God maintains His transcendental character, in the *Gītā* text, while maintaining His transcendental character, He quite often lurks into the immanent region of the human world. He incarnates Himself; He meddles with the human affairs, punishes some and rewards others. In the *Gītā,* the supreme power has grown quite friendly with man. In the foregoing quotes, God has been given at least seven names, Puruṣa, Virāṭa, Brahman, Ātman, Īśvara, Bhagavān and Nārāyaṇa.

What is the God-man relation? On this issue commentators of scriptures vary widely. Commentators draw their conclusion on the testimony of the three apex scriptures, namely, Upaniṣads, *Brahma-Sūtra* and the *Gītā.* Technically, these three apex structures are called the three *prasthāna*s (*prasthāna trayī*). There are more than fifteen acknowledged commentators on the three scriptures. But seven of them are highly acknowledged ones. The first and the foremost of these commentators is Śaṅkarācārya. He talks of unqualified monism. According to unqualified monism, only the *Brahman* is true. The creation is illusion, and substantially the *jīva* is

98. Ibid., 15.1.
99. Ibid., 15.12.
100. Ibid., 15.17.

*Brahman.*[101] There is no duality between the two. As such the question of worshipper and the worshipped between the *jīva* and *Brahman* does not arise. Both are one and the same.

But other *ācāryas* do not agree with the position held by Śaṅkarācārya. Rāmānujācārya talks of Viśiṣṭādvaita (qualified monism). According to him, there is no essential difference between *Brahman* and *jīva*. But non-essential difference between the two certainly exists. To explain his position, he takes the analogy of gold and ornament. Though gold and ornament essentially come in the same category, non-essentially ornament is different from gold. So is the case with *Brahman* and the *jīva*. As such *jīva* attains the ultimate goal of life by devotion to *Brahman*. Nimbārkācārya's Dvaitādvaita and Vallabhācārya's Śuddhādvaita posit almost the same view on the relation between the *jīva* and *Brahman*. Madhva, however, talks of pure dualism. He maintains that the *jīva* and *Brahman* come into two clear-cut categories and they are never equivalent to each other. *Brahman* is the Lord and *jīva* is the devotee. Svāmī Dayānanda Saraswatī comes out with triadism (*Traitavāda*). According to him, there are three inter-related substances, viz. *Brahman, jīva* and the *prakṛti*. Caitanya Mahāprabhu talks of incomprehensible dualistic monism (Acintyabhedābheda).

According to the commentators of the three scriptures, there are two paths that lead to man's *summum bonum*, the path of knowledge (*jñāna-mārga*) and the path of devotion (*bhakti-mārga*). The path of knowledge consists in the perception of unity between the *jīva* and *Brahman*. The moment a seeker of truth develops such a vision, he perceives no difference between himself and *Brahman*. He perceives cosmos in the chaos. He perceives unity in diversity. The knower of *Brahman* becomes *Brahman* itself.[102] The path of devotion is easy for a

101. *brahma satyam jaganmithyā jīvo brahmaiva nāparaḥ.*

102. *brahmavit brahmaiva bhavati.*

common man. In this path, a devotee is dependent on the mercy of God. There is dualism between God and man. God is all powerful and the devotee is totally powerless. It is through the grace of God that *jīva* attains his cherished goal. Rāmānujācārya talks of *prapatti-mārga* (path of total surrender). In *prapatti-mārga* the devotee totally leaves himself on the mercy of God. Further, the doctrine of *prapatti* takes two forms, *markat-nyāya* (monkey-principle) and *mārjārī-nyāya* (kitten-principle). In *markat* form of *prapatti,* devotee (baby-monkey) clasps his mother and mother also extends her supporting hand to the baby-monkey. The devotee (baby-monkey) lies on the mercy of his mother (deity). In kitten form of *prapatti* (*mārjārī-nyāya*), the baby-kitten (devotee) is absolutely dependent on its mother. It is entirely mother's responsibility to look after the baby-kitten.

Vallabhācārya in his pure monism (Śuddhādvaita) talks of *puṣṭi-mārga* (path of grace). According to him devotion to Lord Kṛṣṇa elevates man to his desired goal. Nimbārka, Madhva, Rāmānanda and Goswāmī Tulsīdās eulogize *bhakti.* Goswāmī Tulsī Dās is very categorical on this point. According to him, the relationship of deity and devotees is a *must* between God and man for the latter's ultimate good. Let it be mentioned here that in Hinduism, worship is primarily personal and idol-centred. Sometimes it is collective and recitative. As against this, in Semitic religions (Judaism, Christianity and Islam) worship is essentially collective and non-idolatrous.

Hindusim is different from all other religions of the world on one important point. Hinduism is like a banyan tree with one trunk and several trunk-like branches. The trunk of Hindusim consists in Vedas. The branches consist in several sources making up the body of the Hindu scripture and Hindu belief-system. Hinduism is not founded by one single man as other religions of the world are. Other religions of the world are like common trees with single trunk.

## The Semitic Religions

The Semitic religions (Judaism, Christianity and Islam) may be seen as a bunch of three units. Though each of the three religions has grown into full-fledged autonomous and independent ecclesias, an invisible bond binds them together. The genesis of the bond is traceable to a man called Abraham. In distant past, Abraham founded a religion which emphasized two things: (i) God is one and He must be worshipped by man, and (ii) idolatry must be viewed as taboo. Abraham and his son Ismail raised a house of Allāh in Mecca called Ka'aba. At Ka'aba, Arabs paid obeisance to Allāh. As centuries passed, the religion founded by Abraham degenerated into polytheism and idolatry. Ka'aba became a seat of religion other than the one founded by Abraham. The house of Allāh was flooded with the idols of several deities numbering 360. It is said that on each day of the year, each deity was specially worshipped in the Ka'aba.

Abraham had two sons, Ishak and Ismail. In the progeny-line of Ishak, Lord Moses was born. He founded a new religion called Judaism. Lord Moses is called Kaleemullah. Kaleemullah is a person with whom the supreme deity Yahveh likes to converse. Yahveh taught Torah to Moses for the benefit of mankind. He also gave him the taboos and mores in the form of Ten Commandments. Thus two Semitic religions parallel to each other came into being — the religion founded by Abraham and the religion founded by Moses (Judaism). In Judaic as well as in Abraham's religion, animal sacrifice was in vogue. Jews sacrificed animals to propitiate Yahveh also called Jehovah. So did followers of Abraham to propitiate Allāh.

With the passage of time, there arose a schism in Judaism. There were some who abhorred the sacrifice of innocent animals. They opposed the barbarous practice of animal sacrifice. They called their sect Essene. Members of Essene sect lived like hermits. They bade good-bye to animal sacrifice and lived as recluses. Celibacy and non-possession were the reigning values of their lives. They abstained from wine and flesh and led a monastic life. They frowned marriage and householders' life. Essenes were inspired by the Greek philosopher of the sixth century BCE named Pythagoras.

The Essene sect of Judaism came into being nearly two hundred years before Jesus was born. Jesus though born in a Jewish family, falling in the progeny-line of Abraham, Ishak and Moses, he developed a soft corner for the Essene way of life. So Essene was the mid-stone between Judaism and the religion which assumed shape after Jesus, the Christ. Christianity exhibits several traits of Essenism: monasticism, celibacy, and affront against animal sacrifice. Taboos and mores in case they proved detrimental in the path of service to the mankind were freely overstepped. Almost all these traits of Christianity have been borrowed from Essene world-view.

Scripturally speaking, Judaism and Christianity are very much like Siamese twins. The holy Bible has two sections namely, the Old Testament and the New Testament. Old Testament belongs to the Jewish faith and the New Testament to Christianity. Judaism is regarded as the parent faith of Christianity. If not a Siamese twin, Judaism and Christianity may at least be seen as a dyad bound by the common lace of historicity. Whereas Lord Moses is called Kaleemullah, Jesus is called Roohallah (The soul of the supreme deity).

Islam is the third major member of the Semitic trio. Hazrat Mohammed, the founder of Islam was born in the progeny-line of Ismail. Out of the three religions that existed before him, his favoured religion was the one founded by his progenitor Hazrat Abraham. The religion Hazrat Mohammed most detested was Christianity. He loathed the very idea of a man being God's son. He openly declared, "God neither begets, as He has no wife nor is He begotten as nothing precedes

Him." Hazrat Mohammed, however, aligned himself to some extent with Judaism. Like Judaic God Yahveh, Allāh is all merciful and just but unlike Him, he is not vindictive, demanding and revengeful.

Hazrat Mohammed, however, did not approve of Abraham's religion as it was handed down to the Arabic society of his time. Abraham's religion has by then degenerated into polytheism and idolatry which was the very negation of the religion Abraham taught to the people of his time. So Hazrat Mohammed took the pledge to revive Abraham's religion in its original form. After he was established as Rasulallah (Messenger of God), he broke all the 360 idols enshrined in the Ka'aba for worship. Let it be mentioned here that Hazrat Abdullah, father of Hazrat Mohammed was the caretaker and the head priest of Ka'aba. Hazrat Mohammed, however, spared one idol called Sang-e-Aswad, the why of which still remains a riddle, a mystery, an unresolved and unexplained event. The new religion called Islam was nothing but the original version of the religion preached centuries back by Hazrat Abraham. Hazrat Mohammed did not claim to have founded a new religion. He simply weeded out the pollutants of an already existing religion as commanded by Allāh and ushered it as the reigning religion of the Arabian society, which later assumed world stature. All the three Semitic religions are monistic in temperament.

In the three Semitic religions, the borderline of transcendence and immanence is clearly demarcated. Each world ruthlessly guards its borders. Intrusion into one by the other is never permissible. God is transcendent and man is immanent. Each remains confined to one's own world. Transcendent God, however, intrudes into the immanent world of man through His media, say angels. But this is done only for the good of man. As man cannot follow the proper path to his destination without any help from the transcendence, God sheds light on his path, so that he may get along. In Hinduism, however, the boundaries of the transcendent and the immanent world are not so clearly defined and demarcated. Godhood often descends to manhood and guides him to his proper goal. Man too sometimes through his acts elevates himself to the level of God.

**Zoroastrianism**

Zoroastrianism, Shintoism and Taoism are theocentric religions. Like Hinduism and Semitic religions, adherents of these religions pray to God and worship Him to gain His favour. Confucianism is a religion which though essentially theocentric is homocentric in spirit. It is a religion which de-emphasizes ontology and lays heavy emphasis on ethico- moral issues. The reason behind such an emphasis is to elevate human society to a higher ethical plane.

**Homocentric Religions**

Jainism and Buddhism are homocentric religions. Jain religion proceeds with certain ontological assumptions. Following are the major assumptions of Jain ontology.

(i) The world has no creator. It is beginningless and endless. It has ever been existing; it will ever exist.

(ii) Everything changes with the passage of time. Things appreciate and depreciate.

(iii) In spite of changes, continuity is also there. Every change has a continuity aspect and every continuity has a change aspect.

Let it be mentioned here that Jain philosophy does not believe in the existential entity of time. It regards time as devoid of entity.

Usually in theocentric religions, God has two functions.

(i) Creation, maintenance and dissolution of the cosmos and (ii) Guiding man to his goal, rewarding and punishing him for his good and bad deeds. But Jainistic assumptions make God redundant. In Jain view, cosmos ever exists; it does not require any creator. Further, a man's actions can elevate him to the stature of God; he does not require any help from outside. *Jīva* can rise to the height of God on his own initiative. *Jīva*s get the results of their good and bad deeds without the mediation of God. *Jīva* attains onliness (*kaivalya*) through his own efforts of *saṁvara* and *nirjarā* (checking the inflow of *pudgala*s and weeding out the already deposited *pudgala*s). Those who attain *kaivalya* becomes *arhat* or *nirgrantha* (knotless). *Arhat* is equivalent to God. *Arhat* transcends the cycle of birth and death.

Buddhism like Jainism attaches no function to God. How this world came into being, is not man's concern. Man should concentrate on his own actions. His actions can make or mar him. If he is full of lust and falls prey to the worldly pleasures, he is bound to fall in the cycle of birth and death (*bhavacakra*). *Bhavacakra* entails endless agony of birth, old age, disease and death. The only way to get rid of these agonies and sufferings is *nirvāṇa*. In the state of *nirvāṇa*, all lust (*vāsanā*) dries up; all thirst (*tṛṣṇā*) is satiated. *Nirvāṇa* lifts *jīva* from the ocean of sufferings. *Jīva* or *ātman* in Buddhism is not an eternal being; it is a flow of consciousness. Lord Buddha attained enlighten-ment on his own initiative through his own concerted efforts. No God came to his help. According to Buddhism, man shapes his own destiny through his good or bad acts.

Later, Buddhism split into three *yāna*s (vehicles) — Arhat or Śrāvaka Yāna, Pratyekabuddha Yāna and Buddha Yāna. Adherents of Arhat Yāna were interested in their own *nirvāṇa*. Protagonists of Pratyeka Buddha Yāna were interested in the *nirvāṇa* of their near and dear ones in addition to their own.

Adherents of Buddha Yāna were committed to the *nirvāṇa* of each and every *jīva*. In the entire scheme of *nirvāṇa*, God has no role to play. In fact, existence of any external substance, *ātman* or God, does not fit in with the basic premises of Buddhism as enunciated by Lord Buddha. After Lord Buddha, his basic preachings were lost sight of and in their stead, new premises were interpolated in the system of Buddhistic philosophy. In later literature, Lord Buddha was portrayed as God himself in the form of Amitābha Buddha. According to *Saddharmapuṇḍarīka*, Buddha is all powerful God. Māyā is under him. According to yet another book *Sukhāvatīvyūha*, *Sukhāvatī* is a special heaven where Lord Buddha resides as Amitābha Buddha. Those who worhsip Amitābha Buddha attain this heaven after *nirvāṇa*.

Such absurdities are galore in Mahāyāna literature. One Vimalananda Saraswati, a Daśnāmī Saṁnyāsī of Vārāṇasī in his book entitled *Baudhāyana*, has written that while in the mother's womb, Lord Buddha was provided with all the heavenly luxuries and amenities by the divinity.[103]

"Manhood ascending godhood" (upward journey) no doubt characterizes Jainism and Buddhism but such a view of manhood is not foreign to the Hindu belief system either. In Hinduism, there are two images of God, Upaniṣadic and Paurāṇic. In the Upaniṣadic image of God, *jīva* is essentially *Brahman*. Due to the veil of ignorance (*avidyā, adhyāsa*) *jīva* fails to identify this reality. The moment *jīva* dispels this ignorance, he is established godhood. The veil, therefore, between *jīva* and *Brahman* is ignorance. Through his meditative efforts, *jīva* dispels his ignorance and rises to the level of godhood. This is his upward journey. Exponents of monism are very emphatic on this point. According to them, unity of *jīva* and *Brahman* is possible only through the removal of ignorance of dualism

103. Vimalanand Saraswati, *Baudhāyana*, Varanasi: Central Institute of Higher Tibatan Studies, Sarnath, 2004, p. 9.

between *jīva* and *Brahman* (*ṛte jñānanna muktiḥ*). The *ṛṣi* of Puruṣa-Sūkta (*Yajurveda*) declares unequivocally that the only path of emancipation is the path of knowledge (*nānyaḥ panthā vidyate yanāya*). In the Upaniṣadic literature, there are several great sayings (*mahāvākyas*) which highlight the essential unity between the *jīva* and *Brahman*. Some of such sayings are given here: That thou art (*tat-tvam-asi*); I am *Brahman* (*aham brahmāsmi*); I am that (*so 'ham*); and the *ātman* is *Brahman* (*ayamātmā brahma*).

Rāmānujācārya, the exponent of qualified monism (Viśiṣṭādvaita) talks of upward journey of man through the path of devotion. According to him, there are four stages of proximity which man can attain with godhood. These proximities are : ascendance to the *loka* of divinity (*sālokya*), proximation to the godhood (*sāmīpya*), attainment of god-like attributes (*sārūpya*) and lastly union with the godhood (*sāyujya*). In *sāyujya mukti, jīva* is united with the godhood. He becomes the part and parcel of godhood.

According to the Purāṇic image of godhood, god's descendence or incarnation is not confined to human race only; He descends even to lower species such as fish and tortoise. But along with the descendence of godhood, there are several myths in Purāṇas which talk of ascendence of manhood to godhood. Triśaṅku was physically transported to the heaven by Viśvāmitra. Nahuṣa rose to the high position of Indrahood by his virtuous deeds of exceptionally high category. There are many more myths with such a theme in the Purāṇas.

## Another Classification of Religions

Religions of the world may broadly be classified into two categories, namely, proselytisive and insulative. Adherents of proselytisive religions propagate the messages of their religion among the people and induct them into their fold with a view to increasing its size. Adherents of insulative religions, however, concentrate on the quality of their native fold and are least interested in increasing its size. The three major proselytisive religions are Buddhism, Christianity and Islam. Votaries of Buddhism, particularly kings and powerful people, took the key-message of Buddhism beyond the frontiers of India. Major countries, which came to be enamoured by the charms of Buddhism, were Tibet, Nepal, China, Ceylon (Sri Lanka), Indonesia, Korea, Japan and several other countries of South-East Asia. Buddhism moved from countries to countries with typhonic speed. Later, Christianity followed in the footsteps of Buddhism and covered almost the whole globe. The Christian missionaries spread the message of Christ almost everywhere. Islam, in the seventh century, rose from the soil of Arabia and covered the Middle East, Asia, Northern Africa and some European countries. Along with persuasion, votaries of Islam also adopted pressure tactics for the spread of their religion in the middle ages. Now, in addition to proselytization, they raise the number of their believers through procreation. Huntington highlights this point in the following words: "In the long run, however, Mohammed wins out. Christianity spreads primarily by conversion, Islam by conversion and reproduction."[104]

The remaining seven religions of the world come in the insulative category. Zoroastrianism contains the maximum insulatory tendency. Because of this suicidal tendency, this community is fast heading toward extinction.

Hinduism does not believe in proselytization but keeping in view the growing menace of proselytization by other religions such as Christianity and Islam, it is resorting to reconversion. Further, it is trying to assimilate different tribal religions into its fold in response to the challenges posed by proselytisive religions.

104. Samuel P. Huntington, *The Clash of Civilizations and the Remaking of World Order*, New Delhi: Penguin Books, 1997, p. 65.

8

# God : A Human Creation

*Bashistha Narayan Sinha*

God is a human creation. It is astonishing enough to know that God is a human imagination, because we are habituated to hear that God is the creator, and he has created the whole universe. Theists may be annoyed and angry after knowing this statement. Though it is well-known and well-accepted that God is the creator, sustainer and destroyer of the world, it cannot be neglected and negated that God is human-made. It is man who says that there is God and also it is man who says that there is no God.

Theism and atheism are the main principles in the religio-philosophical thinking. Theism accepts the existence of God while atheism refutes it. But even in theism concept of God has been imagined by the theist thinkers. This may be known by going through the beginning of the Vedic philosophy which is considered as the strong pillar of theism. There have been propounded the following four theories concerning ultimate reality.

1. Naturalistic-Anthropomorphic-Pluralism
2. Henotheism
3. Monotheism
4. Monism

The Vedic philosophy begins with Naturalistic Anthropomorphic-Pluralism, and step by step reaches to Monism, through Henotheism and Monotheism, which may be seen in the following way.

**Naturalistic-Anthropomorphic-Pluralism**

Man living in the lap of nature feels various pleasures and pains created by the different constituents of nature. He likes pleasure but not pain. So, in order to enjoy pleasure and to be free from suffering he imagines different gods and goddesses in the garb and powers of nature. He imagines gods in an earth, water, fire, and sky. He provides human shape to all of them. He prays to them and expects to be blessed by them. Gods and goddesses imagined by man are many in number. Thus naturalistic-anthropomorphic- pluralism has been established.

**Henotheism**

Because there are several gods and goddesses, the question arises: who is the supreme one? To solve this problem, man declares the supermacy of god according to time and place, i.e. according to his need. Suppose he suffers either from heavy rain or drought and he wants to be blessed by Indra, god of water, he prays to Indra as the Supreme God or the Supreme Reality. In case of being troubled by fire he worships the god of fire as the supreme one. In the case of being troubled by earthquake he assigns the god of earth as the Supreme God, so on and so forth.

This theory of accepting the Supreme God according to time, place and need, has been named *henotheism* by Max Müller. Henotheism is very popular in Hinduism. Somebody goes to Viśvanātha-temple, Rāma-temple, Kr̥ṣṇa-temple, Durgā-temple, Hanumān-temple, etc. one by one and he repeats, according to time and place, the same prayer to all gods and goddesses in the different temples.

> O god/goddess,[1]
> You are my mother, you are my father
> You are my brother
> You are my friend
> You are my wisdom
> You are my wealth
> You are my all in all!

## Monotheism

There are many gods and goddesses, and the supremacy goes to them according to time and place. The supremacy moves from one to the other. So the question arises: Who is the permanent Supreme God in the true sense? Then, man imagines a Supreme God who is the head of all gods and goddesses. He is known as the universal (*viśvātmā*) or the supreme soul (*paramātmā*). All gods and goddesses are known as the organs of the supreme God.[2] He is only one, but scholars name Him differently.[3] He is the golden-seed (Hiraṇyagarbha) and the creator of this Universe. In this way monotheism is propounded.

## Monism

Later, monotheism has been converted into monism. Man is found not satisfied with the monotheistic God, because he does not know His form, figure and dwelling place. He becomes very curious to be acquainted with them. But he fails to be so, and he imagines a Supreme Reality (*parama tatha*)

---

1. *tvameva mātā ca pitā tvameva,*
   *tvameva bandhus ca sakhā tvameva,*
   *tvameva vidyā ca draviṇam tvameva,*
   *tvameva sarvam mama deva deva."*
2. *"Ekasyatmanoarya derah pratyasigani bhavanti"* Bharatiya Darshana, Vacaspati Gairota, p. 32.
3. *ekam sadvipra bahudhā vadanti.*

instead of Supreme God (*parama deva*). This reality is named as *Brahman* which is absolute, non-dual and impersonal. But the absolute *Brahman* is of no use for the world in which man is living. So, again he imagines *Īśvara* the personal aspect of the impersonal *Brahman*. The personal aspect of *Brahman* is known as *Saguṇa Brahman* while impersonal *Brahman* is known as *Nirguṇa Brahman*.

Śaṅkara like Kant, believes that God cannot be proved by our finite thought. All attempts to do so end in failure. They lead to what Kant has called antinomies.[4]

This is because God has been imagined. Tulsīdās, a renowned theist has said,

*jākī rahi bhāvanā jaisī* ।
*prabhu mūrati dekhī tina taisī* ॥

It means man perceives God according to his own idea and feeling. He imagines in his own way. One may conclude two things from this statement.

1. Man has created God according to his own will and need.
2. Man has provided his own shape to God.

## God According to Human Will

Man has been facing several problems since he is on this earth, and he finds himself unable to solve them. Even other beings are not capable to solve human problems and to make the human life pleasant and peaceful. Therefore man has imagined such a powerful element, which is quite able to solve all the problems of human life. He has called that element God. God has all characteristics adhering to human needs which may be known in the following ways:

4. C.D. Sharma, *Indian Philosophy*, p. 396.

(a) ***Eternal*** — God has been imagined as immortal because man himself is mortal. In case of God being mortal no difference between man and God may be seen. But God should be superior to human being in all spheres. Moreover, problems of birth, death, mother and father may arise. The followers of atheism also ask who is the creator of God, if God is the creator of this universe. So to be free from all these problems, theists have declared God as eternal.

(b) ***Omniscient*** — God is known as omniscient. Why? Because, God's devotees reside in different parts of world. They live in India, America, Japan, China, Britain, etc. They all, when in trouble pray to God, in order to be saved by Him. But how can he know the sufferings of the numberless devotees living at different places very very far from one another, if his knowing capacity is limited. That is why God has been imagined as onmiscient, so that he may know the problems of all his devotees easily.

(c) ***Omnipresent*** — Supreme God is omniscient, He knows the difficulties of these devotees, but like human being, He is unable to rescue devotees from the calamities they are suffering from. Therefore he has been imagined as omnipresent so that he may be present in time at all places wherever these devotees are in trouble.

(d) ***Omnipotent*** — (i) God knows the sufferings of his devotees. He even makes his presence felt at all places where his devotees are in trouble. But if He himself is weaker than the enemies of his devotees, then how can he save them? Therefore, God has been imagined as omnipotent.

(ii) Moreover, man produces small things such as pen, pencil, chair, table, etc. but he cannot create mountain, river, forest, etc. So man has presented God as the almighty creator.

(iii) God is also known as the controller of this universe. A weak controller cannot control it properly because it is full of numerous difficult problems. Therefore, He has been imagined as almighty.

(e) ***Transcendental*** — God is known as transcendental, i.e. beyond universe. Persons living together are treated as equals. But how can God be equal to human being? In order to maintain His supremacy, He should live beyond the world in which all beings are living. So man believes that God lives in *Viṣṇuloka, Vaikuṇṭhaloka, Brahmaloka,* etc. Even the Greek philosopher Plato has said that God is the *universal* of all universals and He lived in a separate world which is beyond this world.

Not only this, but man wants to get children, property, prestige, etc. by praying and pleasing God. So, man has provided all capabilities and all abilities to God.

**God in Human Shape**

Man has imagined God not only according to his will and need but also in his own shape. Though he has declared God as the resident of some other world, he wants Him sometimes in his own world. So he has established the theory of incarnation. God incarnates when the order of this world is disturbed by evil elements. Śrī Kṛṣṇa has announced in the *Śrīmad Bhagavad-Gītā* that He incarnates in this world when righteousness deteriorates and irreligion develops, with a view to destroying the evil persons, to protect saints and to re-establish religion.[5] In this way man has brought God to a human level. God is born by human parents. He passes through childhood. He goes to some teacher for being educated. He becomes young and gets married. He, like man, decorates himself with fine clothings and valuable ornaments; he even weeps when separated from his wife.[6] He uses different weapons against his enemy. Sometimes he is killed also by some human being as Kṛṣṇa is killed by a hunter.

Man has provided his own shape to God. So God has hands, legs, nose, ears, eyes and mouth like a human being. He takes meals. He sleeps and awakes. When a statue of God is established (*prāṇa-pratiṣṭhā*) in some temple life is given to that idol, otherwise that statue is not considered worthy to be worshipped.

It is man who has accepted God, as creator, sustainer and destroyer. The materialists like Cārvāka, Karl Marx, etc. and many scientists negate the existence of God. They never feel any need of God. Even the religions like Jainism and Buddhism have been going on very smoothly without God.

Therefore, without any doubt and discussion God should be treated as a human creation.

---

5. *yadā yadā hi dharmasya glānirbhavati bhārata abhyutthānamadharmasya tadātmānam sṛjāmyaham.*

6. *Ghana ghamanda nabha garajata ghorā* ।
*Priya hīna darapata mana morā* ॥
— *Rāmacaritamānasa,* Kiṣkindhā Kāṇḍa, Gosvāmī Tūlasīdāsa.

# 9

## The Non-Existent God

*Satya Prakash Mittal*

As per the *Compact Oxford Reference Dictionary*, God means "The Creator and supreme ruler of the universe." He is supposed to be omnipotent, omniscient and omnipresent. How do we know that there is such a being? There is no reliable evidence and proof. Science does not assume such a power as it deals with causes and effects of things and forces on other things and happenings. It tries to find out the rule of their behaviour.

There are at least three old religions and cults in India that deny the existence of such a God. They are Buddhism, Jainism and Cārvākism, the former two are supported by their highly developed philosophies. Out of the six schools of Hindu philosophy five (except Nyāya) have no God. Gautama Buddha of India and Pythagoras of Greece were contemporary, belonging to the sixth century BCE. Both were agnostic. I think Gautama Buddha was the first to propound the theory of causation when he declared that there was *duḥkha* and there was the cause of *duḥkha*. The theory is scientific but alas science could not develop in ancient India. The other theory is that supernatural beings and God were the cause of all things and happenings.

In the early stages of man's history, for thousands of years, man was helpless against the various types of calamities of nature such as storms, conflagration, droughts, epidemics, etc.

As late as 2000 years before Christ, the Āryans of India propitiated the various natural forces taking them as powerful beings, like Indra, Vāyu, Sūrya, Moon, etc. They offered food and drinks through various devices including Agnihotra in order to appease them and to gain their favour.

So, not only the tribal folks but the so-called civilized men of India believe in these deities and other various types of ghosts and evil spirits. When such men get afflicted with a severe disease they instead of going to proper medical persons they go to magicians, charmers and diviners.

It was after a long time in man's history that man could think of a single power responsible for the creation and destruction of the world. Man's welfare, his birth and death were in his hands. Yet the smaller gods and deities remained as in-charge of different departments, and representing different natural powers. It were the semitic religions comprising Judaism, Christianity and Islam, that abolished all the other lesser gods and deities.

The well-being of man is uncertain in this world particularly in less developed countries. When a man finds himself in deep crisis he generally fails to know the cause of his plight. So, many a time he finds nothing to depend upon except the so-called God. He finds some consolation in the will of God or fate. Under such conditions man visits abodes of God, and try to appease them. Many times they recover as fate (circumstance) favours them. In such a situation their belief in the fake gods deepens, even blind faith has the power to strengthen man's will. God is a source of support. It is therefore, that some thoughtful persons plead the cause of God as man needs His support.

In the modern world the science has uncovered many secrets of nature. The man now knows the real cause of life and death. He now performs both at his will. He knows very well the sun, the moon, the air and the fire are not conscious beings and have no will of their own. He knows with certainty what cause disease and death. We know the secret of begetting male and female children, and are in a position to limit and regulate our families with the help of various devices of avoiding conception. In former days destiny was God-given, but not in the modern world; man is the creator of his own destiny.

I think poor and weak persons need God very much. But for an enlightened and strong-willed person, God is just a superstition or a thing of decoration. As the borders of knowledge expand, and more and more areas of darkness get lightened, the domain of the God would be decreasing. Actually it has already decreased, which is quite apparent in developed countries. With the further medical advancement and widening of medical facilities covering the common man, together with preventive devices, man will be in a position to conquer death, i.e. unnatural death. Already in many developed countries, such as Japan, Sweden, U.K., U.S.A., etc. man has already conquered death with an average age of over eighty.

God resides in the mind of man, particularly in its dark corners. As the dark areas get lightened there would be no space for the God to reside.

# 10

# God, Music and Psychology

*Balananda Sinha*

## God and Music

IT all started, when I was a child. *Prabhu dātā re, uṭhare mana Rāma bhajana kara* (प्रभु दाता रे, उठरे मन राम भजन कर) — the notes of Rāga Lalita entered my ears and went deep into my soul — my father was, as usual, doing the morning *riyāẓa* (practice). And for the first time, as a child of 5 years, I could feel the presence of God within me!!

And, then, some forty years later, my singing voices started giving me trouble. I could no longer continue my *riyāẓa*. The consequent depression was unbearable. And, then, one night my late father (Sangeet Bhaskar Kumar Shyamanand Sinha) came in my dreams and said, "Son, why are you so worried? Why don't you try singing from one note lower than your *gurujī* (i.e. Pandit Jasraj Ji)?" Next morning I tried the same and all of a sudden I found complete solace as well as ease in singing! And, once again, I felt the presence of God within me!!

And, then, a few years later, the occasion was the prestigious Sankat Mochan Sangeet Samaroh (Varanasi) and the day (i.e. 9 April) was the day of death anniversary of my father. Suddenly, *pujya gurujī* (Pandit Jasraj Ji) asked me to perform independently. I sang, as if, in a trance!! And when it all ended I found myself at the feet of my beloved *gurujī*. And, once again, I felt the presence of God within me!!

And, now, whenever I tune my *Sūramaṇḍala* for my routine *riyāẓa* I seek blessings from my late father (my first *guru*) and *gurujī* (my ultimate *guru*) and as I sing the first note of a *rāga* I feel the presence of God within me!!

**God and Psychology**

Neuropsychologically, experiencing God is dependent upon certain specialized neurons situated in the limbic system (e.g. amygdala and hippocampus) and also the temporal lobe of the brain. In fact, the perception of God is based neurologically on inputs from a variety of different neurons, each contributing some features to the resulting experience of "experiencing" God. That is, in other words, there are neither "demon" neurons or "God" neurons but rather neural assemblies in different combinations which interact under certain conditions and produce hallucinations and feelings of "to be in the presence of God!"

Thus, it can be assumed that experiences related to visualizing/experiencing God is internally generated, like a dream and that, presumably and interestingly, they have no basis in external reality. Rather, they only serve the need and desire to survive. That is, there may not be an "out there" or "Heaven" or external "God" in some mystical space, but, rather, an internal Heaven (or Hell) dominated, controlled and produced by the limbic system. The temporal lobes insure the survival of the self by dreaming and hallucinating ghosts, spirits and avenging angels, and promoting the illusion of perpetual and eternal survival (or damnation) if taboos, rituals, and the laws of God are (not) obeyed.

Thus, the source of all types of experience, physical or metaphysical, lies in the brain. *Aham brahmāsmi* (I am the

Cosmos) the Vedic metaphysical assumption, too, conceives of the "Ultimate" in a similar vein!! The difference, however, is presumably in the approach or (of visualizing God) the former being "physical" and the latter "metaphysical." Also, according to the *Bardo thodol* (Tibetan Book of the Dead),

> These realms do not come from somewhere outside thyself. They come from within. . . . they exist from eternity within the faculties of thine own brain. . . . reflections of thine own thought forms. . . .
>
> — Joseph, 1996

## Reference

Joseph, R. (1996), *Neuropsychiatry, Neuropsychology, and Clinical Neuroscience*, Williams and Welkins.

# 11

## God is Love
### A Christian Conception of the Divine

*Francis Gonsalves, S.J.*

> "God is love, and he who abides in love abides in God, and God abides in him" (1 Jn 4: 16). These words from the *First Letter of John* express with remarkable clarity the heart of the Christian faith: the Christian image of God and the resulting image of humankind and its destiny. In the same verse, Saint John also offers a kind of summary of the Christian life: "We have come to know and to believe in the love God has for us." . . . Being Christian is not the result of an ethical choice or a lofty idea, but the encounter with an event, a person, which gives life a new horizon and a decisive direction.

This opening sentence — from the very first encyclical letter *Deus Caritas Est* (God is Love) of Pope Benedict XVI given on 25 December 2005 — summarizes the Christian conception of God.[1] Through the past twenty centuries of the history of Christianity, theology has always trod the thin line between history and mystery, the known and the unknown, and, consequently, expressed the divine reality in terminology that is both cataphatic and apophatic. No wonder theologians have traditionally spoken of God in terms that conceal God as much as they serve to reveal God. Augustine asserted that "it's easier

1. For the full text in English, see *L'Osservatore Romano,* 1 February 2006, special insert.

to think about God than to talk about him," Anselm called God "that thing than which nothing greater can be thought of," and, closer to our times, Protestant theologian, Karl Barth spoke of *Gott über Gott* (God-above-God) in the sense that God is ever "beyond" anything and everything the most intelligent human mind can conceive of.

At the outset it is apt to point out that theology necessarily deals with metaphorical, analogical and symbolic language, and it is always insufficient to fully express, much less, exhaust, the divine mystery. None the less, since Christianity believes that Jesus is "God's son" who revealed God in human history, it must assume responsibility of articulating — even if imperfectly — what, or rather *who,* it believes in. This is the aim of this article. First, it will present a brief historical overview of how theological language about God evolved. Then it will discuss how theologians strive to articulate a God-language consonant with changing contexts. Finally, it will point out present-day possibilities for evolving language about God so as to be faithful to the Gospel of Jesus.

## God-Language Down to the Twentieth Century

No theology has developed in a vacuum. Even when it assumes to be unaffected by the intellectual climate of a particular period, it cannot but be influenced by the popular philosophies and ideologies of that time. The following brief historical overview — down to the twentieth century — might seem simplistic; yet, it will enable us to get a bird's eye-view of the main influences that shaped Christian conceptions of God down the ages.

### EARLY CHRISTIANITY, THE PATRISTIC PERIOD AND PLATONISM

Nascent Christianity evolved out of Judaism and encountered a predominant Greek philosophical culture. The *Gospel* —

literally, "good news"[2] — was the proclamation of Jesus' birth, message and life-death-resurrection. Early Christian apologists proclaimed that the unknown, mysterious God, the creator of the universe, was the God of Abraham, Issac, Jacob, and the Father of Jesus Christ, who is Lord of history and ultimate principle of all realties (Acts of Apostles 2: 22-36; 4: 8-12). With the help of Greek philosophy, especially Platonism and Stoicism, the first Christian intellectuals arrived at a description of the soul as a singular, spiritual and immortal reality. The confrontation of Christian monotheism with gnostic dualism[3] led to the orthodox formulation of the language of the first article of Christian faith — namely, "We believe in God the Father, Almighty, Creator of heaven and earth" — in terms of the absolute singularity and unicity of the divine monarchy, with an unequivocal identification of the God of creation of the old covenant with the saving God and Father of Jesus of the new covenant. The Christian thinkers who were in the forefront of this development were Irenaeus, Tertullian and Origen.

The first four centuries of Christianity in the West can be summed up as a period of integration of Christian theology with the dominant philosophies of the time, uppermost among which was Greek Platonism. Jesus is seen as God revealed in history as "image" and in the "likeness" of the invisible God. This thinking is backed by Scripture, especially by writers like John and Paul (John's Gospel 1: 1-18, Paul's letter to the Colossians 1: 15-20). Augustine could be cited as representative of this period, using the *via negativa* (apophatic theology)[4] to speak about God. His classics *De Trinitate* and "The City of

2. The word Gospel comes from the Greek, *Evangelion,* meaning "good news."
3. Thinkers like Valentius, Marcion and Celsus are representatives of this school of thought.
4. Apophatic theology can be compared to the *neti, neti* of the Indian Upaniṣadic or Vedāntic tradition.

God" bear the marks of Platonism. Here, the "mystery" element of God is retained to a large extent, although God enters history in the form of Jesus, God's only son.

The early centuries of Christianity saw the rise of many heresies that were condemned by the Church Councils that sought to maintain God's unicity, while also accounting for a certain *threeness* since Jesus spoke of God as *Abba* (father), of himself as being related to God as "son" (John 17), and of the Holy Spirit. Suffice it to say that the heresies were in the nature of exaggerated emphasis towards the pole of oneness (more characteristic of the West), as well as trends towards a polytheism, or rather "tri-theism" (more representative of the East). The Council of Chalcedon was a milestone in early Church history in that it reiterated God's mysterious *Tri-Uneness,* so to say.

## THE MIDDLE AGES, SCHOLASTICISM AND ARISTOTELIANISM

The middle ages of Western Christianity saw the development of Scholasticism, with a revival of Aristotelian categories of *esse*-essence, potency-act, substance-accident and causality theory. Methodologically, philosophy was relegated to the position of being "handmaid of theology" with great thinkers like Anselm and Aquinas using the *via positiva* (cataphatic or affirmative theology) to propose truths about God. Scholasticism fused the conception of Christian Platonism (of a God who is the origin and goal of the universe, as the supreme God) with the causal ontology of Aristotle. Aquinas's adaptations of Aristotle are akin to Augustine's of Plato. This period saw the emergence of "proofs of the existence of God" and could be considered a kind of "golden age" of Western theology.

The theology of the middle ages does not fully dispense with the element of "mystery" in God. The horizon of mystery will always be maintained; for instance, the 4th Lateran General

Council (1215), asserted God to be one and unique, true and holy, eternal and immutable, "incomprehensible, omnipotent, and ineffable," and yet language about God will be possible by way of creaturely participation: after all, between creature and Creator both "likeness and unlikeness" obtain, although the unlikeness is "always greater". Thus, theology continues affirming a *Deus semper maior* (God ever "more"), although the language of "proofs" asserts a strong certainty of God's presence, nature and action.

## NOMINALISM, THE REFORMATION AND THE BIRTH OF FIDEISM

Nominalism sounded the death-knell of the certainties of Scholasticism by setting out to divorce faith and reason. In juxtaposing faith and reason as two distinct fields with their own internal logic, they were heralding later modernism. William of Ockham, among others, voiced strong suspicions of the use of reason for positing divinely revealed truths about the nature of God. This suspicion would find fuller expression with the Protestant Reformation and its maxim *sola fides* (only faith). Martin Luther held that, to be saved, one must hold on firmly to one's faith and believe in the eternal salvation already wrought for all humankind by the self-sacrifice of God's son, Jesus.

Protestantism was a "protest" against the excesses and abuses perpetrated by the Catholic Church, especially by the clerics among its ranks. The question of Catholic "Tradition" was contested since Scriptural interpretations of the Church's theologians were seen not merely as arbitrary, but also as dissonant with the basic demands of the Gospel, which was later articulated by Schleiermacher as the "sense of absolute dependence."[5] With different nuances in individual positions, reformers like Luther, Calvin and Zwingli held the primacy of faith and negated the capacity of reason to reach any truth

5. Friedrich Schleiermacher, *The Christian Faith*, T&T Clark, 1928, p. 12.

whatsoever. Humankind had sinned, and this sin had severely affected our human capacity to reach any truth about God whatsoever. Faith alone saves, and this faith — *Fideism,* in its extreme — could at most be expressed through a *theologia crucis* (a theology of the cross) whereby one knows God, and is saved, through the death of God's son on the cross. From the Catholic side, the Council of Trent (1550-65) sought to respond to Protestant positions, albeit largely with an apologetic tone.

## THE ENLIGHTENMENT, RENAISSANCE AND THE RISE OF RATIONALISM

Much as the Enlightenment provided the soil for the birth of the "rational self" with the philosophies of Descartes and Leibnitz, it eroded the epistemic foundations of ecclesiastical authority. Influenced by the impetus received from the Renaissance, religion and ethics no longer needed sanction or legitimacy from any Church, for, one could reflect upon the tenets of faith and the nature of God on the basis of what could be termed as "rational theology." Theological rationalism defended the primacy of moral reason over religious faith, which became merely a quest for moral uprightness (Kant). God could be conceived as an all-perfect nature (Spinoza, Lessing), or, Nature itself could be seen as growing into the fullness of God with the latter undifferentiated from the former. Such thinking would, undoubtedly, lead to pantheistic notions of God.

Hegel took rational theology to its logical conclusion by positing the Great Spirit (*Geist*) or Great Mind, God, innate in historical development and in a yet-to-attain divine fullness together with the created world. While Marx would see God and religion as *epiphenomena* that alienate human beings and engender structures of oppression, Freud's conception of the *Super Ego* served to explain away a transcendent God with morality reducible to societal or parental power-structures that seek to control human behaviour. One could say that the final step to demolish any conception of divinity was summed up by Nietzsche's famous "God is dead!" — or, "Long live Man!" — maxim. We can roughly situate this atheistic type of thinking at the end of the nineteenth century. However, the intellectual climate, as well as the socio-political situation of the twentieth century was to bring in sweeping changes in the way of conceiving God.

### Conceptions of God in Twentieth-Century Theology

As outcome of the Enlightenment and Renaissance, the centuries immediately preceding the twentieth century witnessed the growth of philosophies that excessively emphasized the power of human reason not only to reach truth unaided but also to ensure a better life for those deprived of it. However, the world wars, horrors of Hiroshima and the Holocaust, with its over-idealized conception of "Man" led to a rethinking of human nature and the sureties of human existence. Moreover, the euphoria of industrialized society and the promises of modernity faded amidst the darkness of the factory-system and the hellish conditions in which large sections of humanity eked out sub-human existence. In this context, one can dimly decipher two strands which can be designated (a) theologies of transcendence and (b) theologies of immanence that speak of God.

#### THEOLOGIES OF TRANSCENDENCE
DIALECTICAL-NOUVELLE THEOLOGIE-TRANSCENDENTAL

The theologies of transcendence sought to recover God's transcendence in the context of thinking that either reduced Christianity to an ethical theism or to a pantheistic rationalism, for example, "Liberal Theology" of Protestantism. By contrast, "Dialectical Theology" tried to recover the transcendent moment of the religious experience, the personalism of biblical revelation, and eschatological Cristocentrism in theology. Dialectial method emphasized the abyss between the hidden

God of religion and the revealed God who justifies in grace. Faith does not have anything to do with philosophy. Knowledge of God is possible only in Christ: in his divine word, which reaches us through scripture and the preaching of the Church. The God of Abraham and Jesus engage in a self-revelation as the God who loves us freely. The encounter with the God of faith cannot occur by the dialectical *via* of the analogy of being, but only by the paradoxical way of the analogy of faith, in the encounter with the divine grace that justifies the sinner (Karl Barth). The encounter with the divine word of salvation, in the *kerygma* (preaching), entails the simultaneous discovery of one's own existence: one accepts the challenge to live that existence in authenticity and faith. The cross reveals the meaning of personal authenticity. The programme of a "theology of the word" must be integrated with the use of an existential hermeneutics and a demythologizing reading of Scripture (Rudolf Bultmann).

Another group of theologians, mainly Catholic, like Henri de Lubac, J. Daniélou and Hans Urs von Balthasar are representatives of *Nouvelle Théologie* (French, for "new theology"), that strove to recover the mystical moment in religious experience and the living God of biblical revelation. They viewed human existence in terms of a "history of salvation" (*historia salutis*) rendered present in liturgical action. This thinking endorsed the religious yearnings of the great Eastern religions and sought to understand the religious problem in the universe of secularity and atheistic humanism.

Paul Tillich's "Method of Correlation" — an example of a theology of transcendence — is an attempt to mediate between contemporary culture and historical Christianity as one throws up questions and the other strives to provide answers by using religious symbols.[6] He examines Being (God) in the face of an

6. Paul Tillich, *Systematic Theology*, vol. I, London: SCM Press, 1978, pp. 3-68.

existential question:[7] Human existence has its moments that bring us to the edge of being overwhelmed by meaninglessness, guilt and death. Put abstractly, being is threatened by "non-being." Contrary to this, we have the experience of resisting this threat, which could be termed as the "power of being." This situation raises the question: "Whence comes the power to resist the threat of non-being"? The answer is provided by the Christian symbol "God as Creator."

In his discourse on God, Tillich is careful not to confine God to the human categories of essence. God is *Being Itself,* not a being. The God-symbol must bring people to participate in the power of the divine to which it points. God as living must be seen in symbolic terms. One symbolizes that which is one's utimate concern in terms taken from one's own being. One sees the divine life as personal, dynamic and free because God is one's ultimate concern, and therefore God stands in analogy (*analogia entis*) to that which man himself is. Tillich refuses to speak of the "existence" of God because God is the "ground of being," utterly unconditioned by anything else, while being present to everything. God as "Lord" and "Father" are the only two attributes that one might use: "While *Lord* is basically the expression of man's relation to the God who is holy power, *Father* is basically the expression of man's relation to the God who is holy love. The concept 'Lord' expresses the distance; the concept 'Father,' the unity."[8] In a movement from the "hidden God," Tillich affirms the "revealed God" and asserts that the doctrine of God leads one to affirm the mystery of Christ.

Through transcendental method, Karl Rahner reflects on the idea of God from the basic data of human existence.[9] He

---

7. See ibid., part II: *Being and God,* pp. 163-289, for details on Tillich's idea of God.

8. Ibid., p. 287.

9. See Karl Rahner, *Foundations of Christian Faith: An Introduction to the Idea of Christiantiy,* New York: Crossroad, 1994, pp. 44-89.

investigates the human being as a responsible person and a free subject. Everyone is a transcendental being in that one has a capacity to go beyond oneself, as evidenced in the very act of hearing, reflecting, questioning and willing. Rather than adopt classical positions dealing with perishability, design or finality to "prove" the existence of God, Rahner shows that knowledge of Being is structured into the act of human knowing itself. Beginning with philosophical and existential reflections on the word "God," he discusses the different ways of knowing God; namely, through the light of natural reason, through Christian revelation and through God's salvific activity. Human subjectivity necessitates an openness to mystery, a feeling of being overwhelmed by an ineffable presence. The being of beings is disclosed as limitless, unrestricted or Absolute Being. Hence, that to which knowledge is oriented is the Absolute Mystery which all call God.

After establishing the foundation for the possibility of the Being called God, Rahner holds that through Christian revelation, this Being has indeed manifested Godself. He introduces the idea of "divine self-communication." God has communicated Godself in Christian tradition as Person, as Father. In the course of history, the human "hearer" has heard God's Words (*Logos*), Jesus Christ. God has entered human history and through God's Spirit, has transformed human subjectivity so that it may receive and respond to the Word, Jesus. Aquinas' medieval division between the natural and supernatural order is seen in new light by Rahner who stresses the participational and relational character of the supernatural, with human nature divinely constituted in creation and the human being transformed by grace. This *supernatural existential* confirms the orientation of the human natural order to the supernatural order that God's intention to confer grace presupposes.

## THEOLOGIES OF IMMANENCE (HOPE-MODERNITY-PRAXIS-LIBERATION)

The theologies of immanence stress the presence and action of God in history. This is a movement to decipher God in the ups and downs of human history and in peoples' struggles. The Lutheran contribution is that the God of weakness is affirmed in a paradox of faith (Dietrich Bonhoeffer). There is an eclipse of the sacred in secular culture that seems to function perfectly "as if there were no God" (*etsi deus non daretur*). Later theologians speak of the death of God amidst the darkness of the death of God's people. For example, Jürgen Moltmann's "The Crucified God"[10] focuses on the passion-crucifixion-death of Jesus as the privileged place for knowing God. The God of transcendence is eclipsed by the God of immanence manifested in Christ and history. Here, the categories of Christian Platonism and Aristotelian theism are replaced with a Cristocentric focus on the praxic and historical dimensions. Correspondingly, we have a "theology of hope" with its accent on the "not yet" and its tension between possibility and event (Moltmann).

With the increasing problems of mid-twentieth-century modernity and secularization, Catholic theologians like Hans Küng and Edward Schillebeeckx felt the need to confront the challenge of modernity and secularization by developing a "Theology of Modernity." Schillebeeckx tries to paint a God-image that is both "mystery" as well as "concrete." The former, before which the human being stands, is used in a double sense of the unknown and also of the Greek *mysterion,* a path to knowledge that transforms the subject who undertakes it. The "concreteness" that Schillebeeckx tries to highlight is the human reality, which is increasingly marked by secular trends

---

10. See his *The Crucified God: The Cross of Christ as the Foundation and Criticism of Christian Theology,* London: SCM Press, 1974.

and human suffering.[11] God is put in the "dry dock" by a secular society that tends to believe that science and modernity have all the answers to human aspirations.[12] To put it figuratively, modern society's *gods* seem to negate *God;* and thus, Schillebeeckx strives to maintain the mystery of God and the sovereignty of God's activity in human history. The sovereign God is a God of love:

> God is not merely the foundation of all human values. He is not only sovereignly free in his establishment of the attraction of these values, so that man is induced to gaze longingly towards the silent mystery of God; he has also revealed himself to us as a value; he is the God of salvation, who summons us in grace to a personal communion of life with himself. The call proceeds directly from God. This means not only that God's supereminent value addresses itself inwardly to our sense of value by the stirring of his grace, but, at the same time, that the history in which we are situated is so led and directed by the God of grace, that — in its secular aspect — it tells us more than it could of itself.[13]

In this theology, the sacred and the secular cannot be segregated. God makes humanity's cause a divine cause. God is close to human struggles and sufferings — ever present to us in a mediated immediacy, i.e. mediated through human history and through creation in such a way as to be made immediate or directly present. Here, human experience is taken seriously, and, the close connection between communion with God and action in the world is stressed, which can be

---

11. See Edward Schillebeeckx, *God the Future of Man*, London & Sydney: Sheed and Ward, 1986, pp. 57-61, for an insightful anlysis on the 4-step-process of secularization in the Christian West.

12. Schillebeeckx, *God and Man*, London & Sydney: Sheed and Ward, 1969, pp. 3-17, highlights the problem of secularism and apparent redundancy of God in a chapter enitled "God in Dry Dock."

13. Ibid., 261.

designated as the mystical and the political dimensions of human life and relationship with God. Consequently, Christians are called to a "political holiness" that does not separate the inner life of prayer from the worldly liturgy of betterment of humanity's cause. This dimesion of a "political holiness" is more dynamically developed by the "Theologies of Liberation and Praxis."

"Theology of Liberation" was popularized by Latin American theologians in the late 1960s and early 1970s. Gustavo Gutiérrez, often considered the pioneer of this theology, proposes a *new way* of doing theology that is born out of and critically reflects upon concrete, historical life-situations in the light of faith. In his words, theology is "critical reflection on Christian praxis in the light of the Word."[14] Liberation Theology is distinguished from other theologies in that it places theological emphasis on critical reflection and action (praxis), on committing oneself to the task of transforming the world in the light of the Gospel. There is a specific context for doing Liberation Theology, namely, the context of the poor and victimized of the society. It is in the experience of struggle with this particular group that one comes to a correct knowledge of God and God's plan of salvation.

Gutiérrez and other liberation theologians stress the need for a political theology in the line of Johannes B. Metz,[15] and claim that what is needed today is not developmentalism, but a liberation that will come with a revolutionary, new social and economic system.[16] The Marxist frame of reference and

14. Gustavo Gutiérrez, *A Theology of Liberation: History, Politics and Salvation,* 15th edn., tr. C. Inda & J. Eagleson, London: SCM, 1988, p. 11.

15. See Johannes Baptist Metz, *Faith in History and Society: Toward a Practical Fundamental Theology,* tr. D. Smith, London: Burns & Oates, 1980 also Gutiérrez, pp. 126-30.

16. Gutiérrez, pp. 13-16.

the "dependency theory" are the tools with which society is measured. The predominant God-image is that of Liberator. Central to the community-experience of God is the Exodus event wherein the people of Israel encountered a God who was present, who promised and who inscrutably led them forward towards a fulfilment of the divine promises. Knowing and loving God is only possible if one loves one's neighbour. Indeed, the only criterion for salvation in a passage known as the "Last Judgment" (Gospel of Matthew 25: 31-46) is whether one has loved and served the poorest of poor. Thus, there is no better place for the God-encounter than making an "option for the poor."

Some criticisms have been levelled against Latin American Liberation Theology; for instance, it is alleged that social and economic theories have not been used critically. In other words, Marxist models evolved in European capitalistic societies have been borrowed and transplanted into a largely agricultural Latin American context. Moreover, these theologies have been accused of picking and choosing Bible quotations to suit their purposes. It is beyond the scope of this article to evaluate both the strengths and weaknesses of liberation theologies. However, there is no doubt that this is certainly a "new way of doing theology" that has perhaps made many arm-chair theologians aware of the fact that theology must have a bearing on people's lives or else run the risk of becoming a purely speculative discipline unrelated to the faith-life of a community.

## Perspectives and Possibilities of the Present Times

There is no dearth of theological writing on the question of God in Christian circles. Many of the theologies can be said to be corollaries of the basic assertion "God is Love" mentioned earlier, and, though there is convergence of many conceptions, there is also marked divergence. Among Catholic circles, the Second Vatican Council (1962-65) provided an impetus for renewed thinking and co-operation with other ideologies and disciplines.[17] We briefly examine two recent trends and the possibilities therein.

## CHRISTIAN CONCEPTION OF GOD AND DIALOGUE WITH OTHER RELIGIONS

The growing awareness that the world religions share a common spirituality, and that Indian religious expressions, in particular, are reservoirs of rich religious resources, has led many theologians to dialogue with religions in their strivings to evolve God-language. Since the so-called "prophetic" or "Abrahamic religions" (Judaism–Islam–Christianity) share a common "prophetic tradition," the monotheistic and "personal" character of these three religions allow for a common conception. However, problems arise as to how that personal dimension is understood and interpreted. While Judaism and Islam adhere to a strict monotheism that focuses on God as "Wholly Other," the Christian revelation of God as Trinity necessitates the assertion of a "differentiated monotheism" in that God is Father-Son-Spirit — what has traditionally been expressed as "three persons in one God." This is because Christianity believes in God's special intervention in human history through the Incarnation of God's own Word in Jesus.

The dialogue with the so-called "mystical religions" — Hinduism and Buddhism in particular — has been pursued earnestly in the last few decades of the twentieth century. Mention must be made of Raimundo Panikkar whose

---

17. See, for example, VC II's document "Church in the Modern World" entitled *Gaudium et Spes* (n. 62) which reads: "Theologians are invited to seek continually for more suitable ways of communicating doctrine to men and women of their times. . . . In pastoral care, appropriate use must be made not only of theological principles, but also of the findings of the secular sciences, especially of psychology and sociology."

contributions — especially in explaining God in trinitarian terms of Icon-Person-Mystery (representing Father-Son-Spirit respectively) provides a framework for dialoging not only with classical Hinduism, but also for understanding the dynamics of the prophetic, as well as mystic, religions.[18] He holds that the Trinity is the ultimate paradigm of personal relationships. Between World and Spirit — intelligible structure or form and fluid or dynamic life — there is a never-ending process of interchange that reflects what is experienced in everyday interpersonal relations. Just as the human person is neither monolithic oneness nor disconnected plurality, so the Trinity as pure relation epitomizes the radical relativity of all that there is. In sum, the diversity of human experience is not to be totalized into an overcoming universal theory; it is only to be discerned by entering into the *de facto* proliferation of different putative experiences of God in the world's religions.

There have been other attempts to reinterpret God in Christianity by using terminology of classical Hindu trinitarianism. This trend of Indian Christian theology can be traced back to Keshub Chandra Sen (1838-84) who described the Trinity as "the loftiest expression of the world's religious consciousness."[19] His synthesis comprised of triadic attributes and functions identifiable with the three "persons." Thus, Father (Creator/Still God), Son (Exemplar/Journeying God) and Spirit (Sanctifier/Returning God) were associated with

18. See Raimundo Panikkar, *The Trinity and World Religions: Icon-Person-Mystery*, Bangalore: The Christian Institute for the Study of Religion and Society, 1970; see also his "Toward an Ecumenical Theandric Spirituality", *Journal of Ecumenical Studies* 5/3 (Summer 1968): pp. 507-34.

19. See his lecture on 21 January 1882, "That Marvellous Mystery: The Trinity", in *Keshub Chunder Sen: A Selection*, Madras: Christian Literature Society & Bangalore: United Theological College, 1979, pp. 217-47.

the attributes of Truth (*sat*, being, force), Good (*cit*, love, wisdom) and Beauty (*ānanda*, joy, holiness), respectively. Brahmabandhab Upadhyay gave further deeper meaning to the term *saccidānanda*,[20] extolling the divine attributes in a "canticle,"[21] and believed that, as Greek philosophy inspired Western theology, so must Vedānta enlighten Indian Christian theology. Swami Abhisiktānanda too was fascinated by the Hindu Advaitic experience of the Upaniṣads and tried to show that it is compatible with the Christian experience of Trinity.[22] The Advaitic experience is found also at the root of the Christian experience that holds that God and the world are not two. This Advaitic dimension of Christianity finds an eminent expression in the revelation of the Trinity where the Father, Son and Spirit are alike in non-duality (Advaita) of nature and in communication (*koinonia*) of Persons. This is not just theoretical knowledge, but experiential awareness of God.[23]

> [T]here is no question of theological theorizing or of academic comparison between the terms of the Christian revelation and those in which India has expressed its own unique mystical experience. It is rather a matter of an awakening, an awareness far beyond the reach of intellect, an experience which springs up and erupts in the deepest recesses of the soul. The experience of *saccidānanda* carries the soul beyond

20. See *The Writings of Brahmabandhab Upadhyay*, vol. I, ed. J. Lipner & G. Gispert-Sauch, Bangalore: United Theological College, 1991, pp. 94-145, for further details of the development of his theology.

21. See Julius Lipner, *Brahmabandhab Upadhyay: The Life and Thought of a Revolutionary*, Delhi: Oxford University Press, 1999, pp. 199-204, for the text, translation and discussion on the theology of this hymn.

22. For a concise summary of Abhisiktānanda's theology see his "Notes on Christology and Trinitarian Theology", *Vidyājoti Journal of Theological Reflection* 64/8 (August 2000): pp. 598-612.

23. Abhisiktānanda, *Saccidānanda*, p. 178.

> all merely intellectual knowledge to her very centre, to the source of her being.

While Christian theology has been enriched by classical Hinduism, there are those who feel that it has not sufficiently entered into conversations with other streams of Hinduism and much less with other religions. However, scholars of foreign origin like Michael von Brück,[24] Hendrik M. Vroom[25] and John B. Carman[26] have explored the philosophical aspects of classical Hinduism and Buddhism and drawn parallels with the Christian conception of God. In particular, insights were drawn from Mahāyāna Buddhism and the Buddhist *śūnyatā,* relating them to classical Trinitarian doctrine.[27] While such attempts have been bold initiatives, there is always the danger of simplistically brushing aside differences among religions in the enthusiasm to forge some unity.

## THE DIALOUGE OF LIFE AND "SOCIAL TRINITARIANISM"

Today, there is a growing interest in what is termed "social trinitarianism." The nineteenth-century Russian Orthodox

---

24. See von Brück, "Advaita and Trinity: Reflections on the Vedantic and Christian Experience of God with Reference to Buddhist Non-Dualism", *Indian Theological Studies* 20/1 (March 1983): pp. 37-60; also, "Trinitarian Theology: Hegelian *vis-à-vis* Advaitic," *Journal of Dharma* 8/3 (July-September 1983): pp. 283-95.
25. See Vroom, *No Other Gods: Christian Belief in Dialogue with Buddhism, Hinduism, and Islam,* tr. L. Jansen, Michigan and Cambridge: William B. Eerdmans Publishing Company, 1996; also, "Religious Hermenutics, Culture and Narratives", *Studies in Interreligious Dialogue* 4/2 (1994): 189-213.
26. See Carman, *Majesty and Meekness: A Comparative Study of Contrast and Harmony in the Concept of God,* Grand Rapids, Michigan: William B. Eerdmans Publishing Company, 1994.
27. See, for instance, Michael von Brück, "Buddhist Śūnyatā and the Christian Trinity: The Emerging Holistic Paradigm", in *Buddhist*

→

theologian Nikolai Fedorov had said, "The Trinity is our social programme." In other words, the Christian conception of God as Trinity (Father-Son-Spirit) provides a kind of "ideal" or "model" of human community. This thinking was developed by the proponents of Liberation Theology in Latin America. The work of Leonardo Boff has been influential,[28] and has inspired Asian thinkers too.

In India, Geevarghese Mar Osthathios initially used the analogy of the nuclear family to explain the trinitarian God and the consequent demands of establishing a classless society.[29] Though his approach to the world situation of inequality and injustice incorporates Marxian insights, the society he envisages is more Gandhian since he sees *sarvodaya* (awakening of all) as the ideal of classless society.[30] In a later work, Geevarghese develops his trinitarian theology in terms of a "Sharing God" by using traditional concepts like *koinonia* (communication) and *agape* (love), borrowing from Moltmann and Boff, and incorporating insights from scripture and tradition.[31]

---

→ *Emptiness and Christian Trinity: Essays and Explorations,* ed. R. Corless & P. Knitter New York: Paulist Press 1990, pp. 44-66; also David Tracy, "Kenosis, Sunyata, and Trinity: A Dialogue with Masao Abe", in *The Emptying God: A Buddhist-Jewish-Christian Conversation,* ed. J.B. Cobb, Jr., & C. Ives, New York: Orbis, 1990, pp. 135-54, & John P. Keenan, "A Mahāyāna Understanding of the Trinity", in his *The Meaning of Christ: A Mahāyāna Theology,* New York: Orbis, 1989, pp. 240-59.

28. See Boff, *Trinity and Society,* tr. P. Burns, New York: Orbis, 1988 and *Holy Trinity, Perfect Community,* tr. P. Berryman, New York: Orbis, 2000.

29. See Geevarghese, *Theology of a Classless Society,* Madras: Christian Literature Society, 1980.

30. Ibid., pp. 132-33.

31. See Geevarghese, *Sharing God and a Sharing World,* Delhi: Indian Society for Promotion of Christian Knowledge & Tiruvalla: Christava Sahitya Samithy, 1995.

The danger of "social trinitarianism" is that theology can be used to legitimize any type of society and then the "mystery" dimension of God is either not respected or reduced to some idol of human fashioning that can subserve ideologies like monarchy and imperialism, as has happened in Christian history. On the other hand, a reading of the gospel from the perspective of "the underside of history" warrants reinterpreting God as a God who takes sides with the poor, underprivileged and those on the margins of society.

Speaking of the "dialogue of life," theologians are becoming increasingly aware of the need of dialogue with the various disciplines and *isms* so that a fruitful encounter takes place between theology and the sciences. Interdisciplinary approaches to the study of God ensure that theology is not done in a vacuum but is sensitive to what is known as the "signs of the times and places" — i.e. it tries to decipher God's presence and action in the ups and downs of life as it is lived by God's people irrespective of differences in culture, creed, caste or colour.

## Towards a Conception of God in the Indian Context

From the preceding overview of the historical, philosophical and contextual trends affecting the conceptions of God, an Indian contextual theology would take two realities seriously: (a) the question of deep religiosity and spirituality that is part of the Indian tradition, and (b) the question of widespread suffering in the form of poverty, exploitation, inequalities, gender discrimination, and the like. With its sensitivity to the first reality, on the one hand, it would always strive to maintain the "mystery" aspect of God; and, it is here that dialogue with the "mystical" religions — Hinduism and Buddhism, in particular — could contribute to a fuller understanding of God. On the other hand, responding to the second reality would entail awareness of the working of God in "history." Dialogue with the "prophetic" religions would help Christianity in this sphere. Indian Christian theologians almost unanimously agree that dialogue — with the other religions, disciplines, and ideologies — is indispensable for evolving a relevant theology.

The task of evolving a God-language can never be a finished product in the sense that it is closed to reinterpretation. If one were to take the workings of God's Spirit seriously, one would have to be open to a "process of theology" whereby one ever remains humble and aware that no matter what language one uses for God, God is always greater (*semper maior*). At the same time, the death-resurrection of Jesus Christ stands as the centre of the Christian tradition as its defining characteristic. Thus, to the extent that Christians are ready to undergo what is called *kenosis* (self-emptying)[32] in the footsteps of Jesus, to that extent will it be true to itself and proclaim the God of self-sacrificing love.

Although the word *kenosis* is a Christian term, it has equivalents in other religions — for example, *vairāgya, tyāga, dayā* (Hinduism) and *śūnyatā, karuṇā* (Buddhism) — albeit, with varying nuances. Notably, each of these terms necessitates a movement from the self towards the "other." And, beyond religious belief, *kenosis* can also be the meeting point for peoples where secularization is inventing "idols of the market" and popular *isms* like post-modernism and neo-liberalism are eroding at the foundations of culture and community, which adversely affect the poor. The Italian philosopher Vattimo, who expresses his disillusionment with Christianity as it is practised today, sees in divine *kenosis* a "weak ontology" and asserts that it stands out starkly as a challenge to society's

32. The word *kenosis* (Greek, meaning "self-emptying") refers to the self-sacrifice of Jesus as in Paul's letter to the Philippians 2: 5-11.

violence and power play.[33] In the face of "holier-than-thou" stances and violence unleashed in the name of religion, will it not be appropriate to reinterpret our conceptions of God by employing such concepts and "weak ontology"?[34]

**Conclusion**

While religion is meant to foster peace, harmony and community-building, it has, sadly, especially in the past two decades, been a cause of division and strife. Worse still, we have shed blood to defend what we have constructed as "god" and understood as "religion." Called by any name and worshipped in any form, our ideas of God must lead us to promote Life for all peoples everywhere. If religionists can come together and respond to the larger problems of life based on their experiences of God, and only later, as a second step, articulate their theologies and conceptions of God, we might have a more harmonious society, and religion will have played a pivotal role in fostering peace.

A true believer will never force another to accept her or his way of life. This point is well made in Pope Benedict's encyclical *Deus Caritas Est* (n. 31c): "Those who practise charity in the Church's name will never seek to impose the Church's faith upon others. They realize that a pure and generous love is the best witness to God. A Christian knows when it is time to speak of God and when it is better to say nothing and to let

---

33. See Gianni Vattimo, *Belief*, tr. L. D'Isanto & D. Webb, Cambridge: Polity Press, 1999, pp. 20-68, who develops the idea of *kenosis* within a secularist context, albeit reaching contestable conclusions. Vattimo's understanding of *kenosis* is also premised on a nihilism inspired by Neitzsche.

34. The author has attempted one such approach in his doctoral thesis entitled, "Community and Conflict in India: Trinitarian Theology from a Subaltern Perspective" recently submitted to the University of Madras, Chennai.

love alone speak." Besides such an attitude being totally Christ-like, it will ensure that theology respects the healthy tension between mystery and history, wisdom and word, mysticism and prophetism, mythos and logos.

The mystery of God can neither be encapsulated in some doctrines nor shackled in the confines of some sanctuary. When the great leader Moses came into the presence of God in the form of a burning bush, he was ordered to take off his sandals. Then, God revealed Godself with the help of a cryptic sentence — "I am who I am" (Book of Exodus 3: 14) — that seemed to conceal more than disclose. Perhaps we are always called to take off our sandals and walk humbly before the all-pervading and all-powerful presence of the Divine who approaches us in many forms. Two lines of Sant Kabīr must be remembered:

> O Servant, where does thou seek Me? Lo, I am beside thee. I am neither in temple nor in mosque. Neither am I in rites and ceremonies, nor in yoga and renunciation. If thou art a true seeker, thou shalt at once see Me: thou shalt meet Me in a moment of time.
>
> The devout seeker is he who mingles in his heart the double currents of love and detachment, like the mingling of the streams of Gaṅgā and Jamunā.

After having articulated so much, one can put it all down in just one sentence: "Everyone who loves is born of God and knows God. Whoever does not love does not know God, for God is love" (1st letter of John 4: 7-8). It is only in concrete acts of self-sacrificing love that one can know God.

# 12

## Signs of Allāh
### and His Attributes as per Holy Quran

*A. S. Inam Shastri*

God does no injustice to any of His creatures. On the other hand, God needs no praise, for He is above all praises; He needs no petition, for He Knows our needs better than we do ourselves; and bounties are open without asking, to the righteous and the sinner alike. The prayer is for our own spiritual education, consolation and confirmation.

بسم الله الرحمن الرحيم

"BISMILLAHIR REHMANIR RAHEEM"

The Arabic Words "Rahman" and "Rahim" translated "Most Gracious" and "Most Merciful" are both intensive forms referring to different aspects of God's attribute of Mercy. The Arabic intensive is more suited to express God's attributes than the superlative degree in English.

Mercy may imply pity, long suffering, patience and forgiveness, all of which the sinner needs and God Most Mercifully bestows in abundant measure. But there is a Mercy that goes before even the need arises, the Grace which is ever-watchful, and flows from God Most Gracious to all His creatures, protecting them, preserving them, guiding them and leading them to clearer light and higher life.

For this reason the attribute Rahman (Most Gracious) is not applied to any but God, but the attribute Rahim (Merciful) is a general term, and may also be applied to men. To make us contemplate these boundless gifts of God, the formula: "In the name of God Most Gracious and Most Merciful", is placed before every *Sura* of the Quran (except 9th).

It is God who causeth the seed-grain and the date-stone to split and sprout. He *causeth* the living to issue from the dead, and He is the one to cause the dead to issue from the living. That is God: then how are we deluded away from the truth?

It is He who made the sun to be a shining glory and the moon to be a light (of beauty), and measured out stages for her; that ye might know the number of years and the count (of time) Nowise did God Create this but in truth and righteousness (thus) *doth* he explain His signs in detail for those who understand.

Among His Signs is this that He created you from dust (in spite of the lowly origin of man's body, God has given him a mind and soul by which he can almost encompass the farthest reaches of Time and space); and then, Behold, Ye are men scattered (far and wide)!

And among His signs is this, that He created for you mates from among yourselves, that ye may dwell in tranquillity with them, and He has put love and mercy between your (hearts):

And among His Signs is the creation of the heaven and the earth, and the variations in your languages and your colours:

> The variations in languages and colours may be viewed from the geographical aspect or from the aspect of periods of time. All mankind were created of a single pair of parents: yet they have spread to different countries and climate and developed different languages and different shades of

complexions. And yet their basic unity is unaltered. They feel in the same way and are all equally under God's care. Then there are the variations in time. Old languages die and new ones are evolved. New conditions of life and thought are constantly evolving new words and expressions, new syntactical structures, and new modes of pronunciation. Even old races die, and new races are born.

And among His signs is the sleep that ye take by night and by day, *the* quest that ye (make for livelihood) out of His Bounty:

And among His signs. He shows you the lightning, by way both of fear and of hope, and He sends down rain from the sky and with it gives life to the earth after it is dead : (To cowards lightning and thunder appear as terrible forces of nature: lightning seems to kill and destroy where its irresistible progress is not assisted by proper lightning-conductors. But lightning is also a herald of rain-bearing clouds and showers that bring fertility and prosperity in the rain. This double aspect is also symbolical of spiritual fears and hopes — fears that we may not be found receptive or worthy of the irresistible perspicuous Message of God, and hopes that we may receive it in the right spirit and be blessed by its mighty power of transformation to achieve spiritual well-being. Note that the repetition of the phrase "give life to the earth after it is dead" connects this verse with the verse — "It is He who brings out the living from the dead and brings out the dead from the living and who gives life to the earth after it is dead". In other words, the Revelation, which we must receive with wisdom and understanding, is a sign of God's own power and mercy, and is vouchsafed in order to safeguard our own final Future.

"And among His signs is this, that heaven and earth stand by His Command and when He calls you, by a single call, from the earth, behold, ye (straightaway) come forth."

In the physical world, the sky and the earth, as we see them, stand unsupported, by the artistry of God. They bear witness to God, and our physical life depends on them — the earth for its produce and the sky for rain, the *heat* of the sun, and other phenomena of nature — they call to our mind our relation to God, who made them and us.

"Among His signs is this that He sends the winds, as heralds of Glad Tidings, giving you a taste of His (Grace and) Mercy, that the ships may sail (majestically) by His command and that ye may seek."

In physical world, the winds not only cool and purify the air, and bring the blessings of rain which fertilizes the soil, but they help international commerce and intercourse among men through sea-ways and now by air-ways. Those who know how to take advantage of these blessings of God prosper and rejoice while those who ignore or fail to understand these signs perish in storms. So in the Spiritual World: heralds of glad tidings were sent by God in the shape of apostles: those who profited by their Message prospered in spiritual gain, and those who ignored or opposed the clear signs perished spiritually.

"Seest thou not that God makes the clouds move gently, then joins them together, wilt thou see rain issue forth from their midst. And He sends down from the sky Mountain masses (of clouds) wherein is hail: He strikes therewith whom He pleases and He turns it away from whom He pleases. (Artists or lover of nature, or observers of clouds will appreciate this description of cloud effects — thin clouds floating about in fantastic shapes, joining together and taking body and substance, then emerging as heavy clouds heaped up, which condense and pour forth their rain. Then the heavy dark clouds in the upper regions, that bring hail. It hits some localities and leaves free others almost interlaced."

"And God has created every animal from water: of them there are some that creep on their bellies; some that walk on two legs. And some that walk on four, God creates what He wills; for verily God has power over all things."

Protoplasm is the basis of all living matter and "the vital power of protoplasm seems to depend on the constant presence of water" (Low Sons, *Textbook of Botany*, Indian edn., London 1922, p. 23).

It indicates that "Living beings always contain a large amount of water."

God's signs are many, and so are His mysteries: Yet each does point to His unity, Goodness, Power, and Mercy. There is none like Him. His teaching is one, and men that split up His Standard Religion are but purusing their own lusts.

# Part II
## SCIENCE AND SOCIETY

# 13

# Boṅgās in Santhal Thought

*Onkar Prasad*

AN attempt has been made here to deal with the Santal* thought with regard to the Boṅgās** (spirits) they believe in. Myths are the major source of entering into thought. Boas represents serious quests for an understanding and explanation of life and nature. King locates in them areas of life where "man postulates a reality beyond that which he can empirically control or predict" (Black 1997: 542).

The Santals believe in Boṅgā, and name them after the place of their association and the range of influence they exert e.g. *Disam Boṅgā* (country spirit), *Ato Boṅgā* (village spirit), and so on. Those Boṅgās, as Archer (1974) has noted, are said to inhabit three distinct kingdoms. The first is largely an underground replica of the upper land. The second is the realm of the dead, a region vaguely located in the sky above the village. . . . The third and the most significant territory is the village, its fields and homes, trees, hills, rocks and air (p. 26). He observed further that there remains another class of Boṅgā, not connected with any special place but vaguely associated

---

* The Santals are a tribe of proto-Australoid origin inhabiting mainly the eastern part of India, and subsisting mainly on agriculture.

** In Santali language the word Boṅgā is used in a variety of senses, viz. "a spirit," or "godling," "an ignorant fool," "wife," "sacrifice," "offer," etc. Here it is used in the sense of "spirit" or "godling" only.

with particular individuals, occasions or functions (p. 27).

As the Santals believe, in the beginning, these Boṅgās lived with Ṭhākura Jiu, the Supreme Being, who created the earth and everything that exists on it. But, in later course, Māran Burū (spirit of the great mountain), represented by this name, who became the chief of other Boṅgās to whom Ṭhākura Jiu gave all his orders and explained his wishes, became discontented. He rebelled against Ṭhākura Jiu saying that they were doing all the work but in return did not even get the name for doing it. So, these spirits tried to take the power from Ṭhākura Jiu. As a result, he drove them away and in hundred thousands, they came down to the earth where they settled down in villages, on every hill, and otherwise living in rivers, springs, water pools, tanks, trees, roots, rocks, etc. Because Ṭhākura Jiu loves mankind, these spirits, as a revenge, decided to seduce men to get them into their power (Bodding 1926: 65).

The Santals generally conceive of three distinct categories and orders of supernatural beings. For example, they consider Ṭhākura Jiu, the creator of the earth and everything that exists on it, belonging to the first category and order; all their Boṅgās (spirits) that control and guide their life activities, belonging to the second category; and other *bhūta*s (ghosts) and *curin*s (lady ghosts) who have not attained full spiritual status due to their accidental death but continue hovering round the world, belonging to the third category and order of supernatural beings. The Santals have made further gradations of their Boṅgās in terms of their importance. The old Santal *gurus* have ranked the Sin Boṅgā (the sun god) that regulates seasons and day and night, as of the highest importance. Then come, in descending order, the Jom Sim Boṅgā (the deity presiding over the communal feast on chickens); Māran Burū (the great mountain); Jaher-era (the lady of the sacred grove); Moreko-Turuiko (the Five-Six); Gosae-era (her ladyship);

Pargana *Haram* (spirit of the region); Manjhi *haram* Boṅgā (spirit of the village headman); Orak Boṅgā (house spirit); and Abge Boṅgā (spirit of the sub-clan). Besides, the *ojhās* (medicine-men) have separate Boṅgā. There are boundary Boṅgās, Boṅgās of the hollowed out water holes in rivers, Boṅgās of the water pools, Boṅgās of tree-roots and stumps, forest Boṅgās and so on (Bodding 1942: 133). In a creation myth, however, it is the Māran Burū who figures most, and hence has assumed the higher status in the hierarchy of the Boṅgās. In fact, Māran Burū is considered to be the factotum of Ṭhākura Jiu, the supreme being (for detail see ibid.: 14-22).

The position or status of the Boṅgās is determined in terms of their roles in the Santal society. They are said to have played various roles as narrated in myths, some of which are as follow.

### Boṅgā as Rearer of the First Santals

In the Santal origin myth, as referred to above, it is said that in the beginning the Boṅgās lived with Ṭhākura Jiu as his servants, and Māran Burū as their chief. When Ṭhākura Jiu created the Earth and a pair of human beings to live on, he entrusted Māran Burū, who served him as chief of the servants, to look after them. It was Māran Burū who first supported them until they grew up. He taught them to work and gave good instructions. Māran Burū also taught the two human beings to dig out medicines, to collect and prepare rice-beer, etc. (Ibid. 1942: 180).

### Boṅgā as Maker of Social Law

According to a Santal origin myth, when the first pair of human beings Pilcu Haram and Pilcu Budhi had seven boys and seven girls, and when mankind multiplied, it was Māran Burū who first gave them races and septs. But the mankind did not follow the rule of the sex and got indulged in sinful acts. At this, Ṭhākura became angry. He, instead of saving the primordial couple, destroyed all by fire-rain. After that when the First pair got children, again they were divided into septs.

Gradually this division proved itself to be insufficient; they could not all get proper mates. Seeing this, Ṭhākura made Māran Burū instrumental in sending them to the Khandanac forest, so that they do not turn bad as they were. Then Ṭhākura, jointly with Māran Burū, separated them further into many septs. Each sept was divided into twelve, which provided the mankind opportunity of marrying. Māran Burū was given over to mankind by Ṭhākura Jiu, and since then he is ruling (see Bodding 1942: 19).

## Boṅgā as Builder of Settlement

Moreko-Turuiko (Five-Six), one of the Boṅgās slightly inferior to Māran Burū but still of great importance, is described in Santal songs to be the owner of the forest and also the builder of the village. On the first day of the *Baha* (flower festival), when the village priest along with the assistant priest and the messenger, and other village boys clear two patches of ground, plaster them with cowdung and also construct two ceremonial huts, one as symbolic of an abode for Māran Burū, Jaher-era and Moreko Turuiko and the other for Gosae-era; it is sung:

> This forest, this forest, whose is this forest?
> This forest, this forest, whose is this forest land?
> This forest, this forest, this forest is of Moreko
> This forest, this forest, this forest land is of Turuiko.
> This forest, this forest, who will cut down this forest?
> This forest, this forest, who will build this village?
> This forest, this forest, Moreko will cut down this forest.
> This village, this village, Turuiko will build this village.
>
> — From Prasad 1992: 26.

## Boṅgā as Teacher of Cultivation

In the Santal origin myth it is told that after the two primordial human beings grew young, Māran Burū, in addition to teaching them to dig out medicines, to collect and prepare the stuffs for fermenting beer, taught them to sow millets (see Bodding 1942: 18).

## Boṅgā as Founder of Santal Religion

Belief in Boṅgās (spirits) and the Jaherthan (sacred grove) are the two impotant factors upon which the Santal religion is founded. The Boṅgās are said to have taught the Santals to observe festivals and founded the sacred grove. A myth related to the origin of the Baha (flower) festival revealing this, runs as follows:

> When there were only Santals, the clan of Tudus did the work of blacksmiths. Two brothers went to the Urmi forest to make charcoal. It became night. They started to go back. On the way they saw three Boṅgā girls dancing. Behind them, the *Five-Six* were dancing, *sogoe* fashion, with their clothes rustling. The Boṅgā girls had *śāla* flowers in their hair. Their clothes were red. There were no buffalo horns or drums. The two brothers were afraid and hid in a hole, in a fig-tree. The Boṅgā girls with the *Five-Six* came near them. They danced round the tree. The younger of the brothers said, "Our lives are gone.There is no chance of saving them. Let us go and dance with them." So the two brothers came out. The younger went dancing, *sogoe* fashion, with them round the tree. He went round three or four times. His hands were smutty with charcoal. He caught a breast of one of the Boṅgā girls, and his touch made it black. The girls saw the black on her breast, and bowed low. The other two bowed down with her. They danced with cockcrow, bending their bodies and swaying their arms. The *Five-Six* danced with them. When it was dawn the Boṅgā girls told the Tudu boys to start a festival because they had danced with them. The Tudu boys asked, "What shall we call it?" The Boṅgā girls said, "Call it the *'Baha'* festival because we danced with flowers in our hair." Then the Tudu boys left them and went to their village. In the village they called the villagers and asked them to start the festival. They told them about the Boṅgā girls but the villagers did not believe them. That evening buffalo-horn sounded in the priest's house and a drum began to beat. No one was playing the horn and the

> drum was beating itself. As they sounded, a man was possessed with the Baha Boṅgā and rushed to the forest. At that time, there was no *jaher* or sacred grove. He swept a patch of trees and went around it. The priest followed him with a vessel of water. They made the first grove. The next day they put stones by the trees in the name of the *Five-Six* and all the village girls came and danced round them, bending down their bodies. They did this once a year for five years. After five years the Baha Boṅgā came on a man and said that they must sacrifice a black calf to *Five-Six* every five years and take a new *dhotī,* a new broom, a new basket, Boṅgā bells, a new earthen pot, and a bow and arrow, an axe, and an iron chain when they went to the grove. Since then they are doing this! — Archer 1974: 239-48

## Boṅgā as Art-Teacher

In the beginning the Santals worshipped no deities, and did not know the use of musical instruments, and could not dance. Two of their members set out on an exploring expedition, and penetrated deep into the heart of the great forest. Towards evening, they heard the sound of music and not knowing what it was, they went to see from whence it proceeded. On nearing the place, they became frightened and in order to see over the brushwood they climbed up a tree and tried to behold Moreko, Jaher-era, Māran Burū and Gosae-era dancing. Suddenly one of the dancers stood still and said "there are human beings near, I smell them." Jaher-era said, "whether you smell men or beasts, do them no harm, but bring them here." The two adventurers danced with the Boṅgās all night, learning both to play and dance. In the morning they were given two drums, and dismissed with the following injunction:

> Go and tell your people all about us. Tell them to venerate and respect us, and annually offer sacrifices to us. You must also instruct them to play music and dance, and we order you to teach the people of Twelve villages every night. This, it is said, they accomplished and in this manner the Santals

> learned the use of musical insturments and the art of dancing. — Quoted from Sattar, 1975: 134-35

**Boṅgā as Teacher of Secret Knowledge (witchcraft)**

The ancestors say that Māran Burū was teaching the men witchcraft, but by a trick, the women got the magic power first. One day, the men sat down in council to consult each other as to what they should do with their scolding women. They said: "We are men, how is it that our word does not count? When we say a couple of words to the women, they commence to scold shamelessly; we will not stand such behaviour." Then they said: "Come along, let us go to Māran Burū; from him we shall learn some kind of secret skill, that we may subdue these women." They then fixed a time, viz. at midnight they shall meet in such and such a forest. They went; they called Māran Burū to come; they called loudly: "O grandfather, do come here, we, a large number of men, have come to thee in distress." Māran Burū came quickly and asked them: "What trouble is it that you have, grandchildren?" They told their grief and they implored him that he should teach them some secret skill to subdue their women.

Māran Burū said to them — "Well, I shall teach you, but only if you make marks with your blood on these leaves." When they heard this, they became very much afraid and said to him: "tomorrow we shall come again and, giving the marks, receive the secret skill." Thereupon, they went away; but their women had come there secretly and had, from a hidden place, heard exactly all that was said: Then they said: "This, as we have heard, is the justice of these men; before they married us, they were continually following after us like dogs; now when we have become wives, they deem us bad; they are thinking of killing us. Well, we shall have a look at them, who of us are able to kill. When they had said this, they quickly went in advance of the men, following a path. On the way, they decided what they should do. The men also came afterwards. As soon as the men came, the women met their husbands with caresses; therefore the men thought: they have become good by themselves; what shall we go there for?

Next day the women prepared excellent rice and curry for their husbands, and in the evening they poured out any amount of beer for them. The men drank themeselves, drunk and tumbled down on the ground. Then the women called on each other and assembled, they dressed themselves in male loin-clothes and turbans, and fixed goat hair on their lips and started to go to the forest to Māran Burū. They called out to him: "O grandfather, please come quickly, our women have been plaguing us day and night."

Māran Burū came at once. Then they said to him: Do bring your leaves out quickly; we shall make our different marks; we are not able to stand the worrying of the women. Māran Burū brought out his *Śāla*-leaves, and they pricked themselves, and with the blood they made the marks of their respective husbands. Thereupon, Māran Burū taught them incantations and charms, and initiated them in the "eating of people." Smiling and laughing they returned home.

As the men were not getting up quickly next morning, the women abused and cowed them in every possible way. The men got up half-blinded, and rubbing their eyes with their hands they awoke from their sleep. The women had not become gentle minded, this they also got to understand. Feeling sick they came together to take counsel together. Then they said: Come, let us go! Whatever Māran Burū may say to us, we must learn the secret skill. Consequently at night they went to the forest, and they earnestly implored Māran Burū: "Do, father, please teach us, the women are tormenting us awfully."

When Māran Burū heard this, he was astonished and said to them: "Why, I have given you the secret skill. What is it you wish to get again and again?" Then the men unanimously said: "How is that, when have you given it to us? Why, since that day we have never come here, you know?" Hearing this Māran Burū became dumbfounded and said them: "I have given it to you, what else have I done? Look here; look at your own marks!" Seeing their different marks the men said: The marks are ours; but we have never made the marks; somebody, who knows, has made our marks.

Then Māran Burū put his hand to his cheek and was thinking it over in his mind; then it suddenly dawned upon him: the women have made a mere child even of me. And becoming angry he said to the men: "Do make marks here at once; we shall see these deceitful women." They made their marks, and he initiated them as *ojhā*s and witch finders, in order that they might be able to find out the witches and punish them. From that time the witches and the *ojhā*s and witch-finders are enemies. But the *ojhā*s and the witch-finders are unable to do anything, because the witches easily subdue their Boṅgās, so that they are unable to catch them quickly; other people emerge in the divination, and being hoodwinked the witch-finders name the other people (Bodding 1972: 162-64).

**Boṅgā as Lover and Life partner**

Archer (1974) who devoted a chapter on the Boṅgā Lover in his writing observed, "During the years preceding marriage, and in fact, throughout a Santal's lifetime, the Boṅgās continually impinge on Santal affairs. The Boṅgās, it is thought, are not invariably strange invisible forces obsessed with Santal life but are sometimes met with in the guise of boys and girls" (Archer 1974: 279).

He further observed that there are a number of tales, which describe in vivid detail the core of the experience. None of them need to be taken too literally, yet they should not be too lightly dismissed. They reveal how deep is the Santal involvement with Boṅgās and how aware most Santals are of the dangers and mysteries as well as of the delights of sex (ibid., p. 280). Here is a story of a Boṅgā girl as lover and life partner:

One night a young man was driving home his buffaloes. He saw a girl standing by a *pīpala* tree. She was a Boṅgā girl who had been expelled from a man and fastened by thorns to the tree. The young man did not like to leave her, so he told her to go with him to his house. He freed her from the thorns and they went to his house. That night his parents gave her a mat and the girl slept apart. The next morning, she rose early, collected the dung from the cowshed, swept the courtyard and fetched the water. The boy's mother was delighted and they decided to keep her as the boy's wife. That night the two slept on the same cot and made their minds one.

Some time later the girl said to the boy, "We are now husband and wife. We are here not for a day but forever. If we ever quarrel, you may beat me with a stick and strike me with your fist but there is one thing you must never do. You must never trample on me or kick me either with your toes or with the sole of your foot. If you kick me, I shall leave you. When the month of November came, the boy put some vermillion on a flower and put it in her hair, and in a year they had a child. The girl settled down and the family grew rich. They had another child. One day the boy drank rice-beer and thus in fun began to quarrel with her and gave her a kick. The girl wept bitterly and upbraided him, "I told you; you must never touch me with your feet. I am taking the two children. I am leaving you." Then she left the house. The boy's father pleaded with her but she said, "your son did not listen. He has sent me away." When she reached the middle of the field, she and the two children burst into flames and vanished in a flash. When the others saw it they were full of fear for they thought she might have eaten them but the young man was overwhelmed with grief. A little later the family grew poor and were never rich again.

### Boṅgā as Source of Power

The Santals believe that a witch derives power for doing harm to a person from the Boṅgā, though the Boṅgā in question need not be Manjhi Haram or Pargana. At least one Boṅgā approved by Pargana Boṅgā must agree to the act. Sometimes if Pargana Boṅgā does not give consent, the witch takes the help of a Boṅgā who is himself the death-dealing agent. In this case the Boṅgā may do harm to a person.

### Boṅgā as Protector and Destroyer

Archer (1974) finds Boṅgās of three kinds — those who are capable of sudden vicious behaviour, those who are either protective or at any rate well disposed, and those who are intimately, even desperately, concerned with tribal welfare and integrity.

The Boṅgās who are naturally spiteful, and from whom inaction is all that can be hoped, include the Boṅgā husbands of witches, the anonymous dispensers of sickness, the boundary Boṅgās, all the Boṅgās of forests, rocks, spirits and tree stumps, whether within or outside the village frontiers, the Rongo Ruji Boṅgā, Hindu festival-Boṅgās, and finally the Boṅgā of the house. Of this vast and miscellaneous crew, a boundary Boṅgā is particularly feared. It causes snakes and leopards to attack men in the fields. The home-Boṅgā is not so hostile but is like a touchy, "testy" woman, quick to take offence and apt to cause disease. The Boṅgās of the forest, hills and springs are liable to spoil the crops or cause accidents and the Boṅgā of a Hindu festiaval may induce a sudden feeling of mysterious insecurity.

The second type of Boṅgā, on the other hand, is altogether beneficent. The Abge Boṅgās (spirits of the sub-class) protect the Santals as individuals; it is above all the Boṅgās of the sacred-grove who supervise them as a tribe. The greatest of these is Māran Burū who is supposed to have dealt with the first Santal. The other two Boṅgās are Jaher-era and Moreko Turuiko. Jaher-era never does any harm; Moreko Turuiko are supposed to preside over the welfare of the village.

The third group of Boṅgās include Gosae-era (the girl connected with Moreko Turuiko), Pargana Boṅgā (who still rules the local region) and Manjī/Haram Boṅgā (the original founder and in-charge of the village).

This group of Boṅgās constitutes the prime concern of the Santals. Other Boṅgās may vex and trouble them, but if the greater national Boṅgās are ignored or outraged the very foundation of Santal life is threatened. To pass their days happily, and to express to the full the joys of tribal existence, Santals must not only attune themselves to village customs but unite in honouring their ghostly protectors.

**Conclusion**

From the presentation of the materials dealing with the idea-system of the Santals regarding Boṅgās, it may be said that in Santal thought they are the cosmic persons identified after the place they occupy, and the range of influence they exert. They are present everywhere in the underworld, the terrestrial or the aerial space.

The Santals follow a system of gradation in respect of the Boṅgās. Compared to Ṭhākura Jiu at the top and the *bhūta*s and *curin*s at the bottom, the Boṅgās occupy an intermediary position. Irrespective of being benevolent or malevolent, personal or impersonal they have to be appeased through sacrifices on ceremonial occasions for peaceful existence. The Santals make further gradation of the Boṅgās in terms of the roles they have played in the mythical past. Māran Burū, in his various roles, viz. as rearer of the first Santal couple, as maker of social law for regulating sex and marriage, as teacher of cultivation and secret knowledge, and as founder of the Santal religion, occupies the highest position and respect whereas other Boṅgās of benevolent nature have the secondary position. Those Boṅgās, who are malevolent, are thought to be inferior to that of the benevolent type. The Boṅgās are thought to be impersonalized entities, viz. Māran Burū, Jaher-era, Moreko Turuiko and Gosae-era associated with the sacred grove, as well as personalized entities, viz. Pargana Boṅgā, Orak Boṅgā, Abge Boṅgā, etc.

Finally, in Santal thought the Boṅgās are a formless entity, but they may assume form (say Boṅgā girl or boy) and exchange their own kind of life for that of the living (here the Santals). Referring to this, Archer (1979) observes that this kind of thinking by the Santals project thereby a kind of alter Santal over the centuries the tribe has felt it necessary to invent. At this stage of consciousness there is a fusion of normal with the sub-normal, the natural with the supernatural thereby revealing their ultimate confidence in life (p. 280).

## References

Archer, W.G. (1974): *The Hill of Flutes: Life, Love and Poetry in Tribal India*, New Delhi: S. Chand & Co. (Pvt.) Ltd.

Black, Mary B. (1997): Belief Systems. In *Handbook of Social and Cultural Anthropology*, vol. I, ed. J. J. Honigmann. Jaipur: Rawat Publications, pp. 509-77.

Bodding P.O. (1926): Meaning of the word Burū and Boṅgā in Santali, *Journal of Bihar and Orissa Research Society*, Patna, 12, pp. 63-77.

Bodding P.O. (1942): *Traditions and Institutions of the Santhals*, Oslo Etnografiske Museum, Bulletin 6.

Prasad, Onkar (1992): *A Case Study of Music and Santhal in Bolpur-Sriniketan Block of Birbhum District*. Unpublished IGNCA Report.

Sattar, Abdus (1975): *Tribal Culture in Bangladesh*. Dacca: Muktadhara.

# 14

# Syncretic Folk Deities of Sundarbans Delta

*Gautam Kumar Bera*

THE landmass called Sundarbans, spread over an area of 9630 sq km, in the districts of North 24 Parganas and South 24 Parganas of West Bengal in India, is the largest delta on earth formed by the rivers Brahmaputra and Gaṅgā. Covering a forest area of 4284 sq km, it encompasses 102 islands out of which 54 islands are inhabited by human population in an area of 5366 sq km.

Ecological and demographic features coupled with the history of reclamation of land lay the foundation for understanding Sundarbans in terms of its spatial and cultural growth. The policy of reclamation of land in Sundarbans with special reference to the trend of settlement in this special type of environment is the fundamental guideline to understand the process of religious syncretism that is under operation here. It was during the colonial period when reclamation of land started to make islands habitable for human settlement. The forest in this part of the country was cleared during the colonial regime by the tribal people brought in from the Chhotanagpur plateau of the present-day state of Jharkhand, and by the non-tribals particularly the caste Hindus and Muslims of Midnapur district of the state of West Bengal. Later a considerable population immigrated to this soil from East

Pakistan (now Bangladesh) as a result of political exodus during the Partition of our country and achievement of national Independence and also later on during the post-war situation in the successive wars in 1965 and 1971.

The Sundarbans posed unique problems to the clearers and settlers. These littoral mangrove forests were completely different from forests in the other parts of Bengal, which, however, challenged taxonomic comprehension. These forests were also infested with man-eating Royal Bengal Tigers. In consequence thereupon the woodcutters were wary of entering the forests without *fakīra*s (ritual specialist mendicants) who possess the powers of propitiating the spirits of tigers and other wild animals. Hence, people depended more on these beliefs and resorted to the specialists for their rescue.

The factors of human settlement and the crises of survival in this ecological condition have brought people together under a common canopy of syncretism, which borrows a myth from the twin faiths of Islam and Hinduism. The resultant force of this mythical spread has formed a common folk cult in this part of Gangetic delta, which has taken roots in all societies irrespective of their religious faith and occupational pursuits. However, there has been a differential rate of the degree of acceptance in different societies, if observed individually, but the uniqueness of this mythical spread is that it lies at the cognitive dimension of the people. Empirical findings suggest that this common cult may have originated in and around this region during the last century or so and had a sacred bond, which now takes the shape of a secular feature where the religious sacraments are guided in the principles of sacred-secular continuum.

The folk cults that dominate in Sundarbans are Bon Bībī, Dakṣin Roy, Shahjangali, Gāzī Bābā, Mānik Pīr, Badar Pīr, Ali Madat, Mai Bībī, Noy Bībī, Śītalā, Manasā, Pañcananda, Peñcokeñco, Pañcu Ṭhākura, Caṇḍī, Kasto Devī, Khwājah Khijir Pīr, Āteśvar and so on. Whereas some are propitiated for survival strategy, the others are venerated for warding off evil diseases like pox, cholera, etc. For understanding the syncretic folk deities of Sundarbans delta region, the present study will be delimited to the cults of Bon Bībī, Shahjangali and Noy Bībī.

While understanding the folk cults of Sundarbans, however, it is felt that the culture that had grown around the original settlers of the last century had waned away considerably in due course of time since, probably, it was felt to be the order of the day. While following the methodology for the purpose of the study and encountering its problems it was observed that the people of Sundarbans devote much of their time and resources on festivals and rituals associated with Bon Bībī and Noy Bībī. Since it was necessary to find out the meaning underlying the rituals, it was understood that these rituals designated something in their life as an idiom of expression of social, political and economic realities. The people devote much time, attention and effort to these rituals since these apparently seemed to be systematic, self-congruent and capable of generating separate meanings. To understand the meaning of festival they took it as a domain in their own right because it exhibits a particular system and structure. This needed an analysis in totality since other socio-political domains were related to this festival as expressed by myths and rituals. The festivals provided an opportunity to understand a culturally constituted domain through analysing ritual action as the expression of total social fact. The purpose of the present study was not confined to the understanding of the culture of a particular locale. It was rather intended to understand the inner dynamism of the culture of Sundarbans and the general characteristics of the peoples' cognition as expressed through folk deity propitiation. At the notional plane, it was intended to understand the phenomenon of sacred-secular continuum and the process of universalization of the folk deity that are under operation here. By sacred-secular continuum it is meant here a continuity of matters related to the religious order to the non-religious sphere, rather to the socio-political affairs that hold the authority structure; and the use of the term secularization has been made here to denote the tending of conversion from sacred to secular uses. In the same vein of thought the term universalization implies here as "the carrying forward and upward, not only of cultural awareness, but also of cultural contents" (Marriot, 1961: 202).

In Sundarbans, Bon Bībī is the deity of the common people across all sections of the society down to the lowest stratum. Today the role of the commoner is peripheral, as much has been swallowed by the administration in the organization of the Bon Bībī festival. The guardian deity of Sundarbans is Bon Bībī who is believed to be concerned with the well-being of the subjects of the Sundarbans. At the same time, she is also the deity of the forest which is responsible for her daily worship and also for the annual festival in her temple. Almost the whole of the permanent population of Sundarbans forest area coupled with its hinterland in particular turn up to attend the Bon Bībī festival. The various aspects of the festival are vicissitudes of the social organization of Sundarbans, the structure of the relationship between the functionaries concerned, such as the deities, the priest and the devotees, the details of the social actions in the form of rituals, the local theogony and the ontogeny of the people of Sundarbans. Through the present study, it was attempted to explicate the idea system and the logic behind the social actions and the symbols in the festivals, which hold the different strata of the society together in definite forms of corporate behaviour. In doing so, indigenous interpretations of ideas and actions have been made to understand in the dialectical relations to the festival of the greater Sanskritic canopy of Hinduism.

Cognitively the people of Sundarbans conceive of the landmass as low area (*nicher dik*) and high area (*oporer dik*). Whereas the former category takes into cognizance the areas under islands and forests, the latter category includes areas attached to the mainland of south Bengal.

Bon Bībī is the predominating cult here, who is considered in lower Sundarbans by the people of *atharo bhati* (area of eighteen low tides) as the daughter of a Muslim saint who became the sole protector of all the people living here irrespective of their religious affiliations. The parallel cult is Dakṣin Roy, the male counterpart of Bon Bībī, who along with her has formed a mythical background that lays the foundation for a common religious belief, socio-economic environment and a historical signal of trans-cultural overlapping. Both of these characters are referred to in *Bon Bībīr Johurnāmā, Dukhe Kahini, Rāymangal* and *Dhana Manar Pala,* in the form of a long story, which says that:

"A Muslim saint Berahim, with his wife Fūl Bībī, spent his married life for long without any children. He remarries Gulāl Bībī to have a child from her despite serious objection from his first wife. It was also conditional for the second marriage that Berahim has to desert his wife after she conceives. In consequence thereupon Berahim deserts his second wife Gulāl Bībī, when she was in the family way, in the deep forested area in the pretext of taking her to a relative's house. In due course of time Gulāl Bībī gives birth to twin babies of either sex in the forest. Considering her son to be more important she deserts her daughter and goes away with her son. The daughter, later named Bon Bībī, gets patronage from four fairies with motherly affection. She survives with the milk of a deer. The son, Shahjangali grows up elsewhere under the care of his mother Gulāl Bībī. At the age of seven they reunite in the presence of their parents. Berahim wants to take back his entire family to the place of his origin, which eventually the children do not like. Berahim takes back his wife Gulāl Bībī leaving behind Bon Bībī and Shahjangali, his children, for ever."

A point arises here which has been observed empirically. The character "Berahim" is named Ebrahim by the Hindus while the Muslims call him Berahim, which eventually means a heartless man as his character portrays.

With the passage of time the siblings grow up in the forest enjoying all the benefits including food and drink that is available there. In their adulthood, they along with Gazi Baba, a saint of Muslim origin, pick-up confrontation over territory with Dakṣin Roy, the tyrant son of a demon named Daṇḍarakṣa and Nārāyaṇī, who also claims Sundarbans as his domain. It takes the shape of a war and as a result Dakṣin Roy and his mother Nārāyaṇī get defeated in the battle. Gāzī Bābā negotiates over their rivalry and a peace accord gets signed with a demarcating line of jurisdiction for each, i.e. Bon Bībī and Dakṣin Roy. Whereas Bon Bībī wins the authority of supremacy of the entire territory of *atharo bhati,* Dakṣin Roy gets his share of territory between Kendokhali and the sea shore.

From the available literatures it is evident that at least three poets namely Munshi Bayanuddin, Munshi Mohammad Khater and Mohammad Munshi Saheb narrated the glory of Bon Bībī in a poetic manner at three different points of time, such as 1877-78, 1881 and 1899 respectively. In the *Bon Bībīr Johurnāmā,* the two kindreds, Bon Bībī and Shahjangali, stand as central characters of interest with paramount importance. The whole account has interestingly elaborated the situations of social reality of a particular geographical territory in a specific time dimension of historical framework. It eventually served the purpose of theistic necessity from the dimension of a particular religious faith and the aesthetic enlightenment of the non-literate credulous folks. Though the cult of Bon Bībī stands here as an insignia of Islamic faith, yet she transcended the barrier of faith and could win the recognition of the people of the entire region through her acceptance as the mother deity of lower Sundarbans delta.

The legend of Bon Bībī is current among all the people who live in Sundarbans. If one looks into the core issues associated with the legend, she/he finds that it is the story of class struggle where a woman, deserted daughter of a commoner, makes the society free from a tyrant ruler. There is a probability that this was a struggle for encroachment of territorial existence in terms of social, cultural and religious supremacy. Dakṣin Roy was an indigenous cult here who has been overpowered by an encroacher. The settlement pattern and development of the area in terms of historicity of people's rehabilitation here has a linkage with the story of Bon Bībī.

Earlier ethnographic records noted during the period of reclamation of land and first settlement from the tribal areas of the neighbouring state and the fringe areas of West Bengal do not show any reference to Bon Bībī. The process of acculturation got accentuated in this part of land after the immigration of Muslim population and the people of East Pakistan (now Bangladesh). It is an acculturation of two predominant faiths, Hinduism and Islam, mainly through direct culture contact and through the easy accessibility of *darbeśa, fakīra and pīr* (all Muslim saints).

The cult of Bon Bībī has been manifested in manifold manner. She has been seen sitting on a roaring tiger in general, but at times she has also been seen sitting on a deer, and at very rare occasions on a wild fowl. In this part of the land there are a host of people who are directly and indirectly associated with their immediate environment, the forest and the river. People who are directly associated with the forest and the river are called *jungle kara lok* (forest goers) and they include *jele* (fishermen), *moule* (honey collectors) and *bauley* (wood collectors) obviously for livelihood. If a person goes to the interior areas by his own mode of conveyance, i.e. boat, cognitively he is referred to as *jungle korte gechhe* (gone to the forest). So, to them, forest is the most important aspect of their life. Hence, the cult of Bon Bībī stands as the most undisputed saviour of the Sundarbans, irrespective of one's religious affiliation. Some idols of Bon Bībī show a male child sitting in the lap of a woman. Worshipping of a female cult with a child in lap directs one's thought towards fertility cult as productive economy. One may presume here the agriculture developed in this part of land at a quite later stage.

All the characters mentioned above have a legend of their own, which sometimes overlap mythical characters and sometimes historical characters. Almost in all cases no sacred text is identified except the references of legendary tales mentioned earlier. However, the day of annual worship (also referred to as festival day) always overlaps important festive days of the Hindu calendar like *Makara Saṁkrānti* (for Hindus and Muslims) and *Basanta Pañcamī* (for tribals). The entire phase of acculturation as a continuous process was all through routed along such a path where the carrier agents were divine or semi-divine characters like sūfīs and saints. The form of Islamic faith which entered India following the tradition of Sufism differs largely with greater Islamic canopy in terms of sacraments prescribed and proscribed in Islam. Hence, the folk tradition borrows a little from established Islam. The same has been reflected in the case of Hindu belief system too. What is interesting part of the legend of Bon Bībī is that today Bon Bībī is *worshipped* as a Hindu deity by a Muslim priest where she is offered *hajot,* instead of *prasāda.* Unlike other Hindu gods and goddesses she sits facing the east and the priest obviously faces the west while *worshipping* her, a tradition that is proscribed in Hindu faith. Moreover, the very term *worship* of an idol does not fit in the normative pattern of Islamic mode of religious sacrament. The acceptance of a Muslim girl, daughter of a Muslim parenthood, as a Hindu deity comes under the purview of the process of syncretism that took birth under the canopies of acculturation and assimilation.

It is, however, felt that the performance of this sort of folk tradition in a localized pocket is an attempt to justify supremacy of good over evil, struggle for territorial existence, where myth, legend and imaginary characters are the carriers of belief system and once this belief system gets a footage, the forces of syncretic process in the religious axis gets strengthened.

Another dimension of Islamic influence is noted in the discussion of Noy Bībī. In the *oporer dik* or high area of Sunderbans the influence of Bon Bībī gets minimized possibly due to the non-forest environment. But the crises of survival take on a different shape in this part of the delta centring particularly on cults and deities associated with either welfare or diseases. Mention may be made of the snake cult of Manasā, disease cults of Śītalā, Jarasur, Jatapatra, Pañcananda, Andha Muni, Noy Bībī and the welfare deity Mai Bībī.

In many villages of this region, particularly at the outskirts, one notices the existence of a precinct specially meant for Noy Bībī. Interestingly enough this type of precinct was also noticed at the courtyard of the *kutchery* (court) of the *zamīndāra* of Raidighi in South 24 Parganas, West Bengal. In reality there are, in total, nine deities in the altar who are related to one another as kindreds. Each of these deities is supposed to be responsible for the outbreak of a particular disease and their appeasement brings relief as a contrary feature. These nine deities or Noy Bībī are Asan Bībī, Ola Bībī, Jhola Bībī, Tola

Bībī, Mari Bībī, Jhari Bībī, Kuruni Bībī, Jhetuney Bībī and Darbari Bībī. Local belief says that these deities were born out of the sweat of the forehead of Allāh. Of them the eldest sister is Asan Bībī, named after *asan,* meaning easy access. This set of deities also get their share of sacred offerings in the form of *hajot* by the Muslim priest who sits facing the west, as is prescribed in Islam, for *worshipping.* The cult of Noy Bībī has a widespread appellation in this part of rural Bengal who are appeased for either warding off epidemics like cholera, pox, measles, dysentery, etc. or for protecting children from other tropical diseases. It is learnt that rural Bengal was once prone to epidemics for which people developed faith on these folk deities who may have entered this soil and got wide acceptance through the preaching of *fakīra, pīr* and *darbeśa* where religion, faith and belief played no bar at all. The Muslim saints also had easy access to folk/ ethno medicine which otherwise helped all to cure the diseases. Probably this seems to be the potential reason to identify a particular disease against a specific deity, called Bībī and a way to get rid of it. The amalgamation of people's belief system and the encroaching ideas probably formed a system that was different from either of the two original cultures. This probably laid the stage for the process of formation of syncretism in this part of lower Bengal.

From the above it is apparent that there was a tendency or effort to reconcile and unite various systems of philosophy or religious opinion on the basis of tenets common to all and against a common opponent. This fusion of two or more inflectional forms, which were originally different as of two cases of religion, has taken a root under the canopy of syncretism. The form of syncrecy as is seen in Sundarbans is an attempt for blending, harmonizing or massing of different or antagonistic elements, which were clearly understandable in terms of the peopling of Sundarbans, habitational pattern, composition of folk songs, belief in saints (particularly Muslim saints), myths and legends that are current among people professing different religions, practising varied occupational pursuits and from the pattern of immigration to this soil.

An important point which is mooted here is that Bon Bībī in Sundarbans has assumed a new dimension with a new social meaning in the changed socio-political environment. Hence, the cults of Bon Bībī and Noy Bībī have been understood here as an integral part of the whole process of social evolution rather than as self-congruent, self-contained domains that generate non-assimilative meaning. It is the phase of a cultural understanding in this part of poly ethnic mosaic where one finds an essence of assimilation, secularization, syncretism and universalization of culture while delineating the cults as a cultural process.

**Reference**

Marriot, Mckim, 1961. "Little communities in an indigenous civilization" in Mckim Marriot, ed., *Village India.* Bombay: Asia Publishing House. (First published in 1955 by the University of Chicago Press).

# 15

# Forms of Proto-devī Ādyaśakti
## In the Shamanic Cosmogonies of some Ādivāsī groups of Eastern India

*Stefano Beggiora*

THE cosmogonic myths of Indian tribal communities (*ādivāsī*) still bear witness to an extremely rich culture. The existence of uncountable regional versions, the continuous interpretation and re-interpretation of the mythological matter, and the changing patterns according to cultural and historical occurrences have made this complex cultural corpus extremely difficult to be systematically arranged. This difficulty is even more noticeable if we consider both the parallelism and the reciprocal influx between tribal beliefs and the Hindu epics (*Rāmāyaṇa* and *Mahābhārata* with all their local variants).

During my fieldwork among the Muṇḍa-speaking Saoras and the Draviḍian-speaking Kondhs of Orissa and the Tibeto-Burma-speaking Apatanis of Arunachal Pradesh, I have tried to trace and individuate the concept of traditional macrocosm in the myth of creation. This study proved to be extremely intriguing as it allowed further consideration on the eschatological beliefs of different people. In particular, I refer to Shamanism, a cultural reality and a *modus vivendi* which — rather than being a mere melting pot of magic and cultural data[1] — shows the features of a primordial, almost pre-religious, thought.

Previous inquiries on the concept of cosmos and the concept of human soul among Indian tribes have revealed a complex but apparently homogeneous pattern of beliefs, though a reasonable amount of variants are present. On a technical level, such analysis caused more than one difficulty. On many occasions, I had to face the reluctance of both shamans and village *pūjārīs* (priests) in telling and commenting on both epic and mythological events as well as the cosmogony of the tribe. This is in contrast with the enthusiastic collaboration of my informants (most of them shamans) on specific subjects such as post-modern beliefs, the nature of the universe, healing techniques and various ritual practices.

By analysing previous reports and academic inquiries and through my own fieldwork, I have been able to observe how these traditions are quickly vanishing. The causes of this process are various — among these, the advent of modernity, the life-style change, movements of social modification among scheduled castes, etc. During the first stages of my work, I noticed the cultural annihilation of many tribal groups which led their own mythological and cosmogonical beliefs towards oblivion. In many cases this was a source of great embarrassment and reluctance for the members of the tribe.

---

1. Some of the most authoritative and recent studies on Shamanism (Basilov 1999: 17-40, Mastromattei 1995) focused on the ritual specialist in order to clarify whether or not she/he is a shaman. What really matters here, however, is that the whole community — regardless of its actual beliefs — shares with the shaman/religious specialist the vision of macrocosm which contains the subtle world and the supernatural powers abiding it. This should imply a lifestyle regulated by nature. Accordingly I suspect it will be possible to look upon these kinds of practices as pre-religious (Beggiora 2003: 66-78, Pandey 1974: 132-35).

Yet looking at previous ethnological reports, though not so temporally distant, I acknowledged the relevancy of the impact of socio-political changes. However, after several years of research, I feel confident to state that, despite all difficulties, tribal people have somehow maintained their cultural heritage. Rather than focusing on the analysis of mythological symbolism, it seems crucial to explore what the concept of "myth" represents for tribal traditions and what is its function within tribal communities.

### The Meaning of Myth and the "Chamber of Myth"

The present study will inquire into the origin of the Indian tribal universe through the analysis of shamanic and shamanic-related ritual practices. Some remarks of tribal myths and myth-telling techniques are thus in order.

First of all, it has to be noticed that tribal people (usually) lack a written language. Accordingly, they transmit their myths by heart from one generation to another. The very same symbols of a certain myth (i.e. the main events and characters) are transmitted constantly and immutably through time. Nevertheless, some of their features and the dynamics which regulate their interaction might show a certain degree of interchangeability, often depending on the development of the cultural environment they refer to.

After more than a hundred years from the colonial wars fought early in the nineteenth century, the Kondhs of Orissa and the Apatanis of Arunachal Pradesh have acquired in their myths historical figures who were actually involved in those events. They became quasi-mythical heroes and ended up substituting the heroes of the previous cycle due to their individual features (either virtual or imaginary).[2] On the one hand, it is possible to acknowledge the absolute lack of any

2. On Kondhs, see Elwin (1954: 601, 639) and Beggiora (2004: 238-39), On Apatanis, see Blackburn (2003: 338ff).

sense of historiography within tribal communities. On the other, the historical heritage of the tribe has been so transmitted that it became the actual mythological corpus. One of the most interesting features of such a process is temporal levelling. Heroes and anti-heroes act in a place and in a time which almost coincides with the primordial time/space. As a matter of fact, in certain myths, it is told that right after the creation of the universe, along with the tribe, there were the British soldiers. Invariably they are rendered either as terrific charactrers or grotesque buffoons. This does not imply that the Kondhs[3] — to name a tribe — believe the universe was actually created in the early nineteenth century. However the same traditional symbols and archaic thematics are maintained, though in a different and, so to speak, updated, version.

I observed a similar case among the Lanja Saoras in Orissa. Catholic missionaries, in their systematic work of conversion of tribal people, well understood the meaning and the power of myth. Accordingly, in order to spread a new religion and a new god, i.e. Christianity and Jesus Christ, they employed almost obsolete local cosmogonic myth and simply substituted local deities and spirits with Biblical characters.[4] The names given by shamans and *pūjārīs* were maintained, but the result

3. After more than fifty years from the end of the Meriah wars, Elwin (1954: 548) reports a legend in which MacPherson, a British officer, was said to have been born in Kondh territory and to have been married to the daughter of a local king. Chronologically speaking, these events belong to the cosmogonic myth, after the first human sacrifice to the goddess was performed.

4. The name Kittung, in Saora language, literally means "god" but it also indicates semi-gods of the epic cycles of the tribe. Today it is the name of Jesus Christ. In 1998, I found evidence of a Christian missionary in Kerala who translated the whole Bible in local language. He attempted a phonetic transliteration of the Saora language and substituted all Biblical names with those belonging to the local tradition. See Beggiora 2003: 58-59 and 153-58. About Kittung in the cosmogonies of Lanja and Sarda Saoras, see AA. VV. 1993.

is an interesting hybrid which allowed Christian religion to penetrate into an (apparently) hostile socio-cultural environment.

The permeability of myth in these contexts is always present. Not only can the same myth be transmitted with slight variations in clusters of villages more or less close, but it is also possible to hear the same informant referring to a deity with one name, and use another one on the very next occasion. Especially in the latter case, benign or malign forms and attributes are described accordingly (Elwin 1993: x-xii). This process can even be observed in a same narrative performance although relevant symbolic events are connected without any apparent logic (Beggiora 2003: 90).

The result of this process is the creation of a mythological corpus characterized by fervid imagination, great activity and, of course, constant adjournment. Different characters and events coexist and are interchangeable in the narration. Their existence is however hermeneutic in explaining a parallel dimension. This is a sort of cultural container which keeps together both the archaic and recent experiences of the tribe. This container is out of place and time.[5] I will call it the "chamber of myth." When such a chamber is "visited" — during scheduled festivals, public occurrences or private session of myth-telling — the story appears always fresh and alive. Narration, in a sense, strengthens its own existence. The community witnesses the mythical event and the epic gests of the heroes collectively. According to a pattern shared by Indian *ādivāsī*s, the traditional corpus not only has to be

---

5. On the cosmogonic myth of American natives, Spagna (1998: 95) says that "the time of the origins is a recurrent time. It is not just placed backward following a linear criterion, rather it flows in an invisible dimension, it is revealed in dreams and it is actualized in the oral tradition of a certain group."

permeable to variants, but it has to be modifiable as well.[6]

## The Cosmogonic Myth among Indian Tribal Cultures

The first narration in a session of myth-telling is always the cosmogony. A shaman who narrates the myth of creation according to the tradition of his/her tribe revives it and, at the same time, celebrates it. It is a complex performance which does not allow any sort of error or omission. This is well acknowledged in South Asian traditions, where the celebration of a ritual — at all levels — implies the recreation of the microcosm in the macrocosm. Such performance strictly connects the shaman with his/her community. In other words, the shaman, the *pūjārī* or the holder of transmittable knowledge in telling myth performs a rite. This must be complete, correctly executed and has to reflect the cosmic harmony it is about to celebrate.

Despite the presence of local variations, it is still unclear why shamans are occasionally reluctant in narrating myths. In general, the stronger the tradition of a tribe is the more it will be easy for a shaman to debate on the dynamics of his/her ritual acts. In the chamber of myth, legends with different origins and contexts can be tightly looked upon as cosmogonies. Collecting myths, tales and legends is thus a formal attempt to set a ritual celebration, especially in a shamanic context.

6. The same features can be recognized in other cultures too. Aristotle stressed the power of the word as interpreter of thought. Accordingly, words are a narration whose deep meanings need to be explored. Language itself, as an instrument of human intellect, is an analytical tool whereas the symbol transcends this pattern because of its own nature (Guénon 2003: 20).

## The Creation Myth of the Kondhs[7]

The story goes back to the origin of the world. The earth was just wilderness. Buṛa Pēnu (the main god of the Kondhs) was travelling with his wife Tari Pēnu (or Dharani Pēnu, as she is also called).[8] He was extremely annoyed by his companion who questioned every word, action and decision of his. So Buṛa Pēnu decided to create man, a creature meant to respect, love and worship him. He collected some earth so as to build a new universe where a new being, man, could live.[9] Yet Tari Pēnu learned about her husband's project and became furious with jealousy. She reached the place where Buṛa Pēnu was preparing the pieces of earth and started to throw them away with furious anger. The sky was created out of the first clod and then hills, rivers, lakes, wildlife, birds, fishes, etc. When Buṛa Pēna realized the destructive power of Tari, he stopped her by putting his hand on her forehead, an act which made Tari barren. Then he picked up the last clod and he threw it away: man was eventually created.

After creation was made, mankind was living in a beautiful but mysterious world. Plant life grew too intricately and there were jungles everywhere. Animals were savage and ferocious. Yet most of all the soil was not fertile either because of aridity or the thick vegetation. (Such a scenario actually resembles the environment of many Orissan areas.) The myth ends up

---

7. Now an independent district, it was a part of the Phulbani territory. My fieldwork was carried on during February 2000, February 2001 and November 2002.

8. "Pēnnu" or "Pēnu" is used by Draviḍian-speaking tribes while "pinu" is a noun belonging to the Tibeto-Burman linguistic family. In both cases it means "spirit," "deity" or simply a supernatural power. In Kui and Kuvi, the two major Kondh languages, Pēnu is a god or a spirit. Among the Kondhs, Bura Pēnu is the Sun whereas Tari Pēnu is the Earth. On many circumstances, they are interpreted as a god and his *Śakti.*

9. See below fn. 27, 28 and 31.

with the description of how men adapted themselves to the surrounding setting, even though this was not the original project of Buṛa Pēnu.

A first version of this myth was recorded by MacPherson (1865: 84-85), a British officer during the Meriah wars (middle nineteenth century). This conflict covered with blood, the whole state of Orissa for almost a century. On the one hand, it cost the British a high price in terms of men and wealth. On the other, it led to an almost systematic genocide of local tribes. I have elsewhere shown how the Meriah wars were fought on strictly colonialist bases (Beggiora 2004 and forthcoming).[10] Nevertheless, it is herein crucial to stress that the alleged reason why the British waged war against the Kondhs was the suppression of the human sacrifice (*meriah*). Yet after more than 150 years from the end of the Meriah wars, when both the British Raj and local dynasties are no more, many variants of the above-mentioned cosmogony survive along with Kondh culture. The land of the Kondh had gone through radical changes on historical, social and political points of view. All the same, it is quite interesting to notice how the only surviving element of this process is the weakest link of the original cosmogonic myth: Tari Pēnu. The myth of Tari is still transmitted and it bears witness to the centrality of the cult of the earth in central Orissa.

MacPherson (1865: 87) recorded some interesting variants of the Tari myth which presents some obscure and controversial points. In particular, he argued the existence of two original Kondh tribes or antithetic cults: the former devoted to the Sun (Buṛa Pēnu), the latter to the mother Earth (Tari Pēnu). I disagree with such hypothesis[11] and even though

---

10. See also Patnaik (1992: 227-378); Padel 2000; Chetti 1982.

11. The antagonism of primordial forces must have suggested the existence of different religious factions, which in a tribal context do not exist. Nevertheless, MacPherson insists that Tari Pēnu is →

some British officers had ethnographic interests and collected from the source many interesting data, their work is almost invariably the product of a cultural and professional misunderstanding.[12]

Apropos of dichotomies and antitheses, some words need to be spent on the gender of specific deities in a shamanic environment. Though in the daily reality of a cult it is possible to tell male and female deities/spirits, in cosmogonic myths androgyny seems to be praxis. More specifically, the divine is invariably believed to have a twofold power of manifestation, male and female. Such androgyny is structurally linked with the cosmogonic dualism which is at the basis of the mythical scenario.[13]

---

→ the evil principle which installed in humankind the seed of sin. Although the idea of the sin as seed is highly evocative — especially if performed by the Earth — the concept itself of sin is not fitting in this context. The fact that Bura Pēnu, the god, accorded men free will as well as the chance to accept or not evil (i.e. Tari), seems highly polluted with Christian missionary beliefs (cf. MacPherson 1865: 86).

12. For the British the *casus belli* was the abolition of the human sacrifice. Accordingly many records tended to increase the number of Kondh warriors and also emphasized the "barbaric" practices of their cults by adding scaring, yet unfaithful, details.

13. Even when this dichotomy is rendered into plain antagonism between a male and female principle, the theme of the reciprocal belonging survives. Elwin (1954: 65) shows how the thundering sky was meant by many tribes as the battlefield of the gods. The thunderbolt, dynamic, fast and elusive, was the female principle whereas the thunder, slower yet mighty, was the male principle, always running after her companion. However, they are both considered as two manifestations of the same phenomenon. MacPherson too recalls more than one myth where the sky is described as the battleground of Tari and Bura Pēnu. A comet, which lightened up the sky of Orissa in the 1840s, was interpreted by the Kondhs as a celestial weapon thrown by one of the two deities towards the other. The exact date of the phenomenon is however missing (1865: 87).

Coming back to MacPherson's ethnographies, he eventually suggests the victory of Tari. Such a conclusion seems to suggest the success of the quasi-Śākta stream. This interpretation is none the less related to a successive phase, when the genesis of the world is already accomplished. In fact, Kondh legends tell about a benign form of Tari, Nirantali, to whom the discovery of agriculture is ascribed.[14]

This myth describes that the goddess while cutting some plants in the deep of the jungle, accidentally cut-off one of her fingers (or hand, according to the source). When the rush of blood flowing from her body reached the earth, this was made fertile.[15] Nirantali called for the shamans of the tribe and asked them to sacrifice her. She ordered herself to be slain and dismembered, and her blood was scattered on the soil in order to make it fertile.[16] The shamans, though, did not dare to sacrifice the goddess and so they agreed to ritually kill in her spite a human being once a year.[17] Such practices are recorded in medieval or post-medieval times yet they are likely to be more ancient. I suspect this particular ritual structure represents the evolution of a mother goddess cult and its further recognition in central Orissa (cf. Mallebrein 1999: 139-45).[18]

In the second part of this cosmogonic myth, it is possible to recognize some cultural elements shared by a good number

14. The fact that Nirantali is also looked at as the goddess who begins the cycle of human sacrifices shows how the concepts of benign and malign are relative.

15. The ancestral evil aspect of Tari is manifested through the blood-shedding theme and the contact of blood with the earth.

16. This is the same ritual technique of the *meriah* sacrifice (Beggiora 2004: 222-29 and 239-40).

17. Patnaik (1992: 227-30). In MacPherson (1865: 121) the goddess in this form is called Umbally Bylee.

18. Since medieval times, the Khonds looked at Tari as a form of Durgā or Kālī while local rulers considered the *meriah* sacrifice as Śākta worship.

of Indian tribes. On the one hand, the self-sacrifice of the demiurge is also found in institutional Hinduism (Puruṣa-Sūkta, *Ṛgveda* 10: 90) and appears in various *ādivāsī* groups where the first being is either a man, a god/goddess or an animal. On the other, the theme of the fertilizing blood proves the power of the (female) nature which is both giver and receiver. Accordingly, the Tari myth results because of her identification with nature, the primeval force. She seems to create and destroy with absolute indifference in that she also incarnates dynamic chaos, the ultimate source of energy (i.e. fertility or barrenness). In Hindu terms, the goddess is *prakṛti.* She completes the *puruṣa* and allows the genesis.

### The Creation Myth of the Apatanis

Arunachal Pradesh is a north-eastern Indian state bordering with Myanmar, China and Bhutan. It is an extremely interesting area for the high rate of tribal groups, most of whom still hold their own languages, traditions and religions. In particular, local cosmogonies tell a number of myths which also present number of variants and historical adjournments.

Among 'the Apatanis of Arunachal Pradesh, myth is presented in a twofold structure: *migung* and *miji* (Bartolucci 2001: 195-203). The former is in prose, the latter is sung. Both of them echo the ancient Apatani tradition yet quite often — especially in the former instance — real historical events are added (Blackburn 2003). Recitation is generally a complex and long procedure. Depending on circumstances, it can last from one up to twelve hours during scheduled festivities or special recurrences. The *niybu* (the village *pūjārī*) wears his ritual paraphernalia for the whole duration of the ceremony. Small animals (usually poultry) are sacrificed in honour of local deities or to the ancestors. The whole performance is structured as a religious ritual and reveals the centrality of the narrative session. Most of the cosmogonies belonging to the tribes of

Arunachal Pradesh do actually mention a Mother-Goddess.[19] The Apatanis refer to a primordial goddess whose self-sacrifice gave origin to the universe.[20] Here follow two versions of the same myth:

> At the first, Kujum-Chantu, the earth, was like a human being: she had a head, and arms and legs, and an enormous fat belly. The original human beings lived on the surface of her belly. One day it occurred to Kujum-Chantu that if she ever got up and walked about, everyone would fall off and be killed, so she herself died of her own accord. Her head became the snow-covered mountains; the bones of her back turned into smaller hills. Her chest was the valley where the Apatanis live. From her neck came the north country of the Tagins. Her buttocks turned into Assam plain. Just as the buttocks are full of fat, Assam has fat and rich soil. Kujum-Chantu's eyes became the sun and moon. From her mouth was born Kujum-Popi, who sent the sun and moon to shine in the sky.
>
> — Elwin 1993: 8-9.

> First of all there was Kenku, but no one can say what it was or what it was like. From Kenku was born a female Wiyu,[21] in the form of an earthen ball. She said to Kenku, "I am Chantu." Kenku said, "You have been born from me. Who will be born from you?"
>
> "I will give birth to Abo Tani" said Chantu. Then Abo Tani[22] was born, Chantu said to him, "I am going to die. You must

---

19. According to the Singphos, the first ever creature was a beautiful girl who appeared in the form of a cloud from the primordial dust. Other myths refer more explicitly to the earth (Elwin 1993: 7).
20. See also the cosmogony of the Adi Gallongs in Beggiora 2003: 94.
21. Elwin employs this term as a synonym of *ui* (or *wuhui*), that is spirit or deity. In Apatani language, the noun *ui* is equated to *pinu* which indicated a superior class of spirits. I will translate *wiyu* as "female spirit."
22. Abo Tani is a mythical character, identified as the first ancestor by the Apatanis and other different tribal groups of the area such as the Nishis, the Adis and the Tagins.

> give birth to mankind." "If you die," said Abo Tani, "where will all man live? Everything will be dark and where will we get our food or water?" Chantu said, "My thighs will become the earth on which you can move about and cultivate your fields. My eyes will become the sun and moon and my blood will become water." —Ibid., 40.[23]

In both versions, Chantu is a supreme entity and is looked at as the earth. She gives origin to the humankind and allows the genesis of the universe. She is a female primordial spirit identifiable as a proto-*devī.* In particular, Chantu is a giantess who lies on the transforming cosmos. The most outstanding symbol of both myths is the self-immolation of a primordial being (cf. the sacrifice of the *puruṣa*). This appears with slight variation in the whole region and expresses the cosmogonic beliefs of local people. Oral tradition here acquires many benevolent traits. The (ab)original sacrifice of the cosmic animal (both a giant or the first human being) is performed for the sake of love towards both the new world and humankind. Many Apatani legends tell about a monstrous female creature (prodigious rather than ugly) who acts for the benefit of mankind. Elwin (1993: 3-7) mentions similar traditions among the Juangs, Bhuiyas and Gonds of central India and the Madigas of south India.

### The Creation Myth of the Lanjia Saoras

The proto-*devī,* especially in her ambiguous aspect, presents some intriguing aspects which have been familiar in a more institutional environment. The presence of ambiguous goddesses in Hinduism is rather common. Among these, Śītalā, the north-Indian hierophany of the South Asian smallpox goddess, has a central position. In eastern India, it is possible

---

23. A third version, which seems rather a synthesis of the first two, can be found in Ghosh & Ghosh 1998: 86.

to find forms of "tribal" Śītalā, often addressed as Ṭhakurāṇī,[24] an ancestral spirit belonging to local shamanic traditions. Among the Lanjia Saoras — one of the major tribal communities in Orissa — the legend of Rugaboi, a local form of Śītalā/Ṭhakurāṇī is worshipped.[25]

At the origin of the time, there were three beautiful sisters, Angaiboi, Yuyungboi and Rugaboi.[26] Ramma-bimma — a Saora epical hero/spirit, possibly derived from the Hindu champion Rama[27] — decided to make a present to the three sisters. The first one was given the moon and the second received the

---

24. Cf. Beggiora 2003: 182. According to Elwin (1954: 641), Ṭhakurāṇī is "[p]roperly, another name for Mother Earth. Now commonly associated with the giver of smallpox and cholera." Around Regingtal, Saora territory, I found evidence of a male smallpox spirit called Rolisum.

25. From fieldwork: October 1998, February 1999, February 2000 and March 2001. Cf. Beggiora 2003: 67.

26. The suffix — *boi* in Saora is a marker of the female gender, while the nouns *angai* and *yuyang* respectively means "moon" and "sun." Although the first two are described as superior deities, they often are androgynous. In both myth and in the living cult, the feminine form of the moon is believed to be the consort of the masculine form of the sun. However, this is not a strict rule, though here the suffix *boi* clearly indicates we are dealing with goddesses. Furthermore, in Saora, *yuyung* is also a term of respect for elder women (lit. "grandmother"). As a matter of fact, the sun, in its feminine form, is addressed as Great Mother.

27. Ramma and Bimma could be local corrections for Rāma and Bhīma, the heroes of the *Rāmāyaṇa* and *Mahābhārata*. In the Saora ancient oral tradtion it is not rare to find two divine figures united in one. Bhima, particularly because of his strength and hot behaviour, is a common figure among many tribes. According to some traditions transmitted in the district of Rayagada, Ramma-Bimma is nothing but an ancient name of Labosim, the spirit of the earth who taught men agriculture. Since early twentieth century, the plateau Sardas started to identify the ancient Ramma-Bimma, or Labosim, with Jagannātha (i.e. Kṛṣṇa as Lord of the Universe), a fact which strengthens the relation with Rāma.

sun. Unfortunately, Ramma-bimma forgot a present for the elder sister, Rugaboi. Her wrath was such that she climbed the earth and started to devour her first sibling, Angaiboi. (For this reason, Saoras believed that during full moon the moon always lacks a small section.) When Ramma tried to defend the moon, Rugaboi assaulted him too. In order to defend himself, he threw against her the twelve seeds he had previously created for mankind. Every single seed, when touching Rugaboi's face, caused a plague or the purulent wound of a viral disease. When the beautiful Rugaboi spotted her face in a river, she realized her aspect had turned into a terrifying mask. Her vengeful rage should have destroyed the whole universe, but Ramma-bimma gave her the most developed and important of the creature, man, in order to devour him.

Rugaboi is in fact believed to eat the vital forces of entire villages when she spreads the seeds of smallpox or other epidemics.[28] Yet once she has been placated, she also protects her devotees from diseases and malign influences. Rugaboi-Śītalā-Ṭhakurāṇī is also a village guardian and presides over the prosperity of the whole community.[29]

The twelve seeds mentioned in the myth are a clear reference to the theme of the discovery of agriculture and the gift made to men. (In this case, this comes from a god and it is interrupted by the irate behaviour of a dreadful goddess.) Not by chance Rugaboi/Śītalā has been equated with the

28. On the same destructive power, yet related to the cult of Śītalā in West Bengal, see Ferrari (forthcoming) and Mukhopadhyay 1994.

29. As a protective-cum-malign deity, her dreadful aspect is a necessity as it allows to keep evil entities away from the village. Such is a common mythology in South Asia. Among the Kondhs, the goddess Komani (or Komani Pēnu) is the protector of the shamans. This is extremely interesting if we consider that shamans are deputed to heal and protect villagers from diseases and epidemics.

ancient Savara[30] form of Sītā, Rāma/Rāmma's sister (not wife), goddess of agriculture. She was an archaic goddess who was born from the tilled soil.[31]

## Conclusion

The cosmogonic myths here analysed are useful samples in that they allow further consideration on tribal India. On the one hand, they show the relation between the chamber of myth and historical events. On the other hand, they bear witness to shared beliefs. Having said that, some questions need to be answered. Is the goddess myth a real cult of the mother? Is the geographical and historical environment relevant? Is human sacrifice (either actual or symbolic) sufficient to identify a Mother-Earth worship? Do we have clues of any distinctive traits belonging to archaic and/or ancestral mother cults?

Apparently the myths of Tari, Chantu and Ṭhakurāṇī are mother/earth cults, yet there are some aspects which deserve more attention. I refer to the dualism which is at the core of the cosmogonic myth. In fact, it does not seem correct to hold that Indian tribes worship an actual mother goddess. Indian tribes are widely believed to be the original inhabitants of the

---

30. Savara is a recurrent term in ancient Hindu scriptures. It designates a non-specified tribal group, most probably some Saora tribe. See Elwin (1955: 1ff) and Saletore (1935: 38-59).

31. See Roy (1927: 295-96 and 298). Some anthropologists refer to some Saora myths where Ramma and Bimma (also Sitaboi) found a secured shelter in the forest among the Saoras. Such an episode echoes *Rāmāyaṇa* 3.74 when the two heroes are hosted in Savari. See Elwin (1955: 21-24). Sitapati (1940-41: 122-23) sees in the Saora myth of Sittabojan, sister of the epic heroes, an antecedent to the epic Hindu Sītā. Hiltebeitel (1991: 387), with reference to Parpola, mentions the melting tendency of certain Vedic rituals belonging to the tradition of the Durgā-Pūjā with ancestral fertility practices belonging to spring celebration of the Saoras.

Indian subcontinent. The Hindi term *ādivāsī* can be translated as the "aboriginal" [of a certain] place." Quite often, yet rather faulty, tribal religions are believed as primeval too because of this denomination and of the difficulty to empirically find an origin of their beliefs. Yet the cosmogonic myth, as an explanation of the origins themselves, can indeed give some more clues and should be investigated accordingly.

In order to achieve such a task, we should trace a genealogy of forms of proto-*devī* or *ādyaśakti*s in Indian culture. The bibliography on this subject is wide. Yet if we limit ourselves to tribal cultures — on both literary and historical points of view — it turns out how difficult it is to find empirical data on oral traditions (Chattopadhyaya 1979: 74ff).

Tribal cosmogonies show some shared patterns which shape the concept itself of godhead. Most of the time, these features are presented before the creation process. Only after the genesis of the universe, the dichotomy male/female is expressed. The same can be said for the hierophany of a certain deity as benign or malignant. Such primordial images are at the very core of the mythological narration. Nevertheless, among Indian tribes it is possible to recognize some ideas and images which belong to other cultures too. These are linked to an archaic religious tradition or — in a shamanic context — a pre-religious thought. This perception is particularly relevant in the present analysis, as it allows further considerations on the antinomy between the unity of the divine principle and its dynamic force. In South Asian shamanic-grounded religions, this differentiation is applicable to both spirits and ancestral deities belonging to the tribal cultural heritage. Supernatural forces are experienced as the cyclical manifestation, stabilization and destruction of the universe. In brief, a deity who is generally imaged as wrathful and terrifying is not necessarily a destructive principle. More specifically, it can be a vehicle of different actions such as change, metamorphosis and fertility.

## References

AA, VV. (1993), *Indigenous Knowledge on Forests, An Enquiry into the Worlds of Kuttia Kondhs & Saoras of Orissa (India)*, Cuttak, Printoverse-Maitree Sarani.

Bartolucci, R. (2004), "Rapporto della prima missione scientifica della VAIS in Arunachal Pradesh — 2001," *Indoasiatica*, 1, pp. 191-203.

Basilov, V.N. (1999), "Cosmos and Everyday Reality in Shamanism: An Attempt to Formulate a More Precise Definition of Shamanism." In Rigopoulos A. & R. Mastromattei (eds.), *Shamanic Cosmos, From India to the North Pole Star*, New Delhi, D.K. Printworld, pp. 17-40.

Beggiora, S. (2003), *Sonum, Spiriti della giungla*, Milano, Franco Angeli.

———, (2004), "Il culto della *Devi* attraverso la tradizione del Meriah in Orissa," *Annali di Ca Foscari*, 43(3), pp. 215-45.

———, (forthcoming), "Le guerre del Meriah (Orissa 1836-62)", *Asiatica Veneziana*, 8.

Blackburn, S. (2003), "Colonial Contact in the Hidden Land, Oral History among the Apatani of Arunachal Pradesh", *The Indian Economic and Social History Review*, 40(3), pp. 335-66.

Chattopadhyaya, S. (1979), *Ethnic Elements in Ancient Hinduism*, Calcutta, Sanskrit College.

Chetti, D. (1982), *A History of the Meriah Wars* 1836-1862, PhD thesis, Claremont Graduate School.

Elwin, V. (1954), *Tribal Myths of Orissa*, Bombay, Oxford University Press.

———, (1955), *The Religion of an Indian Tribe*, Bombay, Oxford University Press.

———, (1993), *Myths of the North-East Frontier of India*, reprint of first edition (1958), Itanagar, Government of Arunachal Pradesh.

Ferrari, F. M. (forthcoming), "Baciami e uccidimi!" Śītalā e le madri ambigue del Bengala: amore materno, ira divina e epidemie", *Indoasiatica*, 5.

Ghosh, G.K. and S. Ghosh (1998), *Fables and Folk Tales of Arunachal Pradesh*, Calcutta, Firma KLM.

Guénon, R. (2003), "Il Verbo e il Simbolo," in R. Guénon, (ed.), *Simboli della scienza sacra*, Milano, Adelphi, pp. 20-24.

Hiltebeitel, A. (1991), *The Cult of Draupadi*, Chicago, University of Chicago Press.

MacPherson, S.C. (Major C.B.) (1865), *Memorials of Service in India,* London, J. Murray.

Mallebrein, C. (1999), "Tribal and Local Deities: Assimilations and Transformations", in V. Dehejia, (ed.), *Devi, The Great Goddess,* Ahmedabad, Sackler-Mapin-Prestler, pp. 137-56.

Mastromattei, R. (1995), *Tremore e potere, La condizione estatica nello sciamanismo himalayano,* Milano, Franco Angeli.

Mukhopadhyay, S.K. (1994), *Cult of Goddess Śītalā in Bengal: An Enquiry into Folk Culture,* Calcutta, Firma KLM.

Padel, F. (2000), *The Sacrifice of Human Being, British Rule and the Konds of Orissa,* New Delhi, Oxford University Press.

Pandey, B.B. (1974), *The Hill Miris,* Hazarika, Shillong, Government of Arunachal Pradesh.

Patnaik, N.R. (1992), *History and Culture of Khond Tribes,* New Delhi, Commonwealth Publications.

Roy, S.N. (1927), "The Savaras of Orissa", *Man in India,* 7, pp. 277-336.

Saletore, B.A. (1935), *The Wild Tribes in Indian History,* Lahore, Motilal Banarsidass.

Sitapati, G.V. (1940-41), "The Soras", *Journal of the Andhra Historical Research Society,* 13(3-4), pp. 113-36.

Spagna, F. (1998), *L'ospite selvaggio, Experienze visionarie e simboli dell'orso nelle tradizioni native americane e circumboreali,* Torino, Il Segnalibro.

# 16

# Who am I Worshipping ?
## Ritual Ambiguity and Female Devotional Practices in a Beṅgālī Hierogamic Celebration

*Fabrizio M. Ferrari*

This paper aims to explore the rituals performed by the female devotees of Dharma Ṭhākura (or Dharamarāja) on the occasion of the *gājan*, the god's annual celebration. Like male votaries, women undergo specific rites of initiation, confirmation and release. These practices are inscribed in a complex structure which involves both sacred and profane performances. Fieldwork data and textual material are herein analysed following a twofold perspective. On the one hand, female ritualism is described as perceived by the community and the performers themselves. On the other hand, the whole ritual agenda is deconstructed to show that every single action is not performed in honour of a male deity (i.e. Dharma Ṭhākura). In fact, the true recipient of both male and female offerings and self-offerings is a female. Dharma's spouse appears as a marginal character in modern *gājan*, yet the whole festival bears witness to the celebration of the ancestral hierogamy in which Dharma was the sacrificial male and the main deity was the Earth. The study of female ritual practices that infringe social strata (low caste Hindus and tribal communities) proves to be extremely useful in the analysis of how local female spirits/ goddesses reacted to the Brāhmanic penetration and how this encountering has developed into variegated patterns of worship.

## Introduction

The distinctive traits of the *gājan* of Dharma (*dharmer gājan*)[1] are transformation and union. The festival, which is celebrated every year after the vernal equinox during the dark lunar fortnight of Caitra (March/April), is a paramount event among the sacred and profane recurrences of the Beṅgālī agricultural year. Although the *gājan* was once extremely popular in big urban centres,[2] it is in the rural areas that it still occupies a pivotal position. In the Rāṛh area of West Bengal,[3] almost every village celebrates its own *gājan*, as well as its own Dharma.

The character of the *gājan* is that of a complex transformative ceremony in which the central theme is represented by the marriage scenario (hierogamy) between Dharma and his consort, the *devī*. But how should we think of this marriage? Is it the apparent wedding ceremony of a solar[4] god (Dharma

1. The term *gājan* is a corruption of *garjana*, "roar," "rumble," with reference to the tumultuous processions (*calana*) and the continuous ululations, invocations (*bandanā*), loud calls (*nām ḍāk*) and cries of the devotees.
2. Duff 1846, G. Chattopadhyay 1935, K. Chattopadhyay, 1935, Banerjee 1989, Oddie 1995.
3. Rāṛh is a geo-political unit of ancient Bengal subdivided into two parts. The southern one (Dakṣiṇa Rāṛh) includes large settlements of the modern districts of Howrah, Hoogly and Burdwan. The northern one (Uttara Rāṛh) is included in the western parts of the modern district of Murshidabad, the entire Birbhum district, small parts of the Santal Parganas, and the northern part of the Katwa sub-division of Burdwan district. The two parts of Rāṛh are separated by the river Ajay.
4. Dharma is identified with Sūrya, the Sun god, and Yama (Yamarāja), Sūrya's son. Among the various titles of Dharma, there are Nārāyaṇa (the solar aspect of Viṣṇu the creator), Nirañjana (the Spotless One, as the sun is), and Śūnyarūpa (the One of the form of the Zero, as the sun is). In *Śūnya Purāṇa* 32, Dharma teaches agriculture through his solar aspect. The twelve Ādityas (the sun beams) are paddy seeds and Dharma lets them sprout giving good crops.

Ṭhākura, the "Lord of Righteousness") with a benevolent and submissive female? Or does its gendered rituals and ambiguous symbolism point at some other conclusion?

I have already explained my theory on the *gājan* as the relic of a hierogamic celebration originally belonging to Munda and Draviḍian-speaking agricultural tribes of eastern India (Ferrari 2005b). Suffice here to say that while ritual acts exclusively performed by men always include bloodshed and piercing acts, ritual acts exclusively performed by women are meant as displays of fertility.[5]

Male ascetic devotees (dharmer *saṁnyāsīs*) seek to become temporary ritual women through:

(a) self-offerings, a way to expiate guilt towards the female world. By piercing their bodies and letting them bleed, men experience the wounded female (the transformation motif),[6] and

(b) the acquisition of the inner nature of women. This is made by experiencing the pain, the anguish and the wrath they inevitably cause to the female world through sexual penetration and ploughing the soil (the

---

5. In the case of ritual acts performed by men and women together, these involve fire and/or heating practices.

6. After initiation (ritual tonsure, wearing of white upper- and lower-garments and sacred thread, taking of copper bracelet and entering into the deity's lineage), men undergo several of self-offerings. Despite the lack of a ritual agenda, these can be divided into (a) piercing acts: *bābui khelā* (self-whipping with thorny ropes), *bāṇeśvarer upar goṛāno* (rolling on the *bāṇeśvara* studded-with-nails plank), *jibhabāṇa* (piercing the tongue), *kāṇṭā jhāmpā* (jumping on thorns), *kāṇṭā khelā* (rolling on thorny branches), *agunbāṇa* (piercing the body with blazing arrows) and *navakhaṇḍa* (piercing nine parts of the body); (b) hook swinging (*dolān sebā* or *caṛak pūjā*), (c) immolation of a male victim (*bolidāna*), and (d) dancing with human corpses (*maṛā khelā*).

union motif).[7]

The process of transformation of women, as they already share the same nature and experiences with the worshipped entity, consists in identification rather than transformation, while union is a confirmation. Female devotees (*mahilā bhaktyās*) identify themselves with the fertility power of the deity and confirm it in that they are able to conceive.[8] They represent generation and regeneration, two aspects which are embodied by the symbolism of blood and water.

Every culture maintains its own taboos about blood, yet

---

7. On the ancestral fear of raping the earth by ploughing it experienced by tribal cultures see Eliade 1958: 246. In Bengal, from the 7th to 11th day (*ambuvācī*) of the Hindu month of Āṣāḍha (June/July), the earth is believed to menstruate and both ploughing and sowing are not permitted. Sinha, Dasgupta & Banerjee (1961: 33) report that among tribal societies as well as Hindu low castes the Mother Earth must not be ploughed while menstruating. "As it is tabooed to have sexual intercourse with a menstruating woman, so it is a taboo to plough Mother Earth during her monthly period. The peasants go even further than that. They keep their ploughs above the ground level, either on a plank of wood or even on the fork of a tree. The same practice is done again during Bandana Kālī-Pūjā festivals, for the welfare of cattle, in the month of Kartika," See also Nicholas 1982: 199 and Bhattacharyya 1996a: 166.

8. The fact that barren women, or women wishing to conceive, are present and ritually involved during *dharma-pūjā* must be considered as part of the provocative-cum-propitiatory ritualism (see below). Women who are without offspring are in fact considered "barren mothers" in the same way that folk goddesses are childless mothers. Their capacity to conceive is believed to be temporarily interrupted. The recovery from this status can be propitiated through correct ritual behaviour. Yet on a deeper level, barren women who act as pregnant reflect once more the apotropaic character of the ceremony.

it is undeniable that some biological facts are universal, omnipresent because they are experienced and re-experienced. Hauser-Schaublin (1993: 83) has analysed in detail these conditions, which can be summarized as follows:

1. blood allows life while its loss determines illness, and eventually death;
2. blood has a certain colour and consistency;
3. blood is expelled by women during the menstrual cycle and retained during pregnancy;
4. blood runs from the mother's body to that of her child through the umbilical cord; and
5. blood is nurture.

Apart from the above biological features, we have to consider the symbolical value of blood in agricultural societies where two factors are core: the presence of rituals of women's initiation and the centrality of women's economic role (cf. Obeyesekere 1985: 641-42). In particular, "the presence of a women's initiation in a given culture is a mark of the importance of women within that culture and of the culture's willingness to recognize this publicly and institutionally" (Lincoln 1991b: 91). In a religious and ritual context, blood represents the cycle of life (birth, death, rebirth/regeneration);[9] it is connected with the chthonic world and, through menstruation, represents purification (Bhattacharyya 1996a: 164-69). Such an ambivalent aspect is represented by the protective-cum-malign aspect of village deities (*grāmya devatā*s), who reflect the nature of the female world as life-giver,

9. This is valid not only for females, yet it is a universal concept, related to the experience of the whole humankind (cf. Devereux 1953: 334-38). As it has been shown in recent ethnographical works, men too are related to the cycle of regeneration (i.e. their offspring) through blood (Busby 1997: 263).

nurturer and annihilator.

All women's initiatory rites are dependent on blood, either symbolically or not. In the *gājan,* women are not supposed to bleed, which in fact they do not. Kinsley is right indeed when he sees in the ambivalence of the goddesses the predatory nature of a female who wants to be recognized in her role (1998: 198). But here women have virtually no necessity to show this "predatory nature."[10] The sacred marriage the community is celebrating put the *mahilā bhaktyā*s in a position of compensation, so to speak. Women are praised for they incarnate fertility. While men have to repent for their crimes towards the female world, by releasing blood and becoming penetrable, women act though the symbolism of water (i.e. blood), which implies pregnancy and delivery.

## Ritual and Psychological Implications in Female Devotional Behaviour

During the annual celebration (*batsarik-pūjā*) of Dharma, female devotees undergo a *rite de passage.* Immediately after the austerities practised by men, women are initiated. Such a ceremony is relevant in that it establishes identification between women and the deity, rather than a "transformation." Women are equated with the deity's nature, while men must be rendered into it.

The ritual making of a *mahilā bhaktyā* is focused on the (temporary) abandoning of her rule in the society and in the taking of Dharma's lineage (*dharmer gotra dhāraṇa*). Unlike men, women do not observe ritual tonsure (*kāmāno*). Under the

---

10. The analysis of the predatory quasi-cannibalesque attitude of female parents towards their offspirng (especially male children) is an interesting way to inquire into the social modifications of agricultural societies. An ethno-psychiatric approach to this tendency has been proposed by Devereux who tried to individuate the presence of fixed patterns (1966: 160-61).

guidance of a *mūla-saṁnyāsinī* (chief female devotee), they embrace an ascetic lifestyle qualified by abstention from eating meat, drinking alcohol and sexual intercourse. Further they are all required to wear white dresses while sacred marks are put on their foreheads during the *ṭīkā pratiṣṭhā* ceremony. Occasionally *mahilā bhaktyā*s can wear the sacred thread (*paitā*) and a copper bracelet.

Although the main hierophany of Dharma is formally acknowledged as a black stone-slab (*dharma-śilā*), as far as it concerns female ritualism, there are two iconographic renderings which deserve further attention: the "board of nails" (*pāṭ*) and the "full pot" (*pūra kalaśī*).

## THE BOARD OF NAILS

The symbolism of the "board of nails" (*pāṭ* or *pāṭ ṭhākura)* is strictly connected to the apotropaic aspect of the deity. This kind of icon is made of a wooden plank (usually 100-170 cm high) on which sharp points are fixed on one side:[11] usually spears (*śalya*)[12] or iron pegs *(kajjali).* Designed to be carried, the *pāṭ* also has four (or six) lateral handles, and occasionally a central hole where a bunch of arrows (*bāṇa*) or tridents (*triśūla*) can be placed.[13] During the apex of the *gājan* (the last night of the festival, *rat-gājan*), fruits are pierced on the nails and they are then thrown towards women as fertility omens (Ferrari 2004: 156). Robinson (1980: 81) interprets the *pāṭ* as an anthropomorphic transformation of Dharma into a (male) god, Śrī Bāṇeśvara, the "Lord of the Arrows." In particular she

---

11. This reflects the majority of cases. I was shown some *pāṭs* with both sides studded with nails.

12. The most used are *bel*/(wood apple) or *gāmāra* (*Gmelina arborea*) spikes.

13. Neither do all the planks present the hole for arrows/trident nor is the *pāṭ* strictly believed to be a *triśūla*-carrying implement.

sees in the *cakra* (wheel) occasionally depicted on the top of the lower half the "energy seats" of the icon (*mūrti*), and in the nailed fruits (mangoes and cucumbers) the representation of a male organ. I agree with that only partially. If the stylisation of a phallus is indeed recognisable, the *cakra* — rather than the "royal symbol of the authority of a ruler in popular Hindu and Buddhist tradition" (ibid.) — more closely resembles female genitals. The presence of turmeric and spikes may in fact suggest a hidden female symbolism. Spikes and sexual female attributes have been the object of deep study. Symbolic representations of the vulva as a slab stone surrounded by nails, thorns and eyes (because of their intruding power) are common,[14] However the definition of the *pāṭ* as either a male or female icon is not satisfying. First, the *pāṭ* is not always phallic shaped. (Bhattācharyya too in 1996a: 237 recognized an androgynous nature in the *pāṭ ṭhākura*.) Second, the studded plank is indeed the "sacrificial male" of an agricultural culture, yet rather than on gender we should focus on symbolic ritualism. More specifically, male symbols (arrows and tridents) and phallic emblems (the fruits) are "impaled" on the vacuum (the *cakra*/vagina). Penetration thus appears as guilt: it reflects the ancestral fears of agriculturalists who interpret it as impalement. The use of turmeric — a deflector of blood — as a cooling offering (Beck 1969: 559) as well as margosa (*Azadirachta indica*) leaves and fruits like limes and cucumbers (Nabokov 2000: 41, 59) is highly significant. What I wish to stress here is the identification of this symbol with the relic of an earth cult.[15] In fact, it can be observed that: (a) the male victim married and sacrificed to

---

14. See the myth of the *vagina dentata* explained in Doniger 1980: 53 and Kripal 1995: 276.

15. The worship of Dharma in the *gājan* and the transposition of the deity's power in the Pāṭ Ṭhākura or Śrī Bāṇeśvara are well attested. Hiltebeitel (1991: 202) observes that the cult of Bāṇeśvara →

the earth is the *pāṭ ṭhākura,* (b) the male is punished (impaled) by penetration, (c) women are offered the "dead" victim in that it will grant offspring, and (d) sharp objects and iron nails convey blood to the earth and keep bad hungry spirits and misfortune away.[16]

The main difference between the *gājan* and tribal customs lies in the fact that, while in non-Vedic cults the feminine-centred ritualism supported by a lower male figure (the impalement stake) clearly appears, in the domesticated *gājan* the *pāṭ* is virtually the living *mūrti* of the god (Sarkar, 1986: 204).[17] He is the recipient of the sacrifice, the power to be awoken and at the same time a portable impalement stake. The plank is also the medium through which devotees surrender to the deity. After carrying it to the pond, letting it float and offering water to it[18] (the process by which devotees become part of the lineage of the god), the *pāṭ-saṁnyāsīs* roll on it and become possessed by experiencing the piercing, just

---

→ is a Śaiva element acquired by the Dharma cult and transformed into Bāṇa Gosāi (the Lord of Spikes), which Dharma devotees worship in form of thorny branches.

16. In Indian folk/tribal societies the presence of studded stones, thorny branches and iron-nailed trees placed in the fields and around the villages is quite common. These icons are placed for apotropaic purposes. Dharma slab stones are also often offered thorny branches.

17. Nowadays the presence on the plank of *triśūla*s (tridents) and *bāṇa*s (arrows) is believed to be a visual representation of the god's weapons. This must, however, be related to the later identification of Dharma with Śiva, as Dharma does not possess weapons.

18. The two kinds of wood employed are extremely light and tend not to sink. This also symbolizes the process of "coming out from below" commencing with the awakening of the deity in the form of a pole (*carak gāch*).

like the deity. Icons like thorny branches of trees (generally *śāla* and *nīma)* growing around the *śilā* occupy a ritual position similar to the *pāṭ* in that Dharma is believed to dwell in them. This is a widespread custom and its origin can be seen in tribal cults. Not by chance, Dharma votaries tend to talk about this nature-icon as a "spirit" (*bhūta*) rather than a *mūrti.*"[19]

THE FULL POT

The *pūra kalaśī* is an earthen vessel full of water, often decorated with auspicious *svastika*s or a stylized human being. The question of the pot as a symbolic uterus has been variously and repeatedly addressed. Robinson argues that "it is impossible and indeed misleading to try to assign gender to the Bāṇeśvars and the *kalaśī* [*sic*] as central symbols. Even though each is a representation of certain of the androgynous god's aspect, there is no reason to assume that the stone slab represents, in Jungian terms,[20] the male principle and the earthen jug the female principle" (1980: 91-92). I agree with that, but it has to be remembered that when in popular religions supreme deities are said to be androgynous, that is an external perception. In the case of the earth, among agricultural tribes, even though the deity can show both male and female aspects, it is strongly perceived as feminine. Through a closer consideration of local interpretation, we can state that so-called androgynous godheads are usually worshipped through a predominant gender even if in mythology this is often mitigated by its opposite. To define the dance of presentation of the *pāṭ* and the *kalaśī* as "a psychodrama of sexual

---

19. The description in *Śūnya Purāṇa* 17, 18 and 36 of the *pāṭ* gives a more domesticated interpretation. By reading Rāmāi's verses, the plank — which is described as full of nails — is described as a royal throne, the seat of the deity. It has neither gender specification nor is it looked upon as god: in brief, it is not a *mūrti.*

20. On the archetypical identification of Mother Goddesses with the water pot, see Neumann 1981: 286-303.

interaction" (Robinson 1980: 92) is therefore not fitting. First because the *pāṭ* is not an exclusively masculine *mūrti*, second because the pitcher rather than being the "female principle" *strictu sensu* is the representation of women's bodies and power. In fact, the ceremony of initiation of female devotees is centred on filling, emptying, and refilling the pitcher, a gesture which proposes on a symbolical level, the power to conceive and deliver.

But in the living cult, as in Dharma literature, not only is the goddess installed in the pot. The vessel is the goddess. In general, Dharma Ṭhākura is believed to be a self-existent male god: his spouse is not a relevant character. Liturgical texts (*Śūnya Purāṇa* and *Dharma-pūjā-vidhāna*)[21] strongly underline this aspect. Dharma's spouse is called Kāminī and/or Muktā, but is also identified with major goddesses like Durgā, Kālī, Śītalā, Manasā, and local Caṇḍīs. Invoked on various occasions by different names and in different forms, the goddess is also present in the liturgical texts of the cult. She is Kāminyādevī (*Śūnya Purāṇa* 30: 9), Muktādevī (Ch. 35), Abhayā in form of a she-jackal (Ch. 46), Nārāyaṇī, the remover of illness (Ch. 30: 8), and Ādyadurgā the primeval *śakti* (Ch. 1: 130). As Kāminī, she is also worshipped in *Dharma-pūjā-vidhāna* (pp. 30, 77, 86-7) where she is invoked for protection from blindness, leprosy and smallpox.[22]

---

21. Both texts are traditionally ascribed to Rāmāi Paṇḍit (twelfth century). However, a careful analysis of their contents and linguistic structure reveals that both *Śūnya Purāṇa* and *Dharma-Pūjā-Vidhāna* are heterogeneous scriptures, the former written between the twelfth and the sixteenth century, the latter belonging to the 18th century.

22. The word *muktā* (lit. pearl) also indicates the marks and scars of smallpox. Such pustules are believed to be the kiss of the goddess (*debir cumu*). But in *maṅgala-kāvyas* the power to heal belongs to Dharma only. See Manikram Ganguli's *Dharma-Maṅgala-Kāvya* 1960: 2.

The etymology of the name *kāminyā* is intriguing. The root of the name is the same as the Sanskrit *kāma* (love, desire). In Sen's *Etymological Dictionary of Bengali* (vol. 1: 142) Kāminyā (spelt *Kāminī*) is the "wife of Dharma Ṭhākura" or more generally, "a woman, a man's wife." In esoteric and popular forms of Buddhism and Hinduism Kāminī is the goddess related to the *svādhiṣṭhāna cakra,* the subtle centre of the genitals and the "dwelling place of the self."[23] It is thus worth considering the creation myth of *Śūnya Purāṇa.*

The story — which occupies the whole first chapter (*sṛṣṭi pattan*) — goes that Kāma, the divine personification of lust, is generated by the sexual desire of Ādyaśakti. He interrupts Dharma's deep meditation, and because of this he is entrapped in an earthen pitcher (*mṛttikāra bhāṇḍa*) full of water.[24] Subsequently, in order to prevent Ādya's desire, water is turned into poison. So the goddess, deprived of her generative power (i.e. castrated), decides to commit suicide and drinks the deadly liquid. Poison, anyhow, becomes nectar (i.e. Dharma's semen) and Brahmā, Viṣṇu and Śiva are eventually conceived. Kāminyā, who is described as a young virgin (*kanyā*), embodies the goddess, the spouse and daughter of Dharma and the primordial womb in the form of a holy pitcher. In *Śūnya Purāṇa* Kāminyā is indeed the Śakti of Dharma, but theologically speaking her figure lacks the proper features of a Purāṇic Śakti. She does not interact with her "husband," nor does she have any complementary power. Conversely, in the living cult, the vessel displays fertility and is an active symbol

23. Kāminyā (or Kāminī) is also identified with Tripurasundarī, one of the ten *mahāvidyās* and is described in detail in many Śākta texts such as the *Lalitā-Sahasranāma, Yoginī Tantra, Tantrasāra* and *Kālikā Purāṇa.*

24. In the living cult the *bhaṇḍala* is the great vessel full of liquor which is offered to the deity at the end of the *gājan.*

of pregnancy. Whatever its content (water, liquor, blood or the head of the beheaded sacrificial victim), the *kalaśī* is the symbol of the pregnancy of the goddess.[25] also, the pitcher is the womb where — during the *gṛhabharaṇā* ceremony[26] — the head of the sacrificial animal (the *luye* goat) becomes a symbolic foetus.

Coming back to iconography, Dharma became a *ṭhākura* (lord) and a *rājā* (king) and ended up being identified with the *Śivaliṅga* and the *triśūla.* In order to justify the social system of the dominating culture, the Kāminyā pitcher remained feminine, but became a Purāṇic goddess, a god's spouse. Nowadays, in folk/tribal villages, the female *grāmya devatā*s are still represented as stones and supported in their sacrificial function by the impalement stake, but they are also represented as small pots or earthen vessels filled with water or liquor. They are worshipped as fertility icons and believed to keep away plagues. Instead of looking at the *śilā* as a male icon (Dharma Ṭhākura) and the *kalaśī* as a female one (Kāminī), I am therefore more inclined to consider them two different hierophanies of the same godhead, both representing different powers of the same female earth goddess. But what really matters here is that through the identification with the *kalaśī,* women do not *become* Dharma. Rather it is Dharma, the impaled male (i.e. the *pāṭ ṭhākura)* who is given to them, his mothers/spouses, and thus undergoes gender transformation. The *gājan* — a matrimony — allows males (Dharma and his *saṁnyāsī*s) to be temporary females and contemporary exalts

25. This is also suggested by the Santali custom of comparing the bride to a *boṅgā* (spirit) when she is carried in a huge basket before the marriage ceremony (Carrin 1999b: 114).

26. A description of *gṛhabharaṇa* is given in appendix to Mayūrabhaṭṭa's *Dharmapurāṇa* (1-16). For details on Kāminyā's worship see ibid., pp. 5-6, Chattopadhyay 1942: 110-27 and Husain 1985: 91-92.

the fertility power of the female world (the goddess, the earth and the *mahilā bhaktyās*).

## FROM SUFFERING BEINGS TO GODDESSES: WOMEN IN THE GĀJAN

After the self-offerings performed by *dharmer saṁnyāsīs*, the *mahila bhaktyās* carry on their rituals by moving in procession (*calan*) towards a nearby pond where they bathe. They present offerings to the *mūla deyāśi* (chief votary) who immerses the wooden *pāṭ* and lets it float. After this introductory ceremony, the devotees return to the pond and the *mūla deyāśinī* (chief female devotee) presents to the priest a small brass vessel (*ghaṭa*). The votary pronounces mantric utterances[27] which are followed by women's loud ululations. He carries out continuous immersion of the pitcher (one for each *mahilā bhaktyā*) while pronouncing the *gotra paribartana mantra* through which women are formally "initiated." They are all invited by the priest to hold the vessel, to fill it and to empty it in turn. At this point the *kalaśī* is the goddess, Dharma's spouse. Interestingly, women are now of the same lineage of Dharma because they are the *kalaśī,* and not because they are (like) Dharma. Unlike for men, the rite is not dramatic as there is no need to transform, rather to confirm. The water contained in the pot is from now called *śānti jala* (liberating water) and it is used for *jala pāvana* (the offering of water) to enhance fertility. The "liberating water" is in fact the symbolic recreation of the amniotic fluid. The ritual is often called *mukti snāna,* "bath of deliverance" (*Śūnya Purāṇa* 37) and it is concluded with the offering of flowers (*phūla*) on the upper surface of the full pot. Interestingly, as it was first noticed by Robinson (1980: 268), the Beṅgālī word *phūla* has the secondary meaning "placenta."

27. *Mantras* are usually taken from *Dharma-Pūjā-Vidhāna* (Ferrari 2005c).

The second part of women's ritual acts involves the presentation of vegetarian offerings to the deity such as fruits, betel nut, *sindūra,* flowers, *ghī,* sweets and milk. Alternatively, some women may want to show a more radical attitude by surrendering their ego. Among the most common practices, there are circumambulations (*pradakṣinā*), covering a distance (usually from home to the village deity's shrine) with continuous prostrations (*aṣṭāṅga praṇāma*) and/or rolling on the earth (*maṭi lūtā*). All these practices are, however, performed separately by men. This ritual behaviour basically aims to "feel the earth" and develop heat. Yet while the *tapas* produced by male devotees is a way of experiencing the wrath and the pain of a female godhead in order to become the goddess, women take the opposite course, though their heating is a vehicle of transformation too. The deity is in fact sympathetic to women as "it is the role of women to suffer injustice and mistreatment at the hands of men. Doing so increases their righteous power and transmutes these women into powerful goddess" (Harman n.d.).[28]

## Women's Role in Dharma Literature

To know the role of women in a society has always been vital for an accurate comprehension of the structure of the society itself. Social hierarchy, religious beliefs, economic development and even psychological attitudes can be studied from a gender perspective.

28. This pattern is quite common in patriarchal and patrilocal societies where women have an extremely limited sphere of action. Nevertheless, in cultural environments where female social and/or economical power have somehow resisted, the position of men is at odds. If in the everyday life we can admit the existence of male envy, in sacred performances reflecting ancestral heritage grounded on female powers, the perspective is inverted (cf. Obeyesekere 1985: 644).

In India, where the Sanātana Dharma developed from the Vedic andro-centric society grounded on priestly and warrior power and caste seclusion, women are still the living proof of a clash between two opposite cultural mainstreams. Nevertheless, male domination did not lead to a complete psychological "domestication." Where a society is still dependent on the earth cycle, ancestral female worship emerges. Interpreting *dharma-pūjā* and all its rituals as a fertility cycle in which the earth and its feminine representation are the leitmotiv explains some still obscured traits of the cult.

In Dharma literature, which includes *Śūnya Purāṇa, Dharma-Pūjā-Vidhāna* and the *Dharma-Maṅgala-Kāvya*s,[29] three feminine characters are portrayed in detail: Rañjābatī (mother of Lāusen, the hero of the *Dharma-maṅgala* saga), Madanā (the wife of the mythical King Hariścandra)[30] and the *āminī*s. The first appears only in *maṅgala* literature, while the other two belong to liturgical texts. All three figures occupy an

29. This kind of panegyric poetry flourished in Bengal in the Seventeenth century. They celebrate single deities, mostly goddesses, belonging to local folklore and reflect the beliefs of the rural population of Bengal. The corpus of the *maṅgala-kāvya*s is a precious source for the analysis of those rituals which upper castes do not consider as belonging to Śāstric Hinduism.

30. The earliest reference to the king is in *Aitareya Brāhmaṇa* (7.13.8). King Hariścandra, of the solar dynasty of Ikṣvāku, was childless, He made a vow that if ever he obtained a son, he would sacrifice him to Varuṇa. Some time later Hariścandra was blessed with a son who was called Rohita. The King did not fulfil the vow and postponed the sacrifice of Rohita. Eventually he had to perform it but Rohita himself refused to be killed and left for the forest. He spent six years wandering in the jungle. There he met a poor *brāhmaṇa* called Ajīgarta, who lived with three sons. Rohita resolved to buy one of the *brāhmaṇa*'s son, Śunaḥsepa, for a fee of a hundred cows. This substitute was approved by Varuṇa and the sacrifice was about to be performed. Ajīgarta received another hundred cows for binding his son to the sacrificial post →

anomalous position in the history of the cult. Rañjābatī is described in the *Dharma-maṅgala*s as immolating herself in order to conceive (first paradox). The *āminī*s are said in *Śūnya Purāṇa* to be female religious experts who *know* the ritualism of the cult, but their position is virtually taken by the *paṇḍita*s, that is brāhmaṇa male priests (second paradox). Only Queen Madanā reflects the actual ritual attitude of the Dharma *mahilā bhaktyā*s.

In the first case, the story goes that under the supervision of Rāmāi Paṇḍit, the first priest of the Dharma cult, Rañjābatī decides to undergo the ultimate penance and practice *kāṭhā-jhāmpā*, jumping on a spear-studded plank (*kaṭārī*). She dies immediately, but is it a real death? As Robinson remarks (1976: 79), the poet Ghanarām refers to Rañjābatī's death as an *ekjanma mariya*, a "death to her first life". Furthermore, in the *Dharma-maṅgala*s, this practice is referred to as *a śāle bhāra*, a trance on the *śāla* tree. But if this is a trance session induced by the high commitment of the Queen and mediated by an institutional religious specialist (Rāmāi), is it right to speak about an actual death "in the chain of rebirths" (ibid.)? I agree with Robinson

→ and a third hundred for agreeing to slaughter him. But Śunaḥśepa was saved as he started to repeat hymns and *mantra*s in honour of various gods. He was rescued and adopted by Viśvāmitra, one of the officiating priests. Different versions can be found in the *Mahābhārata* (2: 11), *Rāmāyaṇa* (Bālakāṇḍa 17-9) and various Purāṇas (*Mārkaṇḍeya, Viṣṇu,* etc.). Referring to *Kauṣītakī Brāhmaṇa* 19.3, Parpola observes that it is likely that the Viṣuvat (the vernal equinox) might have been celebrated through human sacrifice and sacred marriage. He says that the festival of the vernal equinox "seems to have celebrated the incest of the old and barren mother (the Earth, Mahiṣī later Jyeṣṭhā and Kālī) and her young beautiful son (Kumāra = Rudra/Skanda), who had reached warrior's age and sexual maturity (at the age of sixteen) but had not yet had sexual intercourse. This hypothetical sacrifice probably was the proper ritual context of the legend of King Hariścandra and his son Rohita (= Varuṇa and Rudra), doubled by Ajīgarta sacrificing his own son Śunaḥśepa" (1983: 51-2).

when she suggests the possibility of an initiatic death. More precisely I suggest that the dichotomies death/trance and revivification/recovery can be reasonably looked upon as conducive to a higher degree of knowledge. Yet this process is highly polluted by the presence of Vedic/Brāhmanic elements, it is true that Rañjābatī goes through all those "ordeals"[31] which in the *gājan* are performed by men, yet the ritual environment is different. First the blood that copiously reaches the earth is that of a female, and a female *brahmacāriṇī*, as observed in Bhattacharya 1994: 354. According to the Brāhmanic pattern, Dharma must then appear. Second, Rāmāi Paṇḍita here acts as an ordinary brāhmaṇa priest. Neither does he visit the other world to intercede for his client and recover her soul,[32] nor does he heal the patient through divination or oracular techniques. In brief, Rāmāi is no shaman here. Rather he is an actual priest and a ritual supervisor. His instructions are conducive to the development of inner heat (*tapas*) in order to acquire supernatural power (*siddhi*), here employed so that Rañjābatī can conceive. The final act is in fact the ultimate austerity. It is not an offering, rather a command. Rañjābatī gives her body so as to force the deity to grant the requested boon. This pattern is extremely common and it can be inserted into the "miraculous birth of solar heroes" theme (Eliade 1958: 149).

Queen Madanā's role is not particularly relevant to an

---

31. Rather than ordeals *strictu sensu* or self-tortures (*ātmapīṛana*), Dharma devotees refer to these practices as *sevā*, a service to the deity (Ferrari 2005b).

32. In Shamanism and shaman-grounded societies (both agriculturalist and hunting), diseases (like barrenness) are believed to be the result of the loss of a soul. Men and women have more than one soul and often the spirits of the dead can steal one. The shaman is thus called to contact these spirits and either fight with them or persuade them to deliver the soul back. →

inquiry into the origin of the cult. Her role is that of a female devotee who — wishing to conceive — undergoes a ritual vow. Her *dharma-pūjā* is carefully described in *Śūnya Purāṇa,* She brings the deity with vegetarian edible offerings, accompanies her husband to the opening and inspection of the temple (*dharmaghara*), performs ritual circumambulations and endures slight forms of penance like rolling on the earth (*maṭi lūtā*).

The two queens — Rañjābatī and Madanā — represent two patterns of female Dharma devotees yet each of them reflects a different stage of the domestication of the cult and its legend. On the one hand, there is the Lāusen saga which — although popular and localist (i.e. Rāṛhiyā) in its origin — is a version of the solar-hero legend of non-agriculturalist societies. On the other hand, the sacrifice performed by King Hariścandra and Queen Madanā to obtain a son (a story which is present in the Brāhmanic tradition too) reflects non-Vedic elements and is grounded on the celebration of the "sacred marriage" between the earth and the "ploughing male" on Viṣuvat. Madanā quite resembles the role of the *dharmer mahilā bhaktyā.* Her role emphasizes her feminine nature. After accompanying her husband King Hariścandra into the pavilion, Madanā asks for a son (*Śūnya Purāṇa*: 5.1), praises the deity and rolls on earth (ibid.: 33.8), performs hundreds of circumambulations (ibid.: 12), and offers flowers and water (ibid.: 25).

Rañjābatī's role, instead, can be inscribed in the great Purāṇic devotional tradition. Her sacrifice is directed by a brāhmaṇa priest who ultimately convinces her to be fecundated by the god himself. In *maṅgala* literature the studded plank is the fertilising god *strictu sensu* and its power is symbolically displayed through a tragic penetration.[33] The male god directly

33. It is however relevant that just as the earth takes revenge by forcing the "ploughing male" to an ultimate intercourse (the →

fecundates the queen by violent contact. This aspect is completely absent in both liturgical literature and *gājan,* while the motif of the contact between phallic emblems of gods and female devotees (often after austerities) is well attested in Sanskrit-Purāṇic literature and is considered to be a supernatural way to conceive.

It is different with the *āminī*s. The identification of woman with magic is strictly connected with her capacity to conceive. Bhattacharyya (1996b: 6-7) suggests that "her organs and attributes were thought to be endowed with generative power, and so they had been the life-giving symbols." Furthermore, "the fertility of the soil retained its immemorial association with the women who had been the tillers of the earth and were regarded as the depositories of agricultural magic."[34] In non-Vedic cultures as well as in many contemporary tribal groups, not only is woman the mother and the goddess who incarnates the fertility and recovery processes, but she is also a medium. She is the shaman who communicates with the chthonic world and administers its power. Death and fertility are different aspects of the same power, which is endowed by the earth and — in the human society — by women.

This very role is played in *Śūnya Purāṇa* by the *āminī*s and partially reflected in the contemporary *gājan* by the *mūla deyāśinī* (chief female devotee).[35] The *āminī*s are frequently

---

→ sacrifice), Queen Rañjābatī too makes the god penetrate her. The theme of violent sexual union is still represented, yet according to the tradition the female character appears vengeful and lethal rather than heroic and devoted.

34. Briffault, R. *The Mothers,* vol. 3, p. 117, quoted in Bhattacharyya 1996b: 8.

35. Sukumar Sen, in his *Etymological Dictionary of Bengali,* translates *āminī* as one (f.) who knows the tradition of a religious cult (i.e. Dharma worship).

mentioned in the *Śūnya Purāṇa* and *Dharma-Pūjā-Vidhāna*. They are always associated with a direction and accompanied by a certain number of followers (*gati*) and a gatekeeper (Beṅgālī *koṭāla* < Sanskrit *koṭāvala*). In the Purāṇized form of the cult expressed by the text, they are:

1. Basuyā (or Bijayā) at the west; the *koṭāla* is Candra,
2. Caritrā at the south; the *koṭāla* is Hanumān,
3. Gaṅgā at the east; the *koṭāla* is Sūrya,
4. Durgā at the north; the *koṭāla* is Garuḍa,
5. Abhaya at the centre (*śūnya*); the *koṭāla* is Ullūka.

These characters definitely have a sacerdotal function, even if they have been traditionally considered simple female devotees on the one hand, and "attendants of the Lord" (Dasgupta 1995: 303), on the other. According to *Śūnya Purāṇa*, the role of the *āminī*s is crucial for the ritual offerings: despite the *koṭāla*s whose presence is functional to their role (i.e. protection), they are fully involved in the arrangements for the ritual. The *āminī*s are described as bringing water for *jala pāvana* and cleansing the Lord (*Śūnya Purāṇa* 2), preparing the sandal paste (ch. 3), providing chickpeas for offerings (ch. 5), arranging for *abiṣyā* ritual diet (ch. 10), attending the fire oblation (ch. 12), announcing the passage from age to age (ch. 24), and receiving the sacrificial victim (ch. 45).

## The Position of the Mahilā Bhaktyās Between Tradition and Modernity

Today the role of women in Dharma cult is not so pre-eminent. Dharma *mahilā bhaktyā*s are present mostly for *kalaśī*-related rituals. They hold it, they worship it and they partake of its nature by being part of it in four manners: (a) by being sprinkled with the vessel's *śānti-jala* (blessing water); (b) by swallowing the fermented rice liquor (*bhāḍala*) contained in it;

(c) by enduring the heat of blazing pots by carrying them on their heads; and (d) by performing a vigil while holding the pot with the decapitated head of the *luye* goat.[36]

Women also practise *brata*s (vows) through singing, drawing stylised pictures (*alpanās*), story-telling (*chaḍā* and *kathā*, rhymes and prose) and presenting vegetarian edibles.[37] Because of the privilege of being women, female devotees do not deal with blood. They partake of the earth's nature anyway by naturally releasing blood through menstruation.

As a relic of the quasi-priestly role of women, Chattopadhyaya reports that the ritual killing of the *luye* goat is conducive to fertility only if the bearing of the head has been correctly performed by women (1942: 11-18).[38] Hiltebeitel too (1991: 307), while considering analogies between the structural function of the Beṅgālī hero Lāusen and the Draviḍian Aravāṇ, refers to the *luye* sacrifice in the Dharma Ṭhākura cult. Initially he believes it to be a "Brāhmanic mythic rethinking of the primal sacrifice." But later, because of the blood offerings, he suspects that the earth is both witness and

---

36. Occasionally the *deyāśī can* place inside the pitcher the decapitated head of a fish (a *māgur*) in spite of the *luye* head.

37. In popular Hinduism, a woman who presents offerings to a deity acts on behalf of her own family. Such a concept is completely different in institutional Hinduism, where women do not have a ritual independent role (*Mānava-Dharma-Śāstra* 5: 147-49). The śāstric perspective, where a man represents his women (whatever the relationship) in the ritual sphere and in public too, is here inverted (Walsh 1997: 647-48). The religious attitude of village women is a ritualised performance in which they are the main actress(es). This is the *brata* (< Sanskrit *vrata)* which has been rightly observed to be non-Vedic (Sen 1920: 247-48; Kramrisch in her Foreword to Jayakar 1990: xvi-xxi and Ṭhākura 1350 BS: 4-6).

38. During the *gr̥habharaṇā* ceremony, when a woman holds the vessel with the beheaded head of the goat, she is called an *āminī.*

recipient of the whole rite. Nevertheless, Hiltebeitel insists on a highly Purāṇized explanation of the ritual. When he looks at Lāusen's *navakhaṇḍa* (cutting of his body into nine parts) and the *luye* decapitation as originally a Kālī sacrifice, he seems not to consider the ancestral, earthly, regenerative feminine power of Kālī-like goddesses.

Other significant, and still living, manifestations of an involved ritual participation of women on the occasion of *gājan* and proto-*gājan* ceremonies can be seen in some dances where male Dharma devotees dress like women. Ritual transvestism is the transposition on a practical plane of a subliminal tendency which, in religious devotional movements, leads a practitioner to be identified externally with either the object of his worship or the spirit he is possessed by. Also, a widespread shamanic practice, transvestism, though described to me as a *khelā* (sport), reveals an unconscious attitude to the divine which is perceived as feminine (cf. Carrin 1999a: 103). Men still perform suspending acts while wearing female garments like saris. In south India, where the tradition is still strong, hanging devotees often carry in their hands a child (Younger 2002: 98). The same attitude has been testified in Bhattacharyya (1977: 61) during *maṛā khelā*,[39] when dancers dress as female ghosts (*petni*).

All of this happens with no active female participation. Male devotees throw flowers and fruits, male votaries immolate the *luye* and co-ordinate the *bolidāna*. Feminine presence is observed in that they receive the flowers, carry

39. Lit. "playing with corpses." It is the last of the male ritual acts of the *gājan*. Devotees dance in the crematory camp (*śmaśāna*) with actual human corpses and head. The dance is believed to be a fertility practice and reveals interesting bonds with ancestral earth worship and the cult of the dead (Ferrari 2005a).

the *luye* head, and compete for blessed water and fruits.

Where the earth releases chthonic presences (ghosts and spirits of the ancestors), which are believed to be part of everyday life, there are shamans. Where the earth is at the centre of a fertility cycle in which the soil is a womb and the dead must be fostered in order to prevent barrenness and diseases, there are women shamans.[40] The original position of women as interpreters of the cult is now obsolete. Female shamans (such as the *ojhā gogos* of the Santals) and votaries, who are able to maintain a direct contact between their communities and the earth, do not belong to Dharma-ism.

Like the women of the Kondhs, Gonds, Oraons, Saoras, Hos, Mundas and Santals, the *āminīs* in the mythology of the Dharma cult occupy a primary position. Beside their natural but sometimes neglected position as mothers and thus goddesses (*Śūnya Purāṇa* 46), they were shamans and healers. In Dharma literature the *āminīs* are never referred to as functional mothers, like protective-cum-malign folk goddesses. Nevertheless they administer the cult and those powers which

40. In South and South-East Asia, where societies are mostly agricultural, shamans are in the great majority women (Vitebsky 1995: 35). This has also been confirmed by Beggiora in his recent (2002-04) fieldwork among Saoras and Kondhs in Orissa (personal communication). On the existence and importance of female shamans in agricultural tribes of India, see Elwin (1952: 59-85), Carrin (1999a: 90-113), Beggiora (2003: 86-94). It is significant that, although the *pūjārī* is invariably male (in both institutional and less-institutionalised cults), shamans, exorcists, healers, etc. belong to both sexes and — in certain tribes — women are indeed prominent. For female oracles see Nebesky (1993: 194, 409, 413). For shamans in Draviḍian folk Hinduism and sorcery see Nabokov (2000: 44-48). On female shamans and gender in shamanism in a pan-Asian context see Choi (2003: 170-85), Czaplicka (1914: 253), Balzer (2003: 243-48) and Mastromattei (1995: 76-103).

allow the fertility cycle and belong to the shadowy realm between the living and the dead.

## The "Envious Male" and the "Proud Female"

Popular religions agree in emphasizing the protective-cum-malign aspect of village godheads. Deities, both male and female, are described as emotionally unstable entities, often inclined towards anger. In Bengal such an attitude is represented by the smallpox goddess Śītalā, the serpent goddess Manasā, the goddess of cholera Olāicaṇḍi, the good-fortune goddess Caṇḍī, and Kālī (especially the Kṣepā Kālīs, Mad Kālīs). Popular Hinduism and tribal religions have plenty of similar divine figures and all of them display the same attitude towards humanity: they can protect from the evil/harm they cause if sincerely worshipped. Yet all these goddesses, though referred to as *mās* or *ammās*, are not functional mothers. They have neither a husband nor a companion. They have no children and are often said to be widows. When they are virgins, procreation seems forbidden to them, and quite often they are barren or represent venereal diseases (Nabokov 2000: 111). If they are worshipped as rescuers from a disease, they are imagined as affected by the same. So the question is: why do women worship with such a strong faith ill/barren goddesses who lack a companion? What do they look for in such a subverted image of Purāṇic goddesses who are pious wives and good mothers?

I have already pointed out that devotional practices performed by women especially stress female-specific power: fertility. Yet in the context of agricultural societies, the importance of the earth, which is always portrayed as feminine, is pivotal. In Jungian terms, the same can be said of ill-giving spirits, which — being formerly related to the dead — are a kind of emanation from the earth. Diseases are the tangible wrath of the earth and in most cases they are feminine too.

The *gājan* reflects these features through its iconography:

- (a) the slab stone is the earth;
- (b) the studded plank is its ill-giving aspect; and
- (c) the vessel is the womb in which the vital fluid is contained (both water and blood).

But if this is valid for all village goddesses, some remarks on Dharma are in order. In my view, the ritual behaviour of female devotees can be labelled as an unconscious challenge in which the envy of the hidden goddess (Dharma's spouse) is provoked. The display of the *pūra kalaśī* and its alternate emptiness/refilling is an act which reproduces the fertility power of women. Such a display provokes anger and heat in the restrained mother (i.e. the "castrated" goddess), in fact this particular deity is not only theologically impeded in procreation, but is also believed and perceived as male. The result of this "doubled castration" is furious anger. The priest has to bathe the *pāṭ*, the aggressive emblem of the deity (the *pāṭ*), and try to cool it. Dharma is now an envious godhead. The plank representing the sacrificial male (the object of the deity's wrath) is covered with iron nails and iron is ancestrally believed to keep diseases and barrenness away. The deity is believed to sweat from the great heat that is developed, and that has to be transformed. While men's austerities are meant to cool Dharma by experiencing the same pain, women identify with the true (feminine) nature of the main deity of the *gājan* and confirm their power by sublimating wrath. In the end, we are speaking of earthly spirits, and not of divine hierarchical gods. So, if men absorb the heat in order to transform their own egos, women employ it as a creative power. After *mukti snāna*, when the priest (who represents now the entire female community) and all the women have filled and emptied the *kalaśī*, the deity, like the vessel, is cold because it is full of *śānti-jala*.

The image of Dharma who is invoked in this and other ceremonies as a white ascetic is thus misleading and possibly a later accretion. The role of women in the living cult sheds light on interesting aspects of the perception of the modern male god. If Dharma Ṭhākura is connected to fertility, regeneration and recovery, why does he have to be depicted as an ascetic with white beard and long white matted hair? My informants told me that Dharma is an all-white deity in that he heals diseases such as poxes and blindness, which are traditionally believed to be conveyed or caused by the sun's rays (*Śūnya Purāṇa* 38: 20-2). Local folklore and liturgical scriptures indulge in descriptions of Dharma as all-white (*śveta-varṇa, śukla-varṇa*) and thus confirm the identification with the Vedic/Purāṇic Sūrya (Bidyābhūṣaṇa 1404 BS: 5). But I suspect that, like pox-deities (Māriāmmā, Śītalā, etc.), Dharma might be connected to whiteness because that is the colour of the benign aspect of the deity. When goddesses are anthropomorphized, they appear as white-complexioned young maidens: they are cold because pacified and they might be given in marriage to Hindu gods (McDaniel 2003: 8). In brief, if black is the colour of their natural state (i.e. hungry and furious), white is the mark of their quiet state. So — following an apotropaic custom — the deity is preferably imagined as white.

## Conclusion

The examination of the ritual acts performed in a hierogamic celebration like the Bengali *gājan* according to a gender perspective gives both the anthropologist and the historian of religions a privileged position. The anomalies occurring in the *gājan* are reflected in both religious symbolism (iconography, rituals, etc.) and in the ritual behavioural sphere, which is often dominated by submerged ancestral cultural heritage. The *gājan* — if examined with the eye of a clinician — is a traumatic and critical occurrence which is built around the crises of Dharma's devotees. The gender of the original recipient deity has changed. What originally was a hierogamic celebration in which the Earth (a female goddess/spirit) was placated through the sacrifice of the male (her son/groom) in order to fulfil a process of compensation/retaliation, has changed perspective. Under the influence of the Brāhmanic penetration — which in north-eastern India was later and slower — the festival acquired an andro-centric perspective. In accordance with the dominant social patterns, the female is now the one who is given to the male.

Coming back to the bond which ties women devotees and Dharma, I wish to stress the subverted image of ritual female behaviour in respect to men. Men (unconsciously) aim to transform their egos and partake of the inner nature of Dharma by developing heat and experiencing the feelings of the deity.[41] Instead, women sublimate all this. They identify the symbol of their functional power (i.e. the womb) in the *pūra kalaśī* and then confirm the power to progenerate by displaying ritual fecundation (filling) and delivery (emptying). The generating force is also heat but women differ from men in that they are able to transform the "envy" of the deity into *śakti* regenerative-cum-destructive power.

While we have very few hints to estimate the role of women in the proto-*gājan*, it seems reasonable to infer that the ritual ambiguity, which so clearly appears in the case of male

41. We are far away from the transgender anxiety of certain devotional Hindu *sampradāyas*. In Vaiṣṇava *bhakti* — to name one — everybody, irrespective of gender, must become "female" in order to be united with Kṛṣṇa. In folk or tribal contexts, where the religious sphere is dominated by pragmatism rather than focused on transcendental aims, biological factors and needs are more evident (cf. Goldman 1993: 386-89).

*saṁnyāsīs*, is less problematic for the *mahilā bhaktyās*. Dharma Ṭhākura is a male deity but the ritualism of the *gājan* tends towards a goddess. On a psychological level, women do not fail in addressing the deity, as female ritualism remains centred on the goddess. Men and women worship a female godhead believing it a male. But while the former succeed in the identification-and-union process neglecting (i.e. transforming) their masculinity, the latter are successful thanks to their gender and bodies.[42] The representation of the *gājan* as a hierogamy does not leave any space to the psychological crises of the *mahilā bhaktyās*. Though addressed towards a male deity, the rituals of the *gājan* remain feminine-centred and women devotees — in their process of confirmation with the goddess nature — still represent the apotheosis of the Earth.

## References

Balzer, M.M., 2003, "Sacred genders in Siberia: Shamans, Bears Festival and Androgyny", in Harvey, G. (ed.), *Shamanism A Reader*, New York & London: Routledge, pp. 235-41.

Banerjee, S., 1989, *The Parlour and the Streets, Elite and Popular Culture in Nineteenth Century Calcutta*, Calcutta: Seagull Books.

Beck, B.E.F., 1969, "Colour and Heat in south Indian ritual", *Man*, New Series, 4(4), pp. 553-72.

Beggiora, S., 2003, *Sonum: Spirit Delta Giungla, Lo Sciamanismo delle trib Saora dell' Orissa*, Milano: Franco Angeli.

Bhattacharya, F., 1994, "The God Dharma, Human Sacrifice and Bhakti in the Dharma Maṅgala", in A. Entwistle & F. Mallison (eds.), *Studies in South Asian Devotional Literature*, Delhi: Manohar, pp. 345-62.

42. In the *gājan*, because of its gender-reversal structure, it is possible to recognize the failure of the traditional values which patrilocal societies assign to marriage. The transition from a situation of disunion into union (i.e. marriage) is a traumatic event for men only, as men have to overcome their own anxieties and guilt (cf. Seaford 1987: 106-107; Sax 1990: 498-501).

Bhattacharyya, A., 1977, *The Sun and the Serpent Lore of Bengal,* Calcutta: Firma KLM.

Bhattacharyya, N.N., 1996a, *Ancient Indian Rituals and Their Social Contents,* 2[nd] edition, Delhi: Manohar.

Bhattacharyya, N.N., 1996b, *History of the Śākta Religion,* 2[nd] edn. Delhi, Munshiram Manoharlal.

Busby, C., 1997, "Permeable and Partible Persons: a Comparative Analysis of Gender and Body in South India and Melanesia", *The Journal of the Royal Anthropological Institute,* 3(2), pp. 261-78.

Carrin, M. (ed.), 1999a, *Managing distress, Possession and Therapeutic Cults in South Asia,* New Delhi: Manohar.

Carrin, M., 1999b, The Sacrifice of Femininity: Female Sacredness at the Hindu/Tribal Frontier in Bengal", in H. Tambs-Lyche (ed.) *The Feminine Sacred in South Asia,* Delhi: Manohar, pp. 114-33.

Chattopadhyay, G., 1935, "Carak Festival in a West Bengal Village", in L.P. Vidhyarthi (ed.), *Aspects of Religion in Indian Society,* Meerut: Kedar Nath Ram Nath, pp. 151-65.

Chattopadhyay, K. P., 1935, "The Cadak Festival in Bengal", *Journal of the Royal Asiatic Society of Bengal, Letters,* 1, 397-406.

Chattopadhyay, K.P., 1942, "Dharma Worship", *Journal of the Royal Asiatic Society of Bengal Letters,* 8 (1), 99-135.

Choi, C., 2003, "The Artistry and Ritual Aesthetics of Urban Korean Shamans", in G. Harvey (ed.), *Shamanism, A Reader,* New York & London: Routledge, pp. 170-85.

Czaplicka, M.A., 1914, *Aboriginal Siberia. A Study in Social Anthropology,* London: Oxford University Press.

Dasgupta, S.B., 1995, *Obscure Religious Cults,* reprint of the 3[rd] edn. (1969), Calcutta: Firma KLM.

Devereux, G., 1953, "Les facteurs culturels en therapeutique psychanalytique", in G. Devereux (ed.), *Essais d'ethnopsychiatrie gènèrale,* Paris, Gallimard, pp. 334-53.

———, 1966, "Les pulsions cannibaliques des parents", In G. Devereux (ed.), *Essais d'ethnopsychiatrie gènèrale,* Paris: Gallimard, pp. 143-61.

*Dharma Purāṇa* (by Mayūrabhaṭṭa) (1337 BS), ed. B. Cattopadyay, Kolkata: Bangiya Sahitya Parisad.

*Dharmamaṅgala* (by Ghanarām Cakrabartī) (1369 BS), ed. P.K. Mahāpātra, Calcutta: Kalikātā Biśbabidyālaya.

*Dharmamaṅgala* (by Mānikrām Gāṅguli) (1960). ed. B.K. Datta & S. Datta, Calcutta: Kalikātā Biśbabidyālaya.

*Dharma-Pūjā-Vidhāna* (by Rāmāi Puṇḍit) (1323 BS), ed. N.G. Bandhyopādhyāy, Calcutta: Bangiya Sahitya Parisad.

Doniger, W., 1980, *Women, Androgynes, and Other Mythical Beasts*, Chicago & London, University of Chicago Press.

Duff, Rev. A., 1846, *A Description of the Durga and Kālī Festivals Celebrated in Calcutta, at an Expense of Three Millions of Dollars*, Troy, New York: Wright Publications.

Eliade, M., 1958, *Patterns in Comparative Religion*, New York: Meridian.

Elwin, V., 1952, "The Saora Priestess", *Bulletin of the Department of Anthropology of the Bombay University*, 1(1), pp. 59-85.

Ferrari, F.M., 2004, "Sri Dharmesvara of Vārāṇasī and the cult of Dharma Ṭhākur of Bengal, Some analogies and discrepancies", *South Asia Research*, 24(2), pp. 149-69.

———, 2005a, "Playing with corpses and worshipping skulls. Bodily modifications and gender transformations in rural West Bengal", *Contemporary South Asia, Annual BASAS Edition*, 14(4).

———, 2005b, "Surrendering to the earth, Male devotional practices in the Bengali Dharma cult", *Fieldwork in Religion*, 1(2).

———, 2005c, "Uselessness of translation in Bengali Dharmapuja: The Shift From Ritual Texts to Living Cult", in T. Hermans (ed.), *Translating Others*, Manchester, St. Jerome Publishing.

Fruzzetti, L., 1990, *The Gift of a Virgin: Women, Marriage, and Ritual in a Bengali Society*, Delhi: Oxford University Press.

Goldman, R. P., 1993, Transsexualism, gender, and anxiety in traditional India", *Journal of the American Oriental Society*, 113(3), pp. 374-401.

Harman, William (n.d.), "Promises Made to Goddesses: Women's Boons and Men's Fears": http://www.uni-koein.de/phil-fak/indologie/kolam/kolam3/mariyamm.html!

Hiltebeitel, A., 1991, *The Cult of Draupadī Vol. 2: On the Hindu Ritual and the Goddess*, Chicago & London: University of Chicago Press.

Jayakar, P., 1990, *The Earth Mother, Legends, Ritual Arts, and Goddesses of India*, rpt. 1[st] edn. (1980), San Francisco: Harper and Row.

*Kālārkarudra bā caṛakpūjāpaddhati* (1404 BS). ed. N.C. Bidyābhūṣan. Kalikātā, Saurendra Dās Mukharjī.

Kinsley, D., 1998, *Hindu Goddesses, Vision of the Divine Feminine in the Hindu Religious Tradition*, Delhi, Motilal Banarsidass.

Kripai, J. J, 1995, *Kālī's Child: The Mystical and the Erotic in the Life and Teaching of Ramakrishna*, Chicago & London, University of Chicago Press.

*Manava-dharma-śāstra.*

Mastromattei, R., 1995, "Le nove porte", in R. Mastromattei (ed.), *Tremore e potere*, Milano, Franco Angeli, pp. 63-103.

McDaniel, J., 2003, *Making Virtuous Daughters and Wives: An Introduction to Women's Brata Rituals in Bengali Folk Religion*, Albany: State University of New York Press.

Nabokov, I., 2000, *Religion against the Self, An Ethnography of Tamil Rituals*, Oxford: Oxford University Press.

Nebesky-Vojkowitz, R. von (1993), *Oracles and Demons of Tibet*, Kathmandu: Tiwari's Pilgrim Book House.

Neumann, E., 1981, *La Grande Madre. Fenomenologia delle configurazioni femminili dell'inconscio*, Roma: Astrolabio.

Nicholas, R., 1982, "The Village Mother in Bengal", in J.J. Preston (ed.), *Mother Worship: Theme and Variations*, Chapel Hill: University of North Carolina Press, pp. 192-209.

Obeyesekere, G., 1985, "Symbolic Foods: Pregnancy Cravings and the Envious Female", *International Journal of Psychology*, 20, pp. 637-662.

Oddie, G. A., 1995, *Popular Religion, Elites and Reform: Hook-Swinging and Its Prohibition in Colonial India, 1800-1894*, Delhi: Manohar.

Östör, A., 1980, *The Play of the Gods. Locality, Ideology, Structure and Time in the Festivals of a Bengali Town*, Chicago & London: University of Chicago Press.

Parpola, A., 1983, "The Pre-Vedic Indian Background of the Śrauta Rituals", in F. Staal (ed.), *Agni: the Vedic Ritual of the Fire Altar*, Delhi: Motilal Banarsidass, pp. 41-75.

Robinson, S., 1980, *The Dharmapūjā: A Study of Rites and Symbols Associated with the Bengali Deity Dharmarāj*. Ph.D. Thesis, Chicago: University of Chicago.

Sarkar, R.M., 1986, *Regional Cults and Rural Traditions: An Interacting Pattern of Divinity and Humanity in Rural Bengal,* New Delhi: Inter-India Publications.

Sax, W. S., 1990, "Village Daughter, Village Goddess: Residence, Gender, and Politics in a Himalayan Pilgrimage", *American Ethnologist,* 17(3), pp. 491-512.

Seaford, R., 1987, "The Tragic Wedding", *The Journal of Hellenic Studies,* pp. 106-30.

Sen, Dinesh C. 1920, *The Folk-Literature of Bengal,* Calcutta: University of Calcutta.

Sen, S., 1971, *An Etymological Dictionary of Bengali: c. 1000-1800* CE, 2 vols, Calcutta: Eastern Publishers.

Sinha, S., B.K. Dasgupta & H. Banerjee (1961), "Rituals in Agriculture", *Bulletin of the Anthropological Survey of India,* 10(1), pp. 29-35.

*Śūnya Purāṇa* (by Rāmāi Paṇḍit) (1314 BS), ed. N.N. Basu, Calcutta: Bangīya Sāhitya Pariṣad.

Thakur, A.N., 1350 BS, *Bāṅglār brata,* Kalikātā, Viśvavidyā Saṁgraha.

Walsh, J.E., 1997, "What Women Learned When Men Gave Them Advice: Rewriting Patriarchy in late-Nineteenth-century Bengal", *The Journal of Asian Studies,* 56(3), pp. 641-77.

Younger, P., 2002, *Playing Host to Deity: Festival Religion in the South Indian Tradition,* Oxford: Oxford University Press.

# 17

## God
### A Sociological View

*Santosh Kumar Mishra*

IN the history of mankind, there are certain beliefs which have existed since ancient times. The belief in "God" is one of them. Through the cultural development of man, many Śāstras have originated and developed. Each of these Śāstras has its own view of God. God has found a unique place in the Śāstras such as Dharmaśāstra, Tarkaśāstra, Jyotiṣaśāstra, etc. Dharmaśāstras have conceptualized God as the Creator, Preserver, Destroyer and Controller of the cosmos. These texts have fashioned God as eternal, infinite, comprehensive, omnipotent, omnipresent, omniscient, almighty and the director of the entire cosmos.

Some people consider God as an absolute or amorphous entity while others see him as a form endowed with qualities. Philosophers conceive God as a ubiquitous entity. Some philosophers try to prove the existence of God through logical statements, definitions and reasons while others accept God in the light of faith and belief. As opposed to this, some thinkers refute the very existence of God through their arguments.

The object of this essay is neither to put forward these arguments nor to come out with any final solution to this riddle of God. Its objective is to analyse the faith in God on the sociological plane. An effort is made here to mark the chronological developments in the thought-processes from the ancient to the modern times in relation to God. From the sociological point of view, there can be three basic reasons behind the origin of the concept of God.

1. Consciousness of being powerless of human beings.
2. Faith and devotion.
3. Transcendence.

Definition of religion given by Haebel contains all these points. Further he illustrates the faith in God and the devotion in different primitive religions. Johnson extends the definition of Haebel. Gillin and Gillin have assumed the supernatural force as the supreme power and have supported the respect and honour shown towards it. They also mentioned different views about its nature.

According to James Frazer, primitive man practised *black art* (magic) or *witchcraft* to exercise control over nature. But inconsistency of these practices forced the primitive man to accept an unseen power which could not be controlled by means of magic or witchcraft.

Emile Durkheim refers to this tendency of the primitive man and divides human beliefs into two categories: (1) Sacred, and (2) Profane.

Profane belief is associated with the worldly practices, while the sacred belief is linked with the transcendental power. To establish this view, Durkheim has evolved the concept of totemism. Various sociologists and anthropologists such as Maclennon, Lubac, Tylor, Spencer, Fryod Robinson, Smith, etc. have explained the origin of religion in their own ways. The study of these views reveals that totem is the driving force behind the belief in God in the tribal religion, for the qualities found in totem (mentioned below) strengthens the concept of God in some way or the other.

1. The transcendental and sacred relation with totem.
2. Totem protects man in crisis. It foretells the future and gives warning.
3. There is a feeling of fear, devotion, respect and reverence towards totem.
4. The feeling of morality is also present in the totem.
5. Totem represents the group, etc.

Some thinkers believe that the concept of God (as supernatural power) has its roots in naturalism. The pioneer of naturalism, Max Müller believes that the primitive man was influenced and overwhelmed by the natural events and started worshipping nature as a supernatural power. Naturalism has been supported by the Sūktas of *Ṛgveda* which has referred to the sun, the moon, stars, air, fire and various other natural elements as God.

The archaeological excavations in Egypt and other places have proved that the primitive man worshipped natural elements. In Egypt "Ra" (the sun) is considered to be the biggest God.

Naturalism on the one hand supports the existence of supernatural power in natural elements whereas, on the other hand it also shows its anger and joy in auspicious and inauspicious functions through obvious natural evidence. The implications of natural elements like fire, water, air, etc. is both encouraging as well as disparaging for mankind. So, it is natural for the primitive man to develop the feeling of fear, awe, wonder, love and devotion towards natural elements. Motivated by these feelings he worshipped them as God. Therefore, we can say that the feeling of divinity for the natural powers can be considered as the primary basis of the idea of God.

Tylor has tried to explain belief in the supernatural power through his concept of Animism. According to him, human souls are of two kinds. One, which remains after the death of the person, and the other one which is celestial. Celestial soul is different from the soul of man. These souls include both the powerful and the sinful souls which are immortal. Can they influence human life? This explanation seemingly implies that the concept of God must have arisen from these divine souls.

Codrington and Marriot, after studying the Melanesian tribe, tried to establish that the transcendental power in which primitive man believed should be appropriately termed as "Mana." According to Codrington,

> *Mana* is a force altogether distinct from physical power which acts in all kinds of ways for good and evil and it is of greatest advantage to possess or to control *chanchal mana*. If it is a power or influence, not physical, and in a way supernatural, but it shows itself in physical force or in any kind of power or excellence which a man possesses then it is not transcendental. It is supernatural in the sense that it is that which works to effect everything, which is beyond the ordinary power of man, outside the common process of nature.

According to Lowie,

> *Mana* was like an electric fluid that could charge persons and things and be diverted from one to another. Any conspicuous success was due to its presence and failure due to its absence or loss.

On the basis of above-mentioned statements, two prime features which characterize *Mana* are:

1. *Mana* is a comprehensive and unique supernatural power.
2. It is non-manifesting and non-physical power which pervades through all the conscious and unconscious

things. *Mana* however may be seen as equivalent to God.

To understand the views of modern social scientists, it is necessary to analyse their ideas on religion in order to explain the concept of God. Among the modern thinkers, Durkheim's concept of religion gives special importance to terrestrial and the visible as compared to the supernatural and the invisible. He says that the definition of the religion of primitive man given by some thinkers in the form of "a belief in supernatural force" does not seem to be logical because it is necessary to assume that the primitive man was skilled enough to understand the difference between terrestrial and supernatural.

Religion is a social fact which is experienced by the people through various collective meets and festivals. Therefore, the "collective power" is the base of religion and God. This statement can be explained by the fact that the complete behaviour of man is divided into two categories: Sacred and Profane. The sacred behaviour relates to the collectivity and divinity, while the profane relates to the day-to-day earthly life of man. Mores, taboos and ideals prevalent in the social system regularize and control human life. Society directs and regularizes them in an abstract manner. On this basis, it can be said that, in Durkheim's concept of God, special importance has been laid on this direction and also on regularization aspects, of social life so far as worship and praying are concerned.

Though thinkers like Malinowski and Radcliffe Brown have supported the functional theory of religion they have not discussed God in their religious thoughts. Yet the concept of God seems hidden in the fact that they find it significant to explain the origin of religion. In their functional theory of religion these two thinkers have tried to establish through the example of the people of Trobrianders Island that when primitive man used to go for hunting or for fishing, they felt that their lives were in danger and hence they were in stress. In the same way, during various situations such as of hatred, greed, anger, love, man experiences both stress and strain. The longer span of stress leads to lower mental stability and thus hurts normal living. Therefore, religion plays an important role in maintaining mental balance in conditions like fear, anger and remorse. This function of religion is only possible when religion is able to connect man with a supernatural or transcendental power and man leaves himself at the mercy of this transcendental power an believes that all the actions are controlled by this transcendental power. This supernatural power gradually takes itself the form of God or Almighty.

It has been mentioned above that to explain the views of the modern social scientists about God, it would be imperative to keep in mind their definitions and explanations of religion. Following the views of Durkheim, Malinowski and Radcliff Brown, the concept of God has been hinted upon.

By looking at the views of Max Weber and Karl Marx on religion it seems that out of two aspects of religion,

1. transcendental, faith-oriented, and
2. pragmatic and rationality-oriented,

these thinkers have emphasized more on the second aspect and believe that the supernatural faith-oriented theory of God seems to be far away from being real while the economic morality, pragmatic conduct and rational organization of religion is logical and more real.

Jokim Wach, explaining Max Weber's religious thoughts says that, "religion has two prime aspects." First is the faith towards God and the relation of every member of the community with the power of God, and the second one is rationality based or pragmatic one, i.e. mutual relationships of every member of the community with each other. These two are mutually interdependent. The rational and pragmatic conduct helps in increasing social relations and with the increase in such relations, the supernatural and faith-oriented aspect becomes strong. In support of this belief, Jokim Wach has presented several examples. Some of them are given below:

### Mythological Praise

These praises propagate religious beliefs and are related with the civilization and tradition of specific group of people which gives rise to a feeling of oneness in them.

### Feelings and Faith

People sharing common faith system, expressing some covert and overt feeling constitute a religious community. This raises a sense of unity among them and they experience a certain kind of spiritual bondage.

### Religious Cult

In a particular religious community, there are several sub-groups. They are known as religious cults. The members of these cults on the one hand are connected with other members of the cult and on the other hand they also stay interlinked with their fellows on the comprehensive religious plane. For example the Vaiṣṇava, Śaiva, Śākta, Kabīr Panth, Dādu Panth, Rādhā Swāmī Panth, etc. which are the sub-cults in the Hindu religion. These cults are bound by the beliefs of their separate cults. At the same time, they are also related with the beliefs of the comprehensive Hindu religion.

### Effect of Worship

Every religious community has a public place for worship which is called the home of God or prayer house like Temple, Mosque, Church, Gurdwara, etc. Everybody is equal in that place and there is no discrimination.

**World in the view of Religion**

Every religion imagines a special kind of relation between God and the World as well as God and the Man and directs that a person who does good deeds comes nearer to God and a person who commits evil distances himself from God. On this basis, religious and social ideals and morality are all systemized.

On the basis of the above-mentioned views of social scientists on the concept of religion and God, it can be said that in sociology, God is not a temporal theme of analysis. As such, it seems impossible to find a clear view of sociology regarding the form, existence, attributes and characteristics of God. In sociology the concept of God is explained with reference to societies. When the contribution of religion, or the role played by the religion in the social life of man is questioned, the sociological view accepts the faith and belief in supernatural power as an important fact, as an implication of the natural feelings of fear, terror, frustration, depression, conflict, insecurity, etc. which are caused due to natural occurrences. The exploration of the concept of God is done in the context of the explanation of this faith and belief. In the historical survey of human civilization, anthropologists and sociologists observe this supernatural power in different forms and address it with different names. This supernatural power, present in all the conscious and unconscious things of the world, influences them and also operates to control them. Some modern social scientists accept the concept of power, its directives and ideal implications but they do not consider it to be supernatural. According to them this power is present and contained in the abstract form of society and applied on the social group. This abstract society is God itself and through this only regulation, control and operations are carried out.

In this way, it can be said that the sociology doesn't accept Godly attributes like omnipotence, omniscience, omnipresence, kindness, affinity, etc. on the basis of which Dharmaśāstra and philosophy establish the concept of God. Sociology lays emphasis on social forces that emanate from religion and create order and conflict in society. Further, sociology of religion also concentrates on the social forces that are responsible for the genesis of religion in a particular socio-cultural milieu.

## References

Codringtion, R.H., 1891, *The Melanesian: Study in their Anthropology and Folk-Lore*, London: Oxford, p. 119.

Frazer, James, 1957, *The Golden Bough*, London (abridged edition) Macmillan & Co. Ltd., p. 459.

Gillin, J.L. and Gillin J.P., 1950, *Cultural Sociology*, New York: The Macmillan Co., p. 461.

Tylor, E.B., 1958, *Primitive Culture*, New York: Harper Torchbooks, p. 426.

# 18

# Contemporary Society and Indian View of the Divine Mother

*Jaya Saraswati*

IT is believed that the concept of Supreme Being originated when humans developed the realization that their life was finite: that they would all die. This resulted in the formulation of the primitive religious beliefs. Societies which relied mainly on hunting by men naturally developed the tendency to worship hunting gods. Those societies in which gathering was more reliable generally created vegetative goddesses. The importance of fertility in crops, in domesticated animals, in wild animals and in the society itself was of paramount importance to their survival. The female life-giving principle was considered divine and a great mystery.

Concept of Mother Goddess predates all known male gods. It is believed to have been originated about 27,000 years ago and encompassed the three continents — namely Europe, Asia and Africa that harboured human population then. It was suppressed about 5000 years ago when a new religion came up with male gods, although Mother Goddess or the earth Goddess is still worshipped today.

> The Goddess is diversity. She represents both the darkness and light and her worship is the reconciliation of opposites. There can be no such thing as a "Good Goddess" or an "Evil Goddess." Death is part of the natural cycle as night

> follows day and we accept it with grace as the final destiny. The search for "Balance" is the goal of her people, and it is achieved by the acceptance of multiple paths and truths. Dion Fortune once commented that all goddesses are manifestations of the One Great Goddess who is identified as the universal feminine spirit of Nature.[1]

In different cultures, there is this universality of the concept of Goddess that she has often been visualized in three aspects: Maiden, Mother and Crone. The Maiden represents youth and emerging sexuality. The Mother symbolizes feminine power, fertility, and nurturing. The Crone is wisdom, the compassion which comes from experience, and the one who guides us through the death experience. The maternal influence was unquestioned in such cultures as it was strongly believed that the Divine Mother preserves moral order and righteousness in the creation and she protects mankind from evil and misery by destroying evil forces such as selfishness, jealousy, prejudice, hatred, anger, and ego.

Hinduism (known as Hindu Dharma in modern Indian languages) is a religious tradition. Any kind of creativity of bestowing of life seems to evoke a symbolism of motherhood in it.

> In India it is believed that there is a goddess in every village, a nymph in every lake. Demonesses stand guard on village frontiers, ogresses howl on crossroads, and untamed forests resound with the laughter of celestial virgins. It is a land of mysterious *apsarases* and seductive *yakṣiṇīs*, of terrifying *ḍākinīs* and wise *yoginīs* — each with a story to tell.[2]

The rivers are seen as nourishing, life-giving natural forces and hence are worshipped as Mother Goddesses in India. In

---

1. http://www.jaguarmoon.org/public/Goddess/Mother.htm
2. Inner Traditions: Goddess in India, http://www.innertraditions.com/

fact, the Mother Goddess comes even before the Trinity — Brahmā, Viṣṇu, and Śiva. This becomes obvious when one considers the story of Satī Anasūyā. Anasūyā (devoid of hatred) was the devoted wife of Atri Ṛṣi. She was very beautiful also. Seeing her exceptional devotion to her husband, the gods in heaven began to fear that some day she might overcome them. Brahmā, Viṣṇu and Śiva came to Atri Muni's Āśrama in the mendicants' disguise. They told her, "We have come here from a long distance as we have heard of your beauty. We wish you to take off your garments and then serve us with food. If you do not comply with this, we shall leave this place without meals." Anasūyā thought and decided, "The guests are like my children," hence I need not think otherwise. Instantly all the three gods were transformed into three newly-born crying babies. She fed them and thus became the mother of the three great gods. She placed them in a cradle, pulled the string and began singing lullabies.[3] It is further told in the story that the gods were lost in the happy presence of their human mother. It is further suggested that they were not powerful enough to regain their Godhood.

The same reason stands behind the practice of worshipping the cow as a mother, because, as a mother, the cow provides the humans with milk. As Sanātana Dharma or a universal tradition: Hinduism recognizes that "the Divine" contains both masculine and feminine attributes. Without giving proper honour to the feminine qualities a religion is incomplete or one-sided. Without recognizing the feminine aspect of Divinity one cannot claim to know God. The recognition of the feminine is necessary to restore wholeness, completeness and universality. To a Hindu, the motherly aspect of God in nature is full of beauty, gentleness, kindness and tenderness, and unconditional love. Such love unites the devotee with God,

3. http://saileelas.org/books/ShriGuruCharitra.doc

like a child with her mother. Just as a child feels safe and secure in the lap of her mother, a devotee feels safe and secure in the presence of the Divine Mother. She is the first manifestation of Divine Energy. Thus with the name of Divine Mother comes the idea of energy which is omnipotent, omnipresent, loving, intelligent, and wise. Just as a child believes her mother to be all-powerful, and capable of doing anything for the child, a devotee believes the Divine Mother to be all merciful, all-powerful and eternally guiding and protecting him with her invisible arms. She is a positive figure of piety and power.

In India the Mother Goddess has many manifestations. As Aditi she is a woman clothed in the Sun and is the mother of all the lights of heaven. As Sarasvatī she is the Goddess of music, poem, science and learning. As Anantā or Sarparājñī she is a serpent Goddess who preserves the God during the periods lying between his incarnations. As *Bhavānī* she has bestowed existence and is evoked by women in child-birth. As Chomolung-mā she is Goddess mother of universe. As Māyā she is the mother of Buddha the enlightened one. As Pārvatī she is the daughter of heaven. As Durgā she is the warrior Goddess riding a tiger and fighting the demons that dare to threaten her children (gods in heaven). As Annapūrṇā she is the provider of food. The list is endless. We come across Draviḍian goddesses, goddesses from Assam, Bengal and elsewhere — each full of sincerity and sense of responsibility blended with immense capacity to love, nurture and protect.

*Encyclopaedia Britannica* is particularly harsh on Kālī whom it associates with *death, sexuality, violence, who paradoxically in some of her later historical appearances, is motherly love.* In my opinion this misconception has its root in European prejudices. God cannot be a woman — that too a dark one. We know Europeans are afraid of black. Kālī is believed to have been born of the fury of Durgā. She manifests earth, hence is black;

She is a mother, hence she is full-breasted. She is the Goddess of fertility, death and regeneration, thus she is the conqueror of time. She is ferocious but only against evil, and evil in Hinduism, whatever may be the mythical manifestations, is nothing but ego.

What is the significance of and relevance of Goddess cult in modern times? Answer to this question lies in the philosophy of Mahatma Gandhi. When he envisaged the idea of non-violence as the way of life to nurture human evolution, he was aware that the future belongs to the non-violent, the ones having immense capacity to love and also who are willing to make sacrifices. In his learned opinion women inherently have these abilities and hence he believed that women will be the future leaders — that feminine forces will be prominent in creating destiny of humankind. Is it happening? A cursory glance tells us that our latest achievements — be it human rights, environmentalism, social security, etc. — each is led by women in a significant way. World is more sensitive towards those vanquished in wars today than ever before. Conquerors have been compelled to show greater responsibility and compassion than ever before. While fighting poverty, governments have found that their efforts bear better fruits when targeted towards women. For example, in almost all instances of microfinancing it has been observed that women pay back the loans more often and in time; they use money more productively and they use it on family (and not on themselves).

Thus it may be concluded that Indian view of Mother Goddess is rich, multidimensional, diverse and full of philosophical insights. While looking for future solutions to existing problems and in our endeavour to build a strong, resilient, just and compassionate society we may dwell into this Indian view.

# The Contributors

**Beggiora, Stefano,** is connoisseur in religions of South Asia. After various years of fieldwork in India he has specialized in the study of Central-Asiatic shamanic religion. Now is lecturer of Social Anthropology in Bolzano.

**Bera, Gautam Kumar,** is an anthropologist interested in tribal studies and associated with Visva Bharati, Santiniketan.

**Ferrari, Fabrizio M.,** is a lecturer in Religious Studies in the University of Chester. He has specialized in the studies of popular religions in Bengali-speaking regions. At present, he is working on a project on the concept of disease, illness and possession in South Asian religions.

**Gonsalves, Francis,** is a Professor of Religion at Vidyajyoti College of Theology, New Delhi.

**Gyatso, Tenzin,** the 14th Dalai Lama, is the spiritual and temporal leader of Tibet's people. A number of institutions have conferred awards on him in recognition of his distinguished writings in Buddhist philosophy. He was the recipient of 1989 Nobel Peace Prize.

**Inam Shastri, A.S.,** is a Professor of Social Work at the Mahatma Gandhi Kashi Vidyapeeth, Varanasi.

**Mishra, Santosh Kumar,** is a research scholar in the Department of Sociology, Banaras Hindu University, Varanasi.

**Mittal, Satya Prakash,** is a renowned scholar of socialism, Swatantrata Senani, and ex-Research Officer in Gandhian Institute, Rajghat.

**Prasad, Onkar,** is an anthropologist and musicologist who deals with the tribal world. He is Professor in Palli Charcha Kendra, Visva Bharati, Santiniketan.

**Sahay, K.N.,** has been a Professor of Anthropology at the Ranchi University, Ranchi.

**Saraswati, Baidyanath,** is an anthropologist and has been UNESCO Professor in Culture and Development at the Indira Gandhi National Centre for the Arts, New Delhi. He is the Founder of the N.K. Bose Memorial Foundation, Varanasi.

**Saraswati, Jaya,** is a scholar of English literature. At present working on a project of Department of Computer Science and Engineering IIT, Powai, Mumbai.

**Sharma, R.C.,** is an eminent Indologist and Director of Jñāna Pravāh, Centre for Cultural Studies, Varanasi.

**Sinha, Balananda,** is a Professor of Psychology at T.M.B. University, Bhagalpur, Bihar and senior disciple of famous vocalist Pandit Jasraj.

**Sinha, Bashistha Narayan,** is one of the reputed Jainologists in India and former Asst. Professor, Department of Philosphy, Mahatma Gandhi Kashi Vidyapeeth, Varanasi.

**Tewari, S.N.,** is a retired Medical Officer-in-charge of E.F.I. Hospital, Jaipur.

**Tripathi, B.D.,** is an eminent sociologist and a former Professor of Mahatma Gandhi Kashi Vidyapeeth, Varanasi.

**Vesci, Uma Merina,** is an Indologist born in Rome, came to India in 1963 to begin a new life that few scholars have courage to undertake, to ponder over the words of ancient Sanskrit.

# Index